HR Leadership

Linda Holbeche

AMSTERDAM • BOSTON • HEIDELBERG • LONDON • NEW YORK • OXFORD
PARIS • SAN DIEGO • SAN FRANCISCO • SINGAPORE • SYDNEY • TOKYO

Butterworth-Heinemann is an imprint of Elsevier

Butterworth-Heinemann is an imprint of Elsevier
Linacre House, Jordan Hill, Oxford OX2 8DP, UK
30 Corporate Drive, Suite 400, Burlington, MA 01803, USA

First edition 2010

British Library Cataloguing in Publication Data
A catalogue record for this book is available from the British Library

Library of Congress Cataloging-in-Publication Data
A catalog record for this book is available from the Library of Congress

ISBN–13: 978-0-7506-8173-5

For information on all Butterworth-Heinemann
publications visit our website at elsevierdirect.com

Printed and bound in Great Britan

10 11 12   10 9 8 7 6 5 4 3 2 1

Contents

A long time has passed since I first met Linda. It was the early -90s and Linda – and her (then) colleagues at Roffey Park Business Institute – undertook some leadership work with my (then) board colleagues. I recall my first impressions. She was an absolute one-off! An obvious academic but one with a practical and down-to-earth mind. And an ability to express herself. Since the early days, our paths have crossed on many, many occasions – in Roffey Park, The Work Foundation and in Chartered Institute of Personnel and Development (CIPD) – and it is my privilege to now regard her as a true personal friend and confidante. Over the years, I have come to recognise her many qualities and understand her logic just a tad more.

Linda is a true ambassador of HR. It was a delight to see her recent well-deserved recognition – from one of the leading HR journals – as one of the most influential academics in HR today. Actually, she has, in my opinion, been that for many years. Her opinions are, at the same time, pragmatic and practical yet radical and, on occasions, even eccentric. But one always gets well-argued views, in all cases backed by powerful argument and challenge. And any book by her is going to be that. Well-argued, powerful, pragmatic and, on occasions, just a little radical and unconventional. That is why I like her so much and why I am so pleased to be invited to write this foreword. I am delighted to be associated with a Holbeche product. Be in no doubt that this book will be worth reading... and rereading. And know that your view on HR... and leadership, will be altered. Maybe for the better. Maybe just differently. But Linda Holbeche will challenge you and your thinking.

In HR, we can get a very precious thing. Especially about our status. Personally I think it's a confidence thing. I never see the same arguments put over by Finance, Sales, Marketing or Buying Directors about their level of influence, their role on the Board, their title et al. But in HR, we make a full-time job out of worrying about our position. Our title. Our level of influence. Whether the Chief Executive listens to us. What a load of tosh. If all that inspires confidence in those we manage, Lord help the next generation of HR leaders. They will be a very bitter, twisted and confused lot. To survive let alone develop, we must get out of this constant cathartic self-analysis. It is indulgent and destructive. It serves no purpose. Not for us or the next generation. I know Linda's views on all this. People like her and many of the individuals cited in this book are those whom the profession can have confidence in leading us out of this doldrum. Some of today's HR leaders – Chapman, Dando, Fairhurst, Kearney, Miller, O'Connor, Orme and Waters to name just a few – are top, top performers. People with an opinion about HR, and the way ahead. People who do it day by day. People who are 'stars' in every sense of the word. And people who have the leadership quality. I admire them, their ability and opinions. Whilst there are people of this ilk to lead, HR can change and get better.

Holbeche's strength is her pragmatism. Her book will not be just another HR theory offering. Yes, it will give academic rigour to Linda's views. But it will also offer something additional. Something that gives a clue. Something that is helpful and practical. Linda says that there has never been a better time to lead from and in an HR role. I agree with her so long as we all take the encouragement to take HR strategic. Too many organisations still look to HR to transact its minutiae. Too many HR leaders allow this to happen. Not the ones I listed earlier, and I dare say quite a few more. But too often I still meet HR leaders who just don't get it.

The trouble is that there are too many practitioners who still regard the profession as one of welfare. When I think back into my 'earliest' working days, the 'staffing' department as it was then, was about all things of people. But it didn't do people. It did paper. Leave cards, payroll, contracts, timesheets, that type of thing. I must say they were pretty good at it too. And expensive. Someone else – usually the manager – spoke with the unions and did something akin to staff communications. Consultation was not so popular then. We all did as we were told. But you know I don't want to be a dinosaur when I say that some may regard it as a clearer model than the one that exists today. For them, my message is simple. Go and do something else. For the rest of us though, we have been through various changes and the function has developed. The leave card and 'chitty' bit is done in another way thankfully! Some organisations have really adopted the full contemporary HR model and made it work – and the type of individuals I named earlier sit in those organisations. For many, there are still remnants of that old 'welfare and staffing' department. Oh dear!

I believe in good HR. Properly enacted, it adds profit and value. David Smith, the ex-HR Director at Asda – and another gutsy and top performer – has a great way of saying it *'The mark of a great HR leader is being as un-HR like as possible.'* I buy that. And I buy Linda Holbeche too. For she has the intellectual gravitas to explain what HR leadership might look like and do in the future.

By now, you will sense that I have the highest respect and affection for Linda. I hope that her book might persuade the doubting Thomases about our future functionality and purpose and the leadership required to pull it off. Certainly, her combination of practical example and well-argued theory is a powerful mix. Amongst the shelves of many, many, many leadership books, I hope that this one might add just a unique dimension that helps to better place our profession. I commend it to you. I commend Linda to you. And I look forward to hear the reactions to a product – promised by her for so long – that puts the Holbeche stamp on our future direction!

Martin Tiplady
Director of Human Resources
Metropolitan Police Service
September 2009

Acknowledgements

I would like to thank the CIPD for supporting me with the writing of this book; in particular, Geoff Armstrong for his encouragement and support and Jackie Orme for her helpful contribution.

Gathering the content for this book has been very much a joint effort. First and foremost, my thanks go to my research collaborator Kelly Morgan of Hay Management who carried out a number of the interviews for this book. Kelly was a joy to work with – her enthusiasm, insights and professionalism made working on this project a real pleasure – thank you Kelly. My thanks also go to Martin Tiplady, HR Director of the Metropolitan Police, who has kindly written the Preface for this book.

Then my grateful thanks go to all the contributors to this book, especially those whose commentary I have directly included. I am immensely grateful for their openness, candour and generosity and I hope that I have done justice to their ideas and contribution. In many cases contributors have submitted themselves to several interviews, in at least one case over a 5-year period! Their willingness to share their experiences and help advance HR practice speaks volumes for them and for the HR profession.

I would also like to thank those contributors whose views I have not specifically referred to, but whose input has also helped shape my thinking at a formative stage of developing ideas for the book. I would include in this group HR professionals such as Neil Hayward, Francesca Okosi, Mary Canavan, Debbie Dear and Dave Gartenberg, as well as many others who took part in CIPD and other focus groups to address key aspects of the emerging HR leadership agenda. I would also include leading academics, such as John Purcell, David Guest and Dave Ulrich, whose work provides much inspiration. Also members of the HR and management press, in particular journalists from *People Management Magazine* and *Personnel Today*. I am grateful to Julia Tybura and the NHS HR Directors from the East of England who have shared their views on the future challenges facing the profession in the health sector. And I would like to thank my friend and collaborator Dr Mee-Yan Cheung-Judge for the use of material generated in our joint articles on organisational development.

And my thanks are also due to my former colleagues at the CIPD, especially members of the department previously known as Research and Policy on whose work I have drawn, and Barbara Salmon, Annie Bland and Dr Jill Miller for their help with sources and references. I would also like to thank researchers who have generated research for the CIPD to which I have referred and also organisations with whom the CIPD has collaborated such as MLab at London Business School to whose thought leadership I make reference.

Producing this book at speed has also required great teamwork from the publisher Butterworth-Heinemann. I should like to thank the former Commissioning Editor, Hayley Salter and Sarah Long who have managed the production process, and everyone involved at Butterworth-Heinemann for moving the project along at pace.

Finally, writing this book would not have been possible without considerable support and some sacrifice on the part of my dear husband Barney and my loving mother Elsie. I'd like to thank them both for their forbearance, kindness and encouragement, which mean a lot to me.

Linda Holbeche

The nature of HR leadership, like the HR contribution more generally, is in a state of rapid evolution. Indeed, the very term 'HR leadership' may seem something of a contradiction in terms to some people. After all, the HR Function is historically criticised for being reactive at best, a costly and cumbersome bureaucratic hindrance to progress at worst.

Given that HR leadership is something of a 'moveable feast', I am not claiming that this book sets out an encyclopaedic definition of HR leadership, as it is and always will be. Rather my purpose in writing this book is to take a snapshot in time about what effective HR leadership looks like now and where it might evolve to next. I also want to supply encouragement and inspiration to people aspiring to an HR leader role from the examples of what real HR leaders currently do.

I am delighted that a number of the people I consider HR leaders have agreed to contribute to this book, making this 'snapshot' something of a shared effort. I have included many of their perspectives and provided illustrations of their approaches. I have also taken into account the views of leading academics throughout the book.

What I have aimed to show is that HR leadership is not only about developing and managing a good HR team but also about making a sustainable difference to the fortunes of organisations, their employees, customers and other stakeholders. After all, that is the point of HR, and the purpose of HR leadership. And there has never been a better time for HR to demonstrate leadership. In today's fast-changing times I believe that HR leadership can be a vital shaping force to organisational success – which makes this an exciting time to be an HR professional. An HR leader perspective is whole organisation, its strategic requirements and capabilities.

I have organised the content of the book as follows: Chapter 1 provides an overview of what I consider to be key elements of HR leadership and of some of the drivers for change in the business environment. The context is significant since it both creates the challenges and provides the rationale for the HR leadership agenda. It also requires HR leaders to be able to both adapt to the changing constraints and also to seize the opportunities the context provides. For me HR leadership is not synonymous with rank or hierarchy, even though many of the people featured in this book have achieved senior or executive positions, in every case by demonstrating HR leadership on the way up the ladder. For me HR leadership is a mindset, one which combines a strategic approach with a pragmatic process orientation and drives change in ways which create sustainable success. The focus is on individuals, organisations and their customers, on today and tomorrow, on developing and realising potential and performance for maximum competitive advantage.

Of course theory is all very well but when organisations are under pressure, action speaks louder than words. And at the time of writing, the pace of change and the challenges arising from the economic crisis mean that in many organisations short-term approaches are rife. So throughout the book I shall illustrate how some HR leaders are managing to both respond to immediate business needs and retain a longer-term perspective resulting in well-focused efforts which should equip their organisations for recovery and growth.

In Chapter 2 I shall introduce you more fully to the HR leaders who will be part of this book's story, describing their journey to HR leadership. This book is not intended to be a hagiography and none of these people would describe themselves as textbook role models of some set of ideal HR leader characteristics. They are real people doing real jobs, often in very challenging circumstances. Indeed, they have openly shared the sometimes painful learning they have experienced along the way. However, each in their own way demonstrates the ability to make a real difference to their organisations' success now, and have also laid the pathway to future success. With their different backgrounds they have amassed experience in all the major people-intensive sectors, in organisations large and small, national, international and global. A brief biography of these contributors appears at the end of this Introduction.

What do HR leaders do and how? What do they focus on? In Chapter 3 we consider the essence of an HR leader perspective and its related strategic HR agenda. On the one hand HR leaders are line managers of their function, accountable for specific functional deliverables. But simply being successful at running an HR operation in the conventional sense is not an automatic qualification for the 'HR leadership' title.

HR leadership is about more than that. It is fundamentally a business driver and enabler. HR leaders need to proactively drive change to improve governance, enhance performance and flexibility, build employee commitment and make their organisation a 'talent magnet'. Their ultimate responsibility is ensuring that organisations have the capacity and the capability to sustain high performance both now and in the future against a backdrop of fast-changing times. And in today's challenging economic climate, proactive HR leadership is needed more than ever, both to protect the organisation against loss of key talent or of productivity and also to equip the organisation for recovery.

HR leaders can change the economics of a business, but that does not usually happen by accident or by the wave of a magic wand. HR leaders are business leaders, as responsible as other business leaders for strategy formulation and implementation. At senior levels, they are strategic advisers of chief executive officers (CEOs) and executive teams, responsible for developing leadership from the most senior levels down throughout the organisation. They have the task of ensuring that their organisations' culture is changeable, customer-focused and stimulates innovation.

To fulfil this role requires HR leaders to be both thought and practice leaders. Theirs is a truly strategic and corporate perspective, based on a deep understanding of what the organisation is and could be. To lead rather than follow, HR leaders approach HR's conventional responsibilities = compliance, talent, leadership, performance and change = in ways which protect and advance their organisations' fortunes in an ethical way. In particular, in order to create and deliver this people and culture agenda, HR leaders need the ability to influence key stakeholders. Any HR leader who lacks a capable and effective HR team will lack the credibility to make a business relevant contribution and therefore cannot really be described as a leader. They will fail the 'why should I listen to you about people management?' test.

Over the following five chapters we consider key aspects of the HR leader agenda. In Chapter 4 we look at how some of our contributors have been transforming their Functions to free up HR to provide value-adding services. They describe how they align their strategies with business goals and how success is measured. In Chapter 5 we look at their approaches to Talent Management. Strategic workforce planning is a key requirement for understanding the organisation's future talent requirements. In planning their talent approaches HR leaders also take account of the needs of the changing and increasingly diverse workforce and have the challenge of creating an enticing employer brand which appeals to different generations of employees. We consider whether employee expectations may be changing as a result of growing unemployment and job insecurity and what employer practices might represent enlightened self-interest with respect to talent management.

In Chapter 6 we consider whether new forms of leadership will be required to lead organisations into their next phase. In particular we shall consider how leaders and leadership can be developed at all levels. In Chapter 7 we focus on HR's role in leading change, both large-scale and incremental. We consider where HR leaders need to focus if they are to build their organisations' readiness for ongoing change. In Chapter 8 we look at the significant role HR leaders need to play in ensuring that business and organisational practice are effective and ethical. Issues such as the part played by executive compensation and 'the bonus culture' in contributing to the recent banking crisis have highlighted the need for HR to exercise a leadership role with respect to how these HR levers such as reward are used. I have included the views of contributors about what they believe can and should be done to ensure that good practice can prevail, without HR simply reverting to company 'police officer' stereotype.

In Chapters 9 and 10 we examine the kinds of attitudes, capacities and capabilities that are needed in an HR leadership role. How do you develop these? What kinds of career paths equip you for an HR leadership role? Most of today's executives came up through the HR ranks in-house and were trained on the job, specialising in HR disciplines or gaining mastery across disciplines. Given the new HR structures and organisations, this career path is likely to disappear. It is probable that the entry point for HR careers will increasingly be with outsourcing vendors or consulting firms, creating more specialists than generalists in future.

Finally, we look into the future to consider where HR may be heading. Increasingly as the importance of people to business success becomes a recognised reality, HR roles are becoming conflated with general management roles and vice versa. There are many more non-HR specialists leading HR functions at senior levels now than in the past and more CEOs are leading the people agenda, with the potential result that the role of HR leader risks being reduced to that of implementer rather than initiator of great people strategy. These scenarios raise questions such as: are HR specialists best equipped to lead HR into the next phase? Are HR specialists best placed to lead businesses? I conclude that leaders of the people dimension must increasingly take an active role in shaping the nature of HR leadership and the development of the profession itself, unless they want others to do it for them – which would of course mean that they are not acting as leaders.

But first let me introduce you to the main contributors to this book. Most of these HR leaders have significant achievements to their name both within and beyond their own organisations. Their diverse industry backgrounds reflect the fact that few, if any, have stayed in the same sector or industry where their career began. Between them, these HR leaders have worked in most of the people-intensive industries of our time whether these are in the commercial, not-for-profit or public sectors. I chose to include them because they are self-evidently HR leaders.

And while in an ideal world I would have interviewed many more of the people whose HR leadership approaches I also admire, time was not on my side. I am very content that the blend of experience represented by these contributors provides rich insights into the evolving nature of HR leadership and I am very grateful for their input.

MAIN CONTRIBUTOR BIOGRAPHIES

Geoff Armstrong CBE, Formerly Director-General, the Chartered Institute of Personnel and Development (CIPD)

Until June 2008, Geoff was Director-General of the CIPD, the HR professional body with over 130,000 members across the UK and Ireland. Throughout his 16 year tenure, Geoff led the development of the Institute into becoming a professional body with considerable international stature. He was responsible for creating the Institute of Personnel and Development (IPD) from the merger of the Institute of Personnel Management (IPM) and the Institute of Training and Development (ITD). He also led the process to achieve Chartered status for the IPD and its members. Geoff also served as the elected President of the World Federation of Personnel Management Associations, representing more than 70 national associations. He has worked internationally at board level in the automobile, engineering and banking industries and has served on a range of government committees and working parties.

Victoria Bird

Victoria Bird began her career in retailing completing a degree in Retail Management and roles at Harrods and Marks and Spencer but she too wanted a creative challenge. After her first management position, gaining a good commercial grounding in retail, she moved to the music division of Time Warner in 1996. Electronic Arts followed where she was dubbed by *Personnel Today* 'A Young HR Professional to Watch'. Currently taking a career break to pursue a Masters in Social Anthropology at SOAS. Victoria's later roles have included an international HR role for Whitbread and more recently HR Director for TSL Education.

Mike Campbell, People Director, easyJet

Mike (1957) joined easyJet in October 2005 as People Director. Prior to this Mike worked at Wedgwood in a broad role as Director of People and Brands and Managing Director for Canada, Australia and Pan-Asia. Previously Mike worked for 14 years at Fujitsu in a variety of development and personnel roles across Europe, Asia, Africa and the Middle East, ending up as Chief Personnel Officer. His early career was in education and research. Mike has a BSC in Mathematics and Masters in Fluid Dynamics. Mike and his team demonstrate the close integration of HR with the business.

Jonathan Evans, Director General HR, Defence Equipment and Support (DE&S) of the UK Ministry of Defence

Jonathan Evans is the Director General HR of the DE&S of the UK Ministry of Defence. He held a number of HR positions in the private sector, including Wiggins Teape, Lucas Aerospace and the Chloride Group. In 1990, he became one of the first 12 employees in a small business that then became Orange. In his 11 years as HR Director at Orange, he oversaw the growth of the company to 30,000 employees and the eventual sale to France Telecom for £30 bn. Before joining the DE&S in 2007, Jonathan also ran a small consultancy and worked with Westminster City Council.

David Fairhurst, Senior Vice President People (Northern Europe), McDonalds

David is **Senior Vice President People** (Northern Europe) reporting to the CEO and Divisional President of **McDonald's Restaurants** Limited. David gained broad HR experience before being recruited by *Transport Development Group (TDG)*. At TDG he created and established their HR function and was involved in a broad range of business issues. From there David joined *H J Heinz Co Ltd* as Area Manager Recruitment/Training and was promoted twice during a 4-year period, becoming the youngest Group Manager appointed by the business.

In August 1997, David has been appointed Director of Recruitment and Leadership Planning – Europe for *SmithKline Beecham*, establishing a large Shared Services department. David then took up the position of Group Resourcing Director *for Tesco Stores Ltd* in November 2000. He was given the additional accountability of Corporate HR Director. David was voted Personnel Today's Number One Power Player in HR in 2007–2008 and in June 2009 readers of Human Resources Magazine voted David the most influential HR practitioner.

Martin Ferber, Executive Director HR, International Region, R&D, Pfizer

Martin Ferber is currently Executive Director HR, International Region, R&D, a role he assumed in mid-2003 following the reorganisation of Pfizer's Global HR function. He is also Director and Chair, Pfizer Pension Trustees Ltd. Martin is a companion of the CIPD and previously held the 2-year post of Vice President International and is now a non-executive on the Board of CIPD.

Philippa Hird, Formerly Group HR Director, ITV plc, now Non-Executive Director, Her Majesty's Revenues and Customs (HMRC) *ITV plc*

After reading PPE at Queens' College, Oxford, Philippa joined ICI as a Management Trainee, moving on to become a Marketing Manager. In 1988, she joined Granada Television where she held a variety of line management posts which included creative programme making departments, the Casting department and the creation of a new Rights Management department.

In 1996, following Granada's takeover of London Weekend Television (LWT), Philippa became Head of Personnel for LWT. In 1997, she became Director of Personnel for Granada Media, which by then had acquired Yorkshire Television, and at the beginning of 2001, Personnel Director for Granada plc. In 2004, Philippa became Group HR Director for ITV plc to manage her fourth ITV merger (Granada and Carlton).

Philippa is a Fellow of the CIPD and was formerly CIPD Vice President with responsibility for Employee Relations. She sat on the Board of Skillset (the Sector Skills Council for the Audiovisual industries) and on the Opportunity Now Advisory Board. She is a Fellow of the RSA and a member of the RTS. Philippa is currently a Non-Executive Director of HMRC and the Polka Theatre and has recently begun to build a portfolio career as a Non-Executive Director and Writer developing a new career direction as a writer and consultant.

Liane Hornsey, Director HR and Staffing, EMEA, Google

The face behind Google's people strategy, Liane Hornsey, started her career outside HR. She has a commercial background in sales and marketing and then moved into change management. '*I had no desire to work in HR whatsoever,*' she says. '*I moved into it because a company I worked for wanted someone to work on organisational change and transition. That transition was about making the company more organisationally focused and I was in sales and marketing so they pulled me to be an internal consultant.*' Hornsey then got involved with organisational design and HR, followed by a move into the function proper in 1992. Previous roles have been with BT as Group Head of Change Management, Bertelsmann Music Group (BMG) as Vice President HR Europe, Ntl Group as Group HR Director and Lastminute.com as Group HR Director.

Anne Minto OBE, Group Director, HR, Centrica Plc

Anne Minto has been Group Director HR for the integrated energy supplier Centrica plc since 2002 and sits on the Centrica Executive Committee. Her main areas of interest are senior leadership succession and development, executive remuneration and organisational change. She is also Chairman of the Centrica Pension Schemes. A qualified lawyer by profession, she worked in Shell for 13 years where she held a number of senior commercial management roles. In 1993, she became Deputy Director General of the Engineering Employers' Federation (EEF), representing the interests of 6000 engineering and manufacturing businesses to the UK Government and the European Union (EU) Institutions. In 1998, she joined the global engineering manufacturer, Smiths Group plc as Group HR Director.

She is a Fellow of the CIPD, FCIM and FRSA. She is heavily involved in schemes such as Year in Industry and Women in Science & Engineering and was a former Chairman of both the Engineering Development Trust and the Institute of Employment Studies. She was awarded an OBE for services to the Engineering Industry in 2000 and appointed a Fellow of the London City & Guilds Imperial College in 2008. She is Patron of the University of Aberdeen Alumni Fund.

Angela O'Connor, National Policing Improvement Agency (NPIA), Chief People Officer

Angela O'Connor is Chief People Officer at the NPIA. She is head of profession for police HR staff in England and Wales and leads on Police Learning, Development and Leadership, People Strategy and organisational development.

Following a number of years in the private sector she has spent the majority of her career in the public sector. She has been in senior HR roles at three London local authorities, Haringey, Hackney and Enfield. Her HR teams have been the recipients of numerous awards for equality and diversity, recruitment and innovative HR practices. She was headhunted from Enfield to the Crown Prosecution Service (CPS) in 2002 where she led a national HR team determined to ensure that the CPS became a world-class prosecuting authority. In 2006 she took up the role of Chief People Officer in the NPIA.

She was named Personnel Director of the Year in 2005 at the Telegraph Business Awards, and HR Director of the Year 2005 at the *Personnel Today* Awards and HR Director of the year in 2007 at the HR Excellence Awards. She is a Fellow of the CIPD and she appears frequently in the lists of the top 'power players'. She is a board director of Skills for Justice and has recently been elected as Vice President of the CIPD's Police Forum. Angela O'Connor is the Past President of The Public Sector People Managers Association and she was the first Civil Servant President in the organisation's 30-year history in 2006/2007.

Jackie Orme, Chief Executive, the CIPD

Jackie Orme has been CEO of the CIPD since April 2008. Jackie has been an HR practitioner for more than 17 years. She has worked across a broad range of sectors and HR specialisms. Her early years were spent in the Department of Employment and the Institute of Chartered Accountants before moving to work in the steel industry based in South Wales.

For the last 12 years, Jackie has worked for PepsiCo – including 7 years leading the UK and Ireland HR functions and sitting on both the UK Executive Board of PepsiCo International and the global PepsiCo International HR Council, during a time of impressive business growth and success.

She also sits on the Board of Shelter, the housing and homelessness charity.

Jon Sparkes, Chief Executive, Scope

Jon joined Scope, the national disability charity in March 2004 as Executive Director HR, moving to become Deputy Chief Executive and Executive Director for Organisational Change in 2006. He was appointed acting Chief Executive in June 2006 and took up the CEO role from the beginning of February 2007.

Prior to working at Scope, Jon was Head of HR at Cambridgeshire County Council. He previously worked in the private sector as HR Director for an international technology company, The Generics Group and was Organisational Development Manager at Southern Derbyshire Training and Enterprise Council and HR Manager at GEC-Plessey Telecommunications.

Jon has also been also a Governor of a Further Education College, two not-for-profit Social enterprises, and a trustee of a Charity on Autism. He is also the co author of the book *Leading HR* with Clive Morton and Andrew Newall.

From the end of 2009, Jon will now be returning to HR as Director of workforce development for the NHS in Cornwall and the Isles of Scilly.

David Smith, Formerly People Director of ASDA

David Smith is an HR Professional who has spent his entire career in the HR sphere. Until 2009, David was People Director of ASDA and a member of the ASDA Executive Board. In 2002, David added the Information Technology function to his Executive portfolio, and in 2004 he also took charge of Loss Prevention for the business. During his tenure, David and his team have introduced ground-breaking initiatives which resulted in not only ASDA being named one of the top UK places to work 5 years running by *The Sunday Times*, *FT* and *FORTUNE Magazine* but also David receiving the Sam Walton Award for his contribution to driving excellence in People Policies. Since then, David and the team have embarked on an exercise sharing ASDA best practice with colleagues in Wal-Mart.

David commenced his career in the Coal Industry and honed his Industrial Relations skills in the crucible of the miners' strike and subsequent restructuring of the Mining Industry in preparation for Privatisation. His career in the Industry spanned 19 years in a variety of locations and positions, where he developed a broad base of experience of the HR problems facing leaders. David has contributed to the Profession around HR by voluntary service as a commissioner with the Equal Opportunities Commission for 3 years and as a Vice President of the CIPD for Organisation and Resourcing. He is now pursuing a portfolio career as a writer and consultant.

Martin Tiplady, Director of HR for the Metropolitan Police Service

Martin Tiplady was appointed Director of HR of the Metropolitan Police Service in December 2001. Prior to that, he was group head of HR (The Berkeley Group plc 1999–2001), Director of HR (Westminster Health Care Holdings Plc 1995–1999) and Director of Personnel (The Housing Corporation 1987–1995). Martin started out in local Government, which he entered in 1969, progressing to the position of Assistant Director of Social Services for the London Borough of Haringey. In 1987, he took up the post of Director of Personnel for the Housing Corporation. From there he moved to Westminster Healthcare Holdings Plc in 1995 to be the organisation's first Director of HR and develop the function effectively from scratch.

Martin is a member of the Association of Chief Police Officers (ACPO) and is the Deputy Chair of the ACPO Workforce Development and HR portfolio. He is a member of various HR think tanks and review bodies. In November 2004, he was named by *The Daily Telegraph* as 'Personnel Director of the Year'. He is regularly named by the HR press as one of the most influential people in HR.

Martin Tiplady is a Chartered Companion of the CIPD. He was – until November 2008 – a Vice President of the CIPD and is also now a non-executive director at Roffey Park Business Institute. He is a member of the MBA Advisory Board for the University of Westminster and a trustee of the Employers Forum on Age and Faith.

Graham White, Director of HR, Westminster City Council

Graham is Director of HR at Westminster City Council, which employs about 4900 staff. Prior to joining Westminster Council, Graham was Head of HR and Organisational Development for Surrey County Council. There Graham was responsible for delivering the entire HR remit for the Council's workforce of 33,000, including Strategic Human Capital Management, Career Succession Planning, Talent Management and Pay & Workforce Planning.

Surrey County Council undertook a fundamental review of HR service delivery with major non value-added and transactional activities either outsourced or operated within a Shared Service Centre approach. This reduced the HR team from almost 400 to just 40 and took 9 million pounds out of the budget. Graham is openly against the business partner model and regularly speaks on the benefits of being in a business not just partnering with it.

His breadth of experience and expertise in HR and Personnel Management covers both the public and private sectors with positions in a variety of commercial, public and financial institutions including manufacturing, service, banking, policing and both central and local governments.

Graham is a Fellow of the CIPD and a Fellow of the Institute of Directors.

Chapter 1

The Time Is Now...

'In today's business climate, the opportunity is there for HR to claim responsibility for the productivity of the corporation through the maximisation of human intelligence, interaction and skill.'

(Losey et al., 2005)

If the economic crisis has taught us anything it is that people and people management practice can make or break businesses and entire economies. We have also learned that conventional ways of doing business are going to have to change. And that has big implications for HR whose leaders will need to equip their organisations for futures which for the time being we can only glimpse at, and which the pace of change dictates will be just around the corner.

The impact of the recession has been so profound that as business leaders start to shift their focus towards the recovery, many are keen to learn how to navigate ongoing turbulence in a way that will help their businesses not just survive but also thrive in the future. What seems clear is that conventional short-term approaches to running business are unlikely to produce success which can be sustained in fast-changing times.

Because fast change is bound to continue, even if perhaps not quite so turbulently as during the crisis, it is to be hoped. Today's organisations will face ongoing cost challenges, increasing competition, tougher regulation and growing skills shortages. Their practices will also be subject to much greater scrutiny than in the past. So how can things be managed so as to avoid a vicious circle of futile change activity?

Leaders and managers in all sectors are going to have to embark on the search for *sustainable* performance. And HR leadership is needed to make that achievable. As one participant in a focus group of HR Directors put it: 'Chief Executive Officers (CEOs) are looking at us now and saying, where do we go when we come out of this? With every downturn there's always an upturn. I think you are going to see top talent come through these times – those that adapt to it very well, and those that are really struggling.'

These business drivers, and the related work practices and cultures required for sustainable performance, are the rationale for HR leadership. The time is right to shift from *reacting* to *proacting*. More than ever organisations need HR leaders with the vision and the deep capability to build organisational cultures and business leadership which are fit for both the present and future.

WHAT IS HR LEADERSHIP?

What is distinctive about HR leadership as opposed to any other form of leadership? At one level HR leaders are just like any other business leader. They are line managers with teams who deliver a service, directly or indirectly. However, HR leaders have a broader playing field – their arena is the organisation as whole. Their time horizon is both the immediate and the medium term. Their products are the processes which add value to the sources of production and successful delivery to customers. Their raw materials are the people who create and deliver these services or products to companies. Their distinctive contribution is how they build their organisation's capability to deliver the business strategy in the short and medium terms.

Leadership Styles

Is there an overall approach which defines an HR leader's style? Of course different leaders have different leadership styles and approaches. Ulrich and Smallwood's (2007) thinking on 'leadership brand' suggests that the results required of leaders should dictate the nature of leadership provided. The nature of the HR leader's task may therefore incline them to certain styles and behaviours. Bens (2007) for instance distinguishes between two straightforward leadership style categories – traditional directive and more facilitative styles. Directive leaders:

- Are task-focused;
- Set direction and make strategic decisions;
- Control work assignments;
- Work with people individually;
- Control information;
- Retain the right to make decisions;
- Place a minor emphasis on people skills;
- Have rank and privileges;
- Relate in a distant and formal style;
- Communicate down;
- Hold few meetings;
- Rarely give or receive feedback;
- Feel that staff work for them; and
- Retain accountability for outcomes.

HR leaders featured in this book can be, and are directive when the situation demands it, or by preference. And in certain situations the directive mode can be very effective, for instance when the leader possesses expertise that is essential to the operation and when staff members need both direction and oversight to do their jobs. They are primarily accountable for the results their people achieve.

However, more generally HR leaders appear to exercise more facilitative leadership styles. Bens argues that these are more appropriate in today's workplaces since most have become more informal in recent years. Facilitative leaders have been increasingly sensitised to age group, gender and diversity issues. Many have worked on teams and have developed their meeting skills. These leaders are communicative and people-savvy. These more engaging leaders are still highly involved in directing tasks, but they combine this with an increased focus on both improving how work gets done and enhancing inter-personal relations. Facilitative leaders offer process and structure rather than direction and answers. They possess the ability to put a process around a challenging situation to help resolve a problem or create an opportunity for their business.

Leadership Functions

In common with other business leaders, HR leaders carry out the following generic categories of leadership functions:

- Provide direction;
- Lead with courage;
- Influence others;
- Foster team working;
- Motivate others;
- Develop others;
- champion change; and
- Learn continuously.

(Adapted from Davis et al., 1992)

As we go through the book, we shall explore how the HR leaders featured in the book exercise these different leadership functions and where and how HR leadership differs from other forms of leadership in the way HR carries out these functions.

THE 'LICENCE TO PLAY'

Since applying the term 'leadership' to the HR function is a relatively new concept, by what rights does HR exercise leadership? Where does an HR leader's authority come from?

Line Managing the HR Function

Of course HR leaders lead the HR function, but a Functional Head is not a leader simply by dint of job title. To be an HR leader means exercising functional leadership in a way which demonstrates new and innovative thinking about how to deliver the strategic and operational imperatives of the business. In the past, HR's stakeholders were all considered to be internal – employees, senior line management or executives. Now HR's key stakeholders are a wider group and include customers, investors and society as a whole, as we shall see in Chapters 3 and 4.

An effective HR leader needs a high-calibre, high-performing HR team, suitably organised to produce key 'deliverables' which matter to key stakeholders. Without great delivery, an HR leader's credibility is shot and HR leaders aim to provide world-class execution. Ulrich and Brockbank (2005) argue that HR professionals must grasp and master the concept of value: '*value in this light is defined by the receiver more than the giver. HR professionals add value when their work helps someone reach their goals. It is not the design of a program or declaration of policy that matters most, but what recipients gain from these actions. In a world of increasingly scarce resources, activities that fail to add value are not worth pursuing.*'

Delivering value-adding services involves generating new models of service delivery and technical solutions, understanding the possible costs and return on investment of changes in operations. This is not just about streamlining HR to achieve cost-savings but also about understanding where and how to impact on operations in a measurably effective way, such that profitability, share price and price/earnings ratios can be directly improved as a result. HR has to balance both short-term requirements and longer-term organisational needs, focusing on local activities and also on corporate integration. This both/and strategic tension requires HR practitioners to combine a pragmatic focus and a can-do approach to excellent short-term delivery with a more strategic orientation and perspective on what will equip the organisation for future success.

Thought and Practice Leaders

Leading an HR team is not an end in itself: it is a means to a bigger end, i.e. to help the organisation as a whole to function well and have the capabilities it requires both now and in the future. As leaders of the people dimension, HR leaders need both deep insight into what makes people tick and also into what can make organisations become the source of sustainable competitive advantage.

HR leadership is about adding value through shaping the organisational agenda – by trading on the leader's insights and having the expertise to back it up. This expertise takes many forms from professional talent management, supporting the change readiness of the organisation or part of it at critical times in its evolution, through to helping the organisation find, for instance, a new solution to pension deficit challenges. We shall explore what it means to develop an influential perspective in Chapter 3.

This requires HR leaders to have an organisational mindset, and be able to act as thought and practice leaders. As thought leaders, HR leaders need a perspective on the key issues facing their organisation and the ability to influence others in ways which result in beneficial action. For Ulrich and Brockbank (2005) this is 'a perspective that is compatible with, and distinct from, other business perspectives. That is, they must be able to understand and value the finance and sales perspectives, but they must also add their own point of view. Without such a unique and powerful perspective, they are redundant and fail in their aspirations as full business contributors'. Equipped with this perspective, HR leaders can make a major contribution to the way their organisation's strategy gets implemented.

To add even more value, HR Directors need to contribute to the strategy process not just at the implementation phase but when the strategy is being formulated. But if their strategic focus is purely with respect to the HR function, their value will be diminished. Their focus must be about the business as a whole (Sparrow et al., 2008). They need to understand the financial implications of their ideas and choices not just for own function but for other parts of the business.

In this fast-changing context, HR leaders need to be future focused and tuned in to changing business, economic and other trends, not least the changing demographics and labour market. As Losey et al. (2005) suggest: 'it is critical for HR leaders to accurately anticipate the future and how such changes may affect their accountability. This anticipatory and initiating capacity marks out a leader from followers. Without the capacity to anticipate and accurately plan for changes in the business landscape, coping strategies cannot be proactive – they can only be reactive – and at a much higher cost.'

Simply scanning the changing context for trends which will affect the business is not enough. HR leaders also need to be 'strategic progenitors', according to Hesketh and Hird (2008), with 'the capacity to lead strategic thinking with the full support and recognition of their CEO and finance director, rather than just following or implementing others' ideas'. To be strategy progenitors, HR leaders need to be innovators, seeing corporate level strategic possibilities before other executives.

Building the Foundations for Sustainable Success

HR leadership fundamentally involves identifying and building the organisational capabilities required for sustainable success. Jackie Orme, Chief Executive of the CIPD, believes that HR's contribution to this is about unlocking competitive capability. According to Ulrich and Brockbank (2005), HR leaders must understand how HR strategies can be geared to helping organisations to continuously pass the 'wallet test'. In other words, how the organisation can continuously create products and services that result in 'our customers taking money out of their wallets and putting it into ours' instead of giving it to our customers?' To do this HR must work back from the needs of investors and customers to understand the organisational and employee capabilities that a company must have in order to respond to short-term and longer-term market demands and seize opportunities to create value.

Above all, a leaders of the people dimension HR leaders need a point of view about how this can be achieved through people. And this insight or perspective allows HR professionals to see and interpret aspects of the business environment in ways which are different from, and go beyond what other disciplines can bring, and add substantially to business success.

Talent

A traditional key capability for any organisation is the quality of its people; how they are managed and developed. And the economic crisis has reinforced that point with many business leaders – that it is the quality and contribution of their people that will drive business performance. They really do mean what they say when they utter the phrase, 'our people are our greatest asset'.

HR leaders are the talent experts. CEOs will look to HR leaders to deliver them both the talent and the infrastructure for competitive advantage through people. Today's talent can be sourced from across the world and in a globalised economy HR leaders should be prepared to manage a global workforce. HR leaders need to be proficient at developing and promoting talent from anywhere and creating the infrastructure to build a high-performing global workforce. Indeed, it could be argued that people and talent have become the new operations of the business since IT and other e-enabled systems and processes are increasingly outsourced.

So is HR leadership ready and able to deliver the talent solutions which organisations need both now and for the future? This will mean managing new types of relationships and adapting to a diverse population in terms of needs, business requirements, and cultural expectations. It will also involve making sure that even during the economic crisis, HR leaders are delivering on their employer brand. As one HRD put it: *'Anyone can come up with a sexy brand, do a great advertising campaign and get people through the door, but if there's no honesty or clarity through that selection process, then you are going to have high turnover.'*

Performance

HR leaders are also performance orchestrators (not only enabling but actually driving performance). The role of HR in driving performance was explored by Ulrich in *The Human Resource Champions* (1997). Hesketh and Hird (2008) argue that HR leadership is about more than articulating or accounting for HR's value proposition; it is more than enabling the business to perform and score card holders to deliver service–critical operations; it is more than generating new models of HR service delivery, or the 'orchestrating of performance-enhancing transformations of people and operations and their underpinning architectural forms'. It is about leading the process of performance transformation with, or ahead of the CEO and other executive colleagues. It involves getting key players to align on their understanding of the underlying strategic, operational, financial and people issues and providing them with a route map to solutions and opportunities.

Building Resilient Cultures

HR leaders understand that even the best talent will not thrive in a toxic or stagnant organisational culture. Many aspects of the economic crisis have flagged up where cultural practices and norms, such as leadership behaviours, standards and governance, need to improve. Conventionally, HR roles involve control and compliance. In today's business environment, compliance and risk management are likely to be even greater areas of focus. However an HR leader does not approach governance and risk management as a mere box-ticking compliance exercise, but as a means of proactively building better business practice and creating healthier, more ethical business cultures.

The crisis has also highlighted the need for greater strategic anticipation, flexibility and speed of response, along with the importance of keeping an intense focus on customers. It has also drawn attention to the need for customer focus and renewal – innovation in products and services, employer brands, ways of working, management styles, organisational structures and processes. A performance-driven culture has flatter structures, characterised by learning, collaboration and team working across boundaries. HR puts the structures and processes in place and helps develop the management approaches to support high performance working.

HR leaders therefore support and challenge business leaders to not only deliver today's business agenda but also to lay firm foundations for tomorrow's success. Since no organisation stands apart from its context, it is to the fast-changing business context, and its related challenges for society, business and individuals that we turn our attention now. Right now, the predominantly short-term focus of many management teams puts the longer-term capability building described above at risk.

A CHALLENGING CONTEXT

Today's ongoing economic turbulence brings to a climax a turbulent decade on the world scene. Epoch-making events such as the attacks on the World Trade Centre in New York on September 11, 2001, terrorist attacks in Bali, Madrid and elsewhere and the 'War on Terror' involving protracted military campaigns in Afghanistan and Iraq. The increasing fragmentation between peoples on the grounds of belief and political ideology is being acted out daily in various theatres of war.

At the same time, there is greater there is greater public awareness than ever. News global connectedness than ever. Thanks to the digital revolution, and the power of the Internet and global media to spread ideas and communication instantly, travels fast and there are few boundaries which cannot be crossed in this way. After all, the 'Facebook generation' is not restricted by age or geography. Consumer tastes everywhere have been shaped by global brands and the power of 'viral' marketing is such that ideas can be shared and acted on via social media within hours, as President Obama puts to good use in his presidential campaign. The customer service revolution has given way to a customer-focused revolution and better use of technology and data to provide increasingly personalised goods and services.

Corporate reputations can be both a major asset and a key business risk, as several major corporations would attest. The use of social media is also enabling individuals and groups to share their concerns, for instance, about the environment and climate change, and the growing awareness of the issues is leading to pressure on national and international governments to act. Similarly, corporate social responsibility has been propelled up executive agendas as consumers and employees desert brands which appear to do more harm than good to the environment or people.

A key underlying economic trend is the seemingly inexorable spread of globalisation, with the balance of global economic power appearing to gradually shift away from the US and Europe in favour of China and India in particular. Technology is enabling small as well as large firms to compete globally, and firms to outsource operations of various sorts to other parts of the world.

The knowledge and service economies have seen major growth in recent years, especially in the US and Europe. Materially, the West has enjoyed a lengthy 'boom time' fuelled by cheap credit. Workers in sectors such as banking and consultancy have benefited from large bonuses, giving them enormous purchasing power and generally pushing up prices and demand for luxury goods.

This period of plenty has meant a tight labour market with low unemployment in countries such as the UK. So great has been the demand for different kinds of labour in recent years that the year 2000 heralded what McKinsey dubbed the 'War for Talent' with organisations competing for much needed highly skilled knowledge workers in fields as diverse as consultancy, medicine and teaching. In the UK, labour supply gaps, particularly for low skilled work, have been filled mostly by migrant workers from the EU accession states. However, as jobs became scarcer in 2009 the UK Prime Minister's promise of

'British jobs for British workers' came back to haunt him. Evidence of growing protectionism in both trade and employment is evident in most developed countries.

A Synchronised Global Downturn

The sheer speed with which the credit crunch and subsequent economic downturn have occurred is hard to credit. In early 2008, the UK economy seemed relatively stable. Then the unthinkable happened. By late 2008, formerly powerful banking brands had crashed and been partially brought into public ownership in some cases, leaving their brands and their leaders' reputations in tatters. For consumers, the era of cheap credit and seemingly endless purchasing possibilities has been replaced by 'new thrift'. As consumer spending declines, more businesses fail, putting further strain on the public purse. At the worst stage of the banking crisis, 500 essentially sound businesses were reported to fail everyday in the UK due to lack of available credit. Car manufacturing in particular is suffering due to a collapse in sales.

Banking has become a pariah industry, criticised for starving small businesses of much needed cash when banks themselves have been bailed out by government funding in many cases. As one senior bank employee put it: '*After the banking crisis started and when I met new people, I stopped saying who I worked for and just said I worked in marketing. It's a bit of a relief now that I can say I'm a civil servant!*' No wonder then that the UK government has sought to discourage the big bonus culture in banking which is thought to be responsible at least in part for the rash and even unethical behaviour which led to the current crisis.

Businesses Under Strain

Managing in a recession does put a special focus on short-term survival. Executives typically focus entirely on the immediate business requirements, and attempt to conserve cash. But alongside the recession, business executives are also wrestling with the ongoing longer-term challenges of globalisation and increased competition, slower growth and declining markets.

There is increased competition and shifting centres of economic activity, with the balance of global economic power appearing to gradually shift away from the US and Europe in favour of China and India in particular. China and India are on the threshold of competing with the West for knowledge-intensive work, becoming major providers of service consultancy alongside manufacturing and outsourced service supply. Technology is enabling small as well as large firms to compete globally, and firms to outsource operations of various sorts to other parts of the world.

The global energy crisis, including environmental costs and impacts, provides ongoing challenges. Technology provides both threats and opportunities, many of which are brilliantly exploited commercially by small, nimble firms operating in the developing world. Similarly, high levels of connectivity are changing how companies advertise and deliver their services, and how they are judged by a savvy global public. The need to provide service excellence and respond to ever-changing consumer demands means that continuous improvement and innovation have to be standard operational features. These are just some of the issues which are reported to keep executives awake at night. (Source: *Future World,* Dec 2008).

No-One Saw It Coming

So why did no one see this economic crisis coming? And while wisdom after the event is all very well, what can be learned from recent events that might protect organisations and the broader economy in the future?

In a funny kind of way, the credit crunch and the subsequent economic crisis have highlighted the need for a major step change in business practice to a more strategic and sustainable approach. If organisations are to become more resilient they will need more robust yet flexible business models that can adapt to changing times Better still, if organisations are to get onto the front foot with respect to economic turbulence and they will need to develop the ability to strategically anticipate and help shape events to produce better outcomes I believe that the leaders at all levels will need to master the art of strategic anticipation, i.e. the ability to look ahead, gather intelligence, test assumptions, plan continuously and execute brilliantly if they want to help their organisations survive and thrive.

Leadership Challenges

Business leaders will need to act as organisational leaders, taking ownership of the capability building for their organisation. Just as pharmaceutical companies and others invest heavily in research and development, so most other organisations must also invest in developing new ways of operating which will equip them for future success.

Organisations will need to be capable of not only reacting to change but also embracing and thriving on it, making and seizing opportunities in the midst of turbulence. In other words they will need to be changeable (i.e. innovative, flexible and agile) and capable of speed, tighter cost management and higher quality. However, speed must not be obtained at the expense of greater risk and risk management is likely to become more challenging as governance processes tighten. Managing both innovation and risk will be just one of many dilemmas managers will need to deal with. Developing measurement and management systems that embrace rather than avoid it will be one way of reconciling seeming dilemmas.

Organisations must also be intensely focused on their customers and deliver value. Margins will be squeezed ever more tightly as businesses compete even harder so the challenge will be to build even greater value while driving for greater efficiency and effectiveness. Organisations will increasingly both compete and collaborate across supply chains and organisational boundaries will become increasingly blurred, especially in the public sector where cost saving requirements will become more intense.

How will leaders lead in the new world? This question does not apply just to financial services – the things coveted in the past, such as short-term delivery, may not be the key attributes we need in our leaders, or the strategies we need to adopt to equip ourselves for the future. As one HR Director from a pharmaceutical company in a *Personnel Today* focus group put it: *'The drugs to treat cholesterol, high blood pressure, asthma, diabetes – the big block-buster ones – are all going off patent in all the large companies at about the same time, between 2011 and 2013, so there's a race to see who is going to replace their pipeline first. The agenda for big pharmaceutical companies is aggressive growth, acquisition pipelines, emerging markets, and also cost reduction. So the situation in our industry is not necessarily survival or massive cost-cutting; there's a longer-term nature to our cost reduction. For example, the 20% cost reduction target across our support functions is over three years.'*

'We are looking at what capabilities it takes to deliver on this sort of strategy. That is quite different to the type of leadership that was rewarded and recognised in the past; it is one where excellent execution capabilities are required, and about how can we speed up some of these timelines that we have in place. Rather than select individuals out, it's more: what do we need to develop now?' Another HR Director commented that *'the additional challenge of getting people on the bus is the fact that the leaders at the top are struggling to know where the bus is actually going, because of how fast-moving, complex and challenging the environment is.'*

Of course, leadership is not reducible to what leaders do, or who they are, or even the capabilities they possess. It is how they do what they do, and who they do leadership with that matters. The challenge is to define and develop good leadership, incorporating leadership capabilities into organisation culture. We shall examine these matters further in Chapter 6.

Ethics – the Need for Trust, Truth and Transparency

But alongside pressures on businesses, and the related leadership and HR challenges, the social consequences of the crisis are no less profound. While this may be a cliché, it is clearer than ever that what happens in the broader economy affects business and society as a whole, and vice versa. And in the case of recession, negative consequences appear quickly. Since workers are citizens too, they will be affected by the growing societal trends, directly or indirectly, and there appear to be some serious shifts in the public psyche taking place.

The crisis has flagged up the need for better corporate, civil and political leadership, since levels of public trust in civil and political and business leaders are generally reported to be at an all-time low. What the crisis has made apparent is that the success of organisations and their leaders are inextricably linked with the performance of their counterparts. The reverberations across the financial services industry, which have toppled previously 'untouchable' corporate leaders and indelibly tarnished personal and corporate reputations, would bear witness to that.

The UK parliament's own procedures came under the spotlight when the MPs' expenses scandal hit the headlines in 2009. The initial reluctance of the former Speaker Michael Martin to open up the issue to public scrutiny seemed to confirm prejudices amongst those who saw parliamentarians as self-serving. Similarly various accusations of 'sleaze' and criticisms of the roles of unelected 'advisers' to Government ministers have done little to allay public concerns. The demands for truth and transparency seem to reflect the loss of trust, with journalists cast in the role of 'seekers after truth'. And while MPs are now subject to stricter controls on what they claim in expenses, the calls for greater transparency and improved standards in public life are being translated into moves towards stronger regulation and tough compliance regimes more generally to fill the 'trust void'.

As HR leaders consider the changing context, they reflect on how the expectations and needs of employees and customers are changing and how these might affect what people want from organisations. Are there bigger shifts taking place in society and what people expect of leaders, as well as of politics, institutions and organisations? If increases in unemployment and a slow-down in recruitment result in large numbers of people who have to draw on public benefits, and young people who despair of making a start on the career ladder or owning their own home, we could be at risk of another 'lost generation' who miss out on career opportunities or never get back on the career ladder. If frustrations bubble over and produce unwelcome attitudes such as hostility towards migrant workers, and even civil unrest, things will prove very bleak indeed.

Towards New Business Practice

Equally, if as a result of greater public awareness of some of the causes of the current crisis there is a step change in perspectives about the role and purpose of business and about the need for ethics and accountability in public life, then some good may come of it. This is likely to generate a continuing debate about how organisations can achieve sustainable performance in every sense. For instance:

- Should organisations be accountable to organisations a wider group of stakeholders than shareholders alone?

- Will leaders have to be more values-led than just market-led?
- What will be the implications of greater transparency for the way business will operate going forward, including how people are rewarded?
- Will employees want and expect different things from their employer?

Demands for Greater Accountability

It could be argued that the days have largely gone when business leaders considered that their only duty was to their shareholders. Now stakeholders are demanding greater accountability. Business leaders can increasingly expect to be held to account for the role of their business in its community; that they will be expected to act as good corporate citizens, and also be able to build and maintain a brand (including employer brand) which is honest and credible.

The need for good governance and greater accountability has been made evident by the recent banking crisis. There is an increasing demand for 'cleaner' business practices, and calls for more effective governance since previous reforms of corporate governance have clearly proved relatively useless in preventing some of the worst cases of excess in the banking sector. The G20 leaders have broadly agreed that a stronger form of international regulation of financial services that will have greater enforcement potential will be required, although specifically what that will entail remain's unresolved at the time of writing.

Fairness and Transparency

Within business organisations the need for fairness and transparency is just as strong, whether the issue is about how pay and promotion decisions are made or why certain people's jobs are being made redundant. Without transparency, organisations are more likely to be subject to 'alternative' whistle-blowers (often disenchanted employees) who make use of a variety of media, including social networks, to get their message out to the public, sometimes resulting in damage to global brands and corporate reputation.

Fairness and transparency are becoming the mantra of those who want to see reform of the system. Market-driven practices are increasingly being criticised and the assumption that markets will self-regulate has been exposed as a myth. Similarly, the extreme disparities in incomes which have been evident until recent times are starting to be questioned, such as top earners being rewarded with salaries and bonuses that in some cases are several 100 times greater than the pay of the lowest earners. The 'rewards for failure' given to corporate leaders have highlighted perceived inequities between corporate leaders and those left unemployed as a result of their actions.

Fairness may also be the rationale for the growing debate about public sector benefits. So far, the private sector has borne the brunt of redundancies (although the public sector will soon follow) and public sector pension rights (final salary schemes, etc.) are now superior to most of those on offer in the private sector. At some point it is likely that politicians will gain the mandate to start reducing public sector benefits. Initially the UK government is more likely to cut back on 'softer' public service targets and 'back office' functions including HR, IT, finance, etc.

With respect to recruitment, Generation Y is stereotypically assumed to be values-driven and ambitious. It is possible that employee expectations of employers may have changed as a result of the crisis, especially if young people are desperate for a job/career, and it would be tempting to focus less on values as part of employer brand. I argue that this will be a mistake and that it will be even more important to act as an employer worthy of trust if you want to attract and retain the best employees.

And the crisis has also raised public awareness that HR systems and processes are a vital element of business success, for good or ill, such as the role of executive compensation in contributing to the creation of the crisis by rewarding the behaviours that led to it. Public disgust at executive so-called 'rewards for failure' and fury about the size of Sir Fred Goodwin's pension pot have made the subject of executive compensation a likely key source of ongoing debate and controversy. While the link between HR practice and the causes of the crisis may be a dubious point of distinction, it nevertheless highlights the need for HR to come of age and for HR leadership to shape new and better practice inside organisations.

The New Talent Crisis

Until relatively recently, talent shortages were crippling certain sectors. Construction, IT and pharmaceuticals were only some of the sectors worst affected. Back in 2007, there was talk of a new 'War for Talent'. Money was apparently no object to secure the best talent, companies developed tailored offers and strong employer brands to compete for the best employees, differentiating themselves on the basis of lifestyle, values, etc. Talent had the power to choose.

What Now?

Choice of job has been replaced by job insecurity for many employees. One-third of companies in Europe are planning to lay off full-time employees in a move which signals the scale of the collateral damage that the financial crisis has inflicted across the European corporate landscape, according to Strack et al. (2009). The UK has the highest proportion of companies preparing a major redundancy program for full-time workers: 57%. In Russia, the proportion is 40%, in Austria and the Netherlands, it is 38% and in France and Spain, it is 37%. In Germany, Europe's biggest economy, the proportion is 32%. Among industries, the automotive, consumer goods and industrial goods sectors have the highest proportion of companies preparing radical cuts in their workforce: 46%, 45% and 44%, respectively.

The UK redundancy situation is changing very fast, with 3 million unemployed in June 2009 with predictions that this figure will rise to 3.2 million by mid-2010, representing 10% of the UK workforce. A particularly marked aspect of the current crisis is the wide range of organisations and sectors affected. At the time of writing most job losses had taken place in the private sector. Various pundits suggest that the employment market is unlikely to recover until the second half of 2010. A potential net loss of some 350,000 UK public sector jobs over the next few years is predicted as public spending 'flat lines' or gets cut.

The rapid rise in levels of unemployment is putting the UK's public purse, already strained to breaking point by the need to bail out the banking system, under even greater pressure. The spectre of unemployment haunts many, and young people are apparently finding it hardest to find employment. The number of potential recruits applying to join the Army has increased significantly over the last 12 months. It is reported that graduates who might have gone into high earning jobs in investment banking or consultancy are now looking at public service jobs. Indeed, so great is the quest for a job and job security that many former City employees are opting for public sector jobs, such as teaching. And while Generation Y may currently have jobs, they are reported to be worried about their parents' job security, when a household's viability is based on two parents' earning power.

That said, there is also increasing evidence that many older workers are being badly affected by redundancies and are struggling to find new roles. Despite employment legislation outlawing discrimination on the grounds of age, ageism is apparently alive and well before the legislation has really been put to the test. For many people, given the poor state of pensions, longer working lives are a necessity, not a choice, and at the very time when people will need to work for longer, they are more likely to be laid off.

HR leadership will need to provide answers to some of the challenging issues arising from the crisis for talent. For while the 'War for Talent' had employers differentiating themselves in the competition for potential recruits on the grounds of the 'deal', on having strong values people can relate to, opportunities for growth, etc., what will happen to employer brands in the current situation? Will employers maintain their focus and determination to live their values, to build their talent base and improve the quality of management and leadership, or will short-term needs push these out of the frame? Will those organisations which remain focused on their values/employer brand be more successful in attracting and retaining high calibre recruits and those which don't?

These are just some of the issues arising from the crisis on which an HR leadership response is needed. Will it be forthcoming?

TOWARDS RECOVERY

The demands on managers arising from the volatile context are enormous. They need to focus on cost, quality, productivity, improving cycle times and speed. They have to keep things going (and customers happy) while changing things. They need to innovate beyond the current way of doing business if they are to achieve breakthroughs. All this, and manage employees through a turbulent period when jobs may be at risk. It would be all too easy to just carry on 'carrying on'. But if we are to find different and more enduring solutions to these challenges, we may need a different approach.

A STEP CHANGE IN (BUSINESS AND HR) LEADERSHIP NEEDED

So, looking ahead to when the recession ends, what will differentiate those organisations able to return to growth mode faster and more successfully from others? The current economic crisis raises more questions than it answers:

- Will the shape and operation of business be different from before? Will business models be more flexible? Will organisations need to collaborate more both within and beyond their own boundaries?
- Will new models of leadership and management be needed?
- Will the way organisations have dealt with their employees during the crisis determine the nature and effectiveness of their recovery?
- How best can HR contribute to providing answers to some of these questions?

For all the many challenges arising from the recession, it has also provided some clues about what organisations will need to do if they want to survive and thrive in such a fast-changing environment. While there may be limits to what any single organisation can do to insulate itself from the risks inherent in a turbulent context, or indeed to optimise potential opportunities, I believe that HR leaders can equip their organisations for sustainable success. A primary focus must be to ensure that business leaders are willing and able to act as organisational leaders who champion the creation of more *changeable* cultures.

- The need for organisational change-ability is now apparent
  Change-ability, i.e. being flexible, resilient, agile and capable of speed and innovation, will need to become embedded in the DNA of organisations bent on sustainable success. This requires cultural alignment so that flexibility, resilience, speed, etc. are reinforced through behaviours, norms, processes, systems, structures, rewards, management and leadership styles. HR is at the controls of many of the levers of culture-building and needs to use them proactively to build corporate agility.

Change-ability requires specific mindsets. The very scale and extensive impact of the downturn has demonstrated that simply reacting to change – swiftly or otherwise – when external events require it, or relying on previous recipes for success, may not be enough to help organisations sustain performance.

- Strategic anticipation and execution

Whilst a complete reinvention of management and leadership may not be required, if organisations are to 'get onto the front foot', leaders will need to be better equipped to both react to, and help shape, events to produce better outcomes for their organisations. They will need to be capable of *strategic anticipation*, i.e., the ability to anticipate what may occur, mitigate and manage risks to protect the organisation, and also be ready to create and seize opportunities for the business. This in itself may require a step change in thinking, since in current circumstances many executives are focused exclusively on the core business and the short term.

Strategic anticipation provides parameters within which organisations can produce innovations which will keep their organisations ahead of the field. In practical terms it involves continuous scanning of the environment, collective intelligence-gathering and processes for involving employees in thinking through the implementation implications of choices that have surfaced.

However, strategic anticipation alone will not be enough. Effective *execution* will be key to sustainable success. In particular, it will be vital that business strategies are adaptable to changing customer requirements, that employees are willing and able to change what they do when needed, that decision-making is speedy and effective with a judicious balance of risk and return and that communication is of a high order and involves employees in helping find effective solutions to execution problems.

HR professionals too will need to demonstrate strategic anticipation and execution, especially with respect to changing workforce requirements and also be able to take a holistic view of how and where employee and manager capabilities can be built and deployed to produce optimal performance now and in the medium term. Specific areas of HR expertise which will increasingly be required to build change-ability include *strategic talent planning*, together with *organisational design*, to create flexible structures which encourage empowerment, accountability and innovation; and *organisational development* to build team-based practices and address issues relating to organisational effectiveness such as line manager and leadership capability, workplace climate, change management, conflict and politics. HR professionals will need to act with speed and reconfigure their resources as they go.

More Agile Business Strategies?

Leaders will need to manage both change and continuity, be able to anticipate problems, take a global perspective and build new opportunities. Building flexible mindsets, behaviours and structures will be a key HR leadership challenge. One example of anticipation and adaptability is demonstrated by easyJet. In common with most airlines, easyJet has found the context of economic crisis a challenging one. They have been assisted to some extent by their adaptable business model, but since nothing is certain looking ahead, building such flexibility can involve a degree of risk. As Mike Campbell, People Director, says:

> 'We're hedged on fuel. This means that when the fuel price rocketed last year to $140 per barrel, our hedging meant that we did not suffer as much as others who were not hedged. The downside is that now the fuel price has dropped to $45 per barrel and last year's hedging is now having the opposite effect and we aren't getting the full benefit of the drop in fuel price – although we are getting some of it! Some airlines, like Southwest hedge much further out, others don't hedge at all.'

Building adaptable business models and strategies requires specific mindsets and risk appetites. Prahalad (2009) and others suggest that this requires moving out of reactive/defensive operational mode into responsive and even *shaping* mode with respect to the business context. This will require building robust yet flexible business models and strategies that can be executed fast and well, helping organisations get ahead and stay ahead of the competition. Leaders will need to reduce the capital intensity of business. Prahalad (2009) argues that these more adaptable business models focus on value (price–performance), reduce risk and are capable of rapid scaling up and down alongside a rapid reconfiguration of the portfolio.

Sustainable success will require a new approach to customers, seeing them as part of an ecosystem in which personalisation is taken to the point of co-creation of products and services with individual consumers. Building agility into how globalised supply chains operate is a speciality of George Stalk (2009). He advocates agile business strategies such as 'Supply Chain Gymnastics' arguing that in most companies 'there is a yawning gap between global demand for shipping and transit-related services—and the available and anticipated supply'. Companies that design their strategies to accommodate and even leverage this reality can gain an unassailable advantage over rivals. He advocates side-stepping economies of scale by creating the 'disposable factory' which is labour-intensive, capital-light and offers high throughput at low cost – and it has been an engine of growth for many competitors from developing economies.

Stalk also recommends dynamic pricing. In many sectors it is now possible to maximise profits by matching pricing to immediate second-by-second demand. And first movers can gain a critical information advantage that's hard to neutralize. The same principles may offer a way for other companies and industries to address the uncertainty inherent in today's shorter product and business-model life cycles.

HR NEEDS TO PLAN FOR THE RECOVERY

This period of economic crisis is a significant opportunity for HR to clarify its deliverables and ensure that organisations not only survive but also prepare for the recovery by ensuring that they have the talent they need and that employees are as engaged as possible with the organisation and their work. What HR professionals do today to make their organisation more changeable will position their organisation to look smart as business conditions improve. If they do nothing, their organsiation may be forces to play catch-up with more agile competitors.

- Leveraging higher performance
  In the economic crisis, many companies are focusing on leveraging higher performance from their workforces. This is done by better goal alignment and higher levels of stretch in targets and more rigorous performance coaching. HR technology investments, shared services and outsourcing accelerate at such times as does a focus on the more cost-effective processes.
- Growing the focus on talent
  There has been a growing recognition amongst business executives of the competitive advantage to organisations derived from their people. And with the deepening of knowledge- and service-intensive work, 'those with the best people win' replaces 'our people are our greatest asset'. Many companies have therefore heeded lessons from the last recession and have tried hard to avoid lay-offs. Managers recognise that making people redundant, while understandable from a short-term cost-cutting perspective, could have a serious and long-term impact on the company. In the last recession, companies cut employees to save money only to discover that they then faced key shortages a few years later.
  Various surveys suggest that despite the context challenges arising from the economic crisis, for most executives the real issues are about talent, especially retaining and developing their top talent. For instance even at the heart of the crisis, the McKinsey Quarterly Survey (March 2009) highlighted the following executive concerns:
  - Intensifying competition for talent;
  - Shortage of technical and managerial skills;
  - Managing change across the organisation;
  - Dealing with diversity; and
  - Need for quicker decision-making.
  The need for effective talent management – a company's ability to attract, retain and motivate employees – is given added impetus by the crisis. Producing a powerful talent agenda will be the base-level deliverable

for HR leaders. Many people-oriented CEOs have taken human capital under their personal remit of driving the future strategic direction and performance of their organisations – with no need for HR at the boardroom table.

- Build sustainable employee relations

   The recession may provide a springboard to more sustainable employee relations. While there have been large numbers of redundancies, there could have been many more without the active partnership approach between trade unions or other staff representatives and HRM to tackling the need for cost-cutting facing companies. Thanks to their active collaboration, many jobs were saved as employees and companies experimented with various alternatives to redundancy, such as pay freezes, short-time and flexible working, deferred recruitments, etc. So how can HR leaders cement these new employee relations as the foundations of a new form of collective and individual employee relationship and a new psychological contract with employees?

- Keep focused on building employee engagement

   Employers may have little choice but to cut costs and jobs. Hard times and diverse employee attitudes will test engagement strategies to the fullest. When change threatens job security, will performance drop? It is possible that for the present, performance may even improve. With an increased emphasis on performance management, poor performers might raise their game. People generally seem to be working hard and are experiencing increased pressure and stress. It is possible that employees may be working hard because they are engaged with their work, and/or because they may be fearful of losing their jobs. However, while this pressurised environment may produce performance gains in the short term we believe performance gains are unlikely to be sustainable if employees end up feeling burned out.

   So how people are treated during the downturn may affect how they feel about the organisation and their own sense of job security. That in turn may affect whether or not they want to continue to give of their best. In that sense, keeping employees feeling engaged with the organisation may be an essential pre-requisite to organisational performance and survival in this fast-changing context but may also be at risk if the process of change undermines employee security and trust.

- Changing employment models

   And what will happen to employment models post-recession? The last decade has seen a gradual reshaping of the workplace to reflect the changing demands of business, especially knowledge-intensive businesses. Various forms of contract working have reflected business needs for cost-effectiveness and flexibility. As the UK and Irish economies become more knowledge-intensive, work which can be 'parcelled up' gets outsourced or delivered through technology. So, will full-time permanent employment give way to more contingent models?

For instance will flexible working become much more widespread in the future than prior to the recession? Similarly, are employee expectations changing about what employers should provide? Will HRM practice and individual engagement strategies prevail over more collective approaches? Is the 'we're all in this together' stance the basis of new forms of collective and individual employee relations which will act as a firm foundation for more rapid and fundamental change post-recession? Only time will tell, but I believe that employer initiatives aimed at keeping people employed and engaged will maintain and grow mutual trust and confidence between employers and employees, even though some job losses may be inevitable in the current conditions.

Flexibility can benefit both organisations and employees and as the workforce ages it is easy to envisage how the demand for greater flexibility will grow to allow people to meet their eldercare needs. The 2004 Employment Act gave parents of young children the right to request flexible working and the trend in recent years has been to extend the right to request flexible working to a wider workforce – those with children under the age of 16. However, at a time when contractors are amongst the first to be laid off and many workers who might wish to work part-time may feel that they might be putting their job at risk by so doing, it is more likely that people will work longer hours, rather than fewer, especially as colleagues lose their jobs. And what happens to work–life balance then?

Where there is a shared sense of purpose and commitment and where all concerned see mutual benefits in collaboration to further the interests for their organisation, we believe this will be a positive outcome of the recession. This new relationship will of course need to be based on well-founded trust, since any reversion to old style adversarial or 'tricksy' behaviour by investors, management or employees may undermine what has begun in the way of shared endeavours. Trust has to be earned and HR needs to be in the vanguard of trust-building, watching out for and dealing with those actions which could undermine trust.

Similarly, the issue of executive pay is unlikely to go away. The recent exposure of the potential role played by market-driven incentives in encouraging behaviours which contributed to the banking crisis suggests that more creative ways will need to be found of attracting and retaining key talent but also responding to investor and other stakeholder requirements for greater accountability and transparency. HR will be in the front line of negotiations on this contentious area. Those organisations that have fair and clear processes for deciding on structures and roles, well developed and genuine communication lines that enable open and honest dialogue, where leaders 'walk the talk' on values, that retain active talent management strategies and make decisions on where to make the cuts with the future in mind will be best placed to weather the storm and to prosper thereafter.

- Building healthy and effective organisations:
  The causes of the economic crisis have shaken public trust in business prac-
  tice, as well as in the quality of leadership in all walks of life. HR leaders
  can play a key role in rebuilding trust within organisations by:
  - Ensuring that role design and performance targets allow for clear
    accountabilities and that managers are trained to manage performance
    effectively.
  - Ensuring that governance practices, and leadership behaviours,
    including operational decision-making are operating to agreed ethical
    standards.
  - Challenging leaders and others who fall short of what is required to
    'walk the talk' on values.
  - Keeping a 'finger on the pulse' of how employees are feeling about the
    organisation and taking steps to meet their needs where possible, as well
    as championing making the employer brand a lived reality rather than
    just rhetoric.
  - Becoming effective non-executives for other companies.
  So, it can be envisaged that HR will need to play a stronger role to help
  build an ethical basis for sustainable organisational performance. We shall
  explore some of these approaches more fully in Chapter 8.

CONCLUSION: ACCELERATING HR'S OWN TRANSFORMATION TO FOCUS ON NEW RESPONSIBILITIES

These are just some of the challenges which HR will need to address. Above all,
the crisis has highlighted many of the underlying trends which will impact on
organisations in years to come, so ignoring them is not an option. Change will
be a constant. Old models will need to be transformed, including HR's own.
This is a time when HR needs to be at the top of its game – acting with speed
and discretion as well as the maximum of fairness and transparency.

Therefore, the HR function will need to demonstrate its own ability to build
and operate as a high performance team, working effectively to deliver key
outcomes across the organisation. Earlier preparation in terms of HR organisation should bear fruit and if the way HR organises itself gets in the way of
delivering value, it should be changed, with the minimum of fuss and the
maximum of clarity for all concerned. Changing role requirements will mean
that the HR profession will need to attract people of the highest calibre who can
rise to these strategic and operational challenges.

HR leaders will need to lead the way, role modelling the behaviours and
values that will help the organisation thrive, installing processes which are fit for
purpose for such a fast-changing context (which is likely to become the norm in
the future). This requires vision, proactivity and courage, and throughout the
book we shall look at how our HR leaders demonstrate and other leadership
qualities to the benefit of their organisations.

This is a great opportunity for HR leaders to rise to the challenge of supporting their organisations through this period and help pave the way to a more sustainable basis for future performance. The critical issue is to focus on *what* needs to be done and *how* best to do it, then deliver in ways which create effective outcomes. As one focus group HRD participant put it: '*If you are emerging from the downturn and you aren't a strategic partner with your CEO, I think you have lost your way. Yes, do the basics and the operational piece brilliantly, but be seen as that go-to person and true strategic partner. There's never a better time to raise the profile of HR in the organisation.*' So the challenge is there: as we move into a new era the opportunities for HR leaders to make a difference are richer than ever before. In the next chapter we shall look at how some HR leaders view the task of HR leadership, and at some of the factors which have shaped them for their role.

Chapter 2

Who Are the HR Leaders?

'The mark of a great HR leader is being as un-HR like as possible.'

David Smith

Who are our HR leaders? In this chapter I want to introduce you to some of the 20 or so HR leaders who were interviewed for this book. We will look at who they are, how they came to be in HR roles, what they are responsible for and at some of the experiences which shaped their thinking and practice.

Even the very notion of HR exercising leadership is a relatively new concept, and a somewhat disputed one at that. HR leadership is about building competitive advantage through people. Is HR leadership restricted to those in the top HR role? Certainly not – leadership occurs at all levels and leadership potential is usually evident early in a person's career. Similarly, HR leadership may be exercised by others than the person in the top HR role, as we shall discuss in Chapter 3. How did the HR leaders featured in this book reach a top HR role? In this chapter we shall consider their career backgrounds, and significant development experiences. Back in 2002, the American Society of Human Resource Management (SHRM) invited a group of senior consultants to discuss where the HR profession was heading. They predicted that in the future, the top HR slot would no longer be the preserve of HR professionals. They argued that a combination of business experience with highly developed consulting skills was required for senior HR roles and that these could be acquired through many different route's.

In practice, they suggested that one of the failings of many HR professionals was their lack of real business understanding and therefore their inability to formulate and deploy HR strategies aligned to business objectives. SHRM argued that marketing professionals might be able to play a valuable role in HR – since they would be able to deploy marketing strategies and techniques (including research, employee segmentation and building an employer brand) to better understand and address the needs of employees.

We will be exploring how our HR leaders go about their roles, and whether or not these predictions apply in practice. We shall look at what they think is the mark of a great HR leader. Of course the people we've interviewed for this book don't fit into neat categories – they are distinctive individuals in their own right. In terms of responsibilities, some are in group HR roles; others manage specialist functions; some have middle-ranking roles; and others have very senior roles whose scope has broadened beyond HR. Two have become Chief Executive Officers (CEOs). In terms of career backgrounds they are just as diverse. However, one thing they all have in common is that they make things happen.

As I've previously stated, HR leadership is not reserved for the person in the functional top spot, although many of the people interviewed for this book are, or have been in such a role. HR leadership is as much a mindset and a way of operating as a role. So how do our HR leaders operate? Why did they move into HR? What matters to them in the role? Let's start off by looking at their early career orientation.

DID OUR HR LEADERS START OFF IN HR?

Where do our HR leaders come from? Did they follow a traditional HR path from the outset? In practice only a few of them did. It appears that for many of our interviewees a career in HR was not deliberately planned. For David Smith money was the initial driver, as he thought HR might be the more lucrative of two choices, HR or accountancy. Others followed very different early career routes. Some, such as Liane Hornsey, Dr Tim Miller and Jonathan Evans, began their careers as teachers, or like Mike Campbell first entered research and then became a teacher. Anne Minto studied law and was a qualified solicitor.

Philippa Hird started her career in marketing. As a young person Philippa had a strong interest in the creative arts and she had wanted to be an actress – or to become the Director General of the UN! She studied politics and economics at Oxford and enjoyed being among bright people. From the outset she had a general interest in business, her father having worked for Glaxo, though she was to the left politically. This twin-track of interests – creativity and politics/business marks much of her subsequent career.

Early in his career Graham White joined the civil service and then went to theological college and was ordained. He was a priest for 10 years before going into general management in textiles in Ireland. Along the way he was also a Finance Director. David Fairhurst was also initially attracted to a career in the Church; 'There are some similarities between that and HR. Both require leadership skills – having a clear understanding of what you want to achieve, and the ability to communicate that to people in a compelling way. Both are rooted in helping people to achieve their full potential. And both have a welfare aspect – supporting people through difficult times'. He graduated from Lancaster University with an honours degree in Social Ethics and Psychology.

Victoria Bird planned to make her career in retailing and having completed a degree in Retail Management which included a year working in Harrods joined the graduate trainee scheme at Marks and Spencer in the early 1990's. Dave Gartenberg of Microsoft started his career as an economic analyst. Jackie Orme 'fell into HR', having wanted to be a journalist. Martin Ferber initially wanted to study medicine but took Zoology at university and ended up focusing his PhD studies on parasitic diseases in pigs. His first role in Pfizer was as a scientist. Angela O'Connor started her career at a young age direct from school at the Department of Health and Social Security, working in reception and moved from there to working for Reed Employment.

WHAT ATTRACTED THEM TO HR?

In some of the HR leaders, a strong sense of personal mission appears to have driven their career choices. One common theme among our interviewees was the desire to develop people, although this manifested itself in different ways. David Smith went to work for British Coal, which was a big employer at the time, and he cut his HR teeth during the miners' strikes in the 1980s. His first big job was in Resourcing and Development, where he discovered the desire to develop people was an intrinsic part of his make-up.

Desire to Develop People

Graham White, Anne Minto, Martin Ferber and Liane Hornsey were highly motivated by the idea of developing people in order to better the business. Graham is very clear that he thinks that people are a company's best resource for success in business. Anne highlighted how important it was for her that Centrica has an interest in its people, Liane mentioned her early socialist views, while Martin was attracted to personnel because there was something essentially valuable about the role that to him was to do with humanity in work.

Social Good

David Fairhurst wanted to work with people: 'I've always believed in the power of people to make a difference'. It was while Angela O'Connor was working in reception at the Department of Health and Social Security that she developed strong views about the way people should be treated and honed her philosophy about the public sector. She learned that when people are in difficulties they can often be isolated from the state and she knew that she wanted to make a difference and where possible assist government agencies in providing better services to the public they serve.

Jon Sparkes wanted to do something of social value and HR was a way of doing that. From his degree in management sciences at Loughborough to his first HR jobs, Jon was half developing as HR professional, doing social change in his spare time. Jon's personal politics were in social change: *'You see things in HR which at least demonstrate the impact of what HR does. In the 1990s, I saw a site of engineering/manufacturing go from a headcount of 5000 to 2500 in two years flat. I saw the social impact – shops in the High St became Charity shops, the level of violence in the town centre went up, you can see the link clearly. If you live in the locality, you can see the impact. It was a defining experience.'*

Jackie Orme too wanted to take the social career route, and do something of social good. Her way of doing this was to help people get into employment. Her first main job at the Professional Executive Recruitment (PER) agency of the then Department of Employment left her somewhat disillusioned. She felt that PER was operating along strong commercial lines, that it was 'really about making money' and in a real way had lost its sense of mission and purpose. That said, it provided a good grounding in recruitment. Jackie followed this with a stint at the Institute of Chartered Accountants (ICA) then took a career break to go on her travels with her husband. On their return, Jackie went into graduate recruitment in the steel industry in South Wales in the first part of British Steel to be privatised, and it became profitable after privatisation.

MORE PRAGMATIC MOTIVATIONS

Headhunted

All of our interviewees have been headhunted or earmarked for specific roles at some point or another in their careers, some quite frequently. David Smith was headhunted into the role of Head of Colleague Relations by ASDA, who wanted him to intervene and sort out the union issues that they were having at the time. He agreed to join ASDA after hearing the then CEO, Archie Norman, speaking. Martin Ferber became interested in business, as well as science. When he went to see Pfizer's HR manager, he was told that they were hoping he would take an interest in a vacant personnel position and would have asked him to apply if he hadn't done so.

Liane got headhunted after moving from teaching into sales and marketing. It turned out that she was exceptionally good at her job and so she was plucked out of marketing department and put to work on running a change programme. Her first 'proper' job in HR was as an HR Director, although she'd worked in very similar things like internal branding and change programmes before.

Liane has been headhunted for nearly every job she's had. She was internally headhunted in her sales position to work in change management and was then headhunted to go and work for BT, to run their transition programme. She was then headhunted again to work in the music industry, NTL, lastminute.com and Google, respectively.

'BY ACCIDENT'

From the Law to HR

Anne Minto had a place to study criminology at Keele but met her future husband and decided it was too far away, so looked around for interesting courses closer by. Anne studied law at Aberdeen University and thereafter took a post-graduate degree in HR. She decided to qualify as a solicitor in Scotland

and for the first part of her career worked in the commercial world using her legal qualifications. She joined Shell, where she worked for thirteen years in commercial general management roles.

She then left Shell and became the deputy director general at the Engineering Employers' Federation (EEF), with a very broad area of responsibility covering employment law and policy, employee relations and health and safety. The Chief Executive of one of EEF's largest member companies, Smiths Group, approached Anne and asked her if she would become his HRD because he wanted somebody who could offer not just expertise in HR but who was a more rounded business person. Subsequently Anne returned to the energy sector to do a larger role in Centrica.

From Sales to HR

When Liane Hornsey went to university, she had no sense at all of what she wanted to do career-wise and she went into teaching for a very short while. She said that she was quite socialist at the time and thought that it was 'a cool thing to do' to teach in a social priority area, with very disaffected kids. She found that a lot of her ideals were really shattered as she couldn't make the difference to her students that she wanted to, and she was influenced by the experience of a friend who worked in sales, which she thought looked a lot easier than teaching.

Liane went to work for a big pharmaceutical company, in sales and then marketing, and was hugely successful, becoming the top sales person in the UK three years running, and from there went into marketing. '*I just found it unbelievably easy to sell after working with disaffected kids. I then totally fell into HR because I was the highest performing person in the company, because it was a very sales and marketing-led company, and I was seen as high potential- very young and very able. It was a US owned company, and they wanted someone to lead an internal change programme. In effect they were told by the States to pick somebody who was high potential, so I was plucked out of the oblivion of the marketing department and I was put to work for the Managing Director (MD) running this change programme. To me that was so painful, because I was so very used to having very tangible results, you know – in sales, sell this product, get this many sales at this price point – in marketing, launch this product, be creative around this product – and I went in to make these improvements through these people, which I just found unbelievably tricky.*'

At the age of 24 she was headhunted to go and work for BT, to run their transition programme, in a very senior position, with 60 or 70 people working for her. She was given more and more responsibility – for quality, organisational development (OD), internal consultancy and development. In the early 1990s, she was sent up to headquarters to work in a strategic think tank role for a couple of years, at which point she was headhunted to go into the music business by Bertelsmann Music Group (BMG). She worked for BMG for about seven years in what she described as her first real job in HR as HRD for UK and Ireland. After a couple of years she became HR vice-president for central Europe, UK and Ireland and then vice-president for the whole of Europe, the Middle East and Africa (EMEA).

Angela O'Connor also found that she was very effective in sales. Early in her career she moved to Reed Employment where she learned about customer service and the bottom line, profit margins and the importance of financial acumen, about the importance of answering the phone within three rings (she still does). She became interested in marketing and sales and the link between good customer service training and excellent outcomes for customers. She recognised that in the recruitment business, people were a commodity, albeit a lively commodity. She discovered that she was good at sales and found that it was easy to make good money and bonuses. She loved working with employers and stayed for five years working as a troubleshooter at branches which were struggling. This meant that sometimes she would have to close down branches and make staff redundant, a process she found initially very difficult to do because of the impact on staff.

Moving back into the public sector with a job in personnel for Haringey Council, Angela's job involved providing personnel advice to grant-aided voluntary sector organisations such as the network for elderly Asian and Caribbean women. This was a time of some turbulence in Haringey, with riots in Tottenham and the first Lesbian and Gay Unit being established by a UK local authority. Angela was keen to get involved in some of the 'meaty' issues but recognised that most of the more interesting work went to men, most of whom had an Industrial Relations (IR) background and personnel qualifications.

From Science to HR

Martin Ferber enjoyed his career as a scientist at Pfizer but found that he was also very interested in the business world outside of his laboratory: '*I had a broader interest in company matters; I always felt slightly more interested in things going on around me than I was meant to be doing. In fact, I was sometimes criticised for being distracted by other stuff that didn't matter. That's one aspect of science which is to keep focused, keep your head down and work on the specific scientific project. There wasn't a lot of chance to get into the commercial side of animal health and medicines, which was another possible area to go into at Pfizer. It was quite hard to make that jump into the commercial side the way we were structured.*' A senior colleague pointed out to him an advert on a notice board for a job in personnel, and a week later he was being offered the job, without really knowing what personnel did.

EARLY CAREER STEPS

Between them, our HR leaders have worked in most sectors of British industry. In many cases they have pursued a typical career route – start off in one direction, realise that it's time for something else and move on to something new.

From Traditional Industry to Supermarkets

David Smith worked at British Coal and credited the miners' strike with helping to develop him as a young executive. David left British Coal after 19 years, having worked in workshops, pensions and insurance and restructuring. He decided to leave as coal mining was becoming a dying industry. David decided that it was time to make a change and signed up to do an MBA at Henley, through distance learning over four years. He thought that it would be an astute move after such a long period of time in one business. Halfway through the MBA he was headhunted by ASDA, who wanted him to sort out some union issues they were having which David felt were well within his capabilities. ASDA was going through a difficult time and was close to bankruptcy. They were bringing in a new management team and board, which he thought made it a fantastic time for him to come and prove himself. David was a 'colleague' (as staff members are called at ASDA) for 16 years.

From Teaching to Management Development to Industrial Relations (IR)

Though originally a school teacher, Jonathan Evans decided he would prefer to teach adults instead and went to work for the paper industry (1975–1985), initially in a management development role for Wiggins Teape. This was a period of economic recession when Wiggins Teape was closing down a number of paper mills. Jonathan joined the closure team and was seconded into the mills to help prepare people for the future, training people in job search and interview technique. During that time Jonathan worked closely with the trades union and gained a strong respect for their efforts to help people. This led to his joining in the IR team, which by 1981–1982 was a tough time to be in IR, and this was a period when unions were at their most powerful. Jonathan's empathy with the plight of workers helped him reach agreement with the unions more often than not.

Still in the paper industry, Jonathan took on his first generalist HRD role in a self-adhesive company in 1985. This meant a steep learning curve, as he had to quickly master a variety of key specialist areas, such as reward. However, Jonathan makes no claims to be an expert in these specialisms. His point is that as HRD you need to know enough but that you need to have good people around you to be an effective HRD. He has therefore always made a point of growing strong teams around him.

There followed a period of finding his way career wise, largely prompted by head-hunting opportunities. First Jonathan allowed himself to be headhunted by Lucas Aerospace in 1987. His job was again to help downsize the organisation. He found the centralised culture did not suit his temperament and that although he had lots of responsibility, he had no authority, so he soon left.

This time he went to work for the Chloride Group, British Leyland in particular, moving back into a management development role. This exposed him to leaders such as Ray Horrocks and Michael Edwardes whose careers also included leadership roles at British Leyland. He learned a lot but he found that working in Manchester while his young family was based in Cambridge made his lifestyle unsustainable, so he took matters into his own hands and became a bespoke outplacement consultant, working from home. It was then that matters took a more surprising turn. He was asked if he would help set up a new business – Orange – just working a couple of days a week! This job was based in Bristol and as things turned out, Jonathan stayed with Orange 11 years, until Orange was acquired by France Telecom. It was hard work and Jonathan admits he made lots of mistakes, but he had the chance to formulate HR from scratch. For more about how Jonathan put HR at the heart of the Orange business, see Chapter 6.

A Gradual Shift

Philippa Hird's early serious ambitions were to go into conceptual/creative work and she initially went in to marketing and advertising. She did well and, being highly ambitious, she wanted a job promising responsibility early on. When Imperial Chemical Industries (ICI) offered her a job based in Manchester, she felt she should say yes. As she says, 'It felt cool to be out of London and the City. At the time ICI was in crisis and had lost a lot of money'. Under Sir John Harvey-Jones, a turnaround strategy was implemented in 1985–1986. Lots of people left, leaving a great deal of work not done. It meant that for the people who were left there were lots of opportunities for progression and travel in Europe.

Philippa took on a role in industrial marketing for a product group of the Dyestuffs division. She learned about the manufacturing process and felt lucky at an early stage to have a substantive role in the development of a big marketing programme to change the way dyestuffs were sold and in the trade sale of a part of the business. She also worked hard on cementing client relationships, running major customer programmes, including a Summer School for children of clients (a private textile business). The remit of Product Management was a broad one and Philippa was able to be heavily involved in the introduction of new Manufacturing Resource Planning systems which involved building good relationships with schedulers and manufacturing. She was fortunate to meet John Harvey-Jones during this time who said that his most difficult decisions were always about people. It didn't motivate he to move into HR at the time, but it stayed with her. After 18 months, Philippa realised that inorganic chemistry was 'not my thing' but she was not sure what was. After all, she was in a creative role but it was still not right for her. Reflecting later on her experience of exiting senior people, Philippa considers it vital to know what it is you want to do if you are going to fulfil your potential as any kind of leader.

Her own career transition was helped by a conversation with a Colour Consultant with whom she worked as part of her Marketing role. She introduced Philippa to the career choice book '*What colour is your parachute?*' On reflection Philippa realised that she was in the wrong job and that she wanted to work in creative organisations but in a management role. 'If you are absolutely clear about what you want, you are more likely to end up doing it'.

Philippa applied for and got the job of General Management Trainee in Granada Television which was, at that time, the ITV Licence holder for the North West of England. She had no hesitation about accepting the role. That said, she had not realised the true extent of her new role at Granada. She found herself managing 80 researchers (a permanent pool of people, mainly graduates, who move from project to project). She got to know them all.

Creative Industries

Victoria Bird started her career in retailing but she too wanted a creative challenge. After her first management position, gaining a good commercial grounding in retail, she moved to the music division of Time Warner in 1996. At the time this was not an obvious move for her. The UK music division was building a new HR function for their record labels. Victoria believed it was somehow fate that she got the job and she learnt a lot from working for Tracey Hough (who had recently arrived from Mars and L'Oreal) in order to develop the function.

The music business was in its heyday – this was before the advent of the Internet, iPods and illegal downloads challenged the profitability of the music industry. It was a tough, yet creative environment and Victoria had plenty of opportunity to hone her business partnering skills working for the label Managing Directors she worked to establish trusting and challenging relationships – which the MDs valued. Also, Victoria relished the job, being personally interested in the industry and coming from a musical family.

Victoria brought retail principles to Warner and spent about 80% of her time on the floor working with people. She admits she was 'not always strong at the detail' but her strengths lay in establishing process, long term thinking and building genuine and influential relationships with people. In particular Victoria created a framework around diversity, not for the sake of it, but because the industry depended on operating according to good diversity principles. This was a period of transition in popular music terms from the Rock genre to R&B.

Victoria discovered that the key to success was getting those making decisions to think differently about their employees, team dynamics and the commercial impact getting it right could have. Warner was a small environment in which any individual could influence a decision. Victoria became the influential partner to the MD, and, though she was still 'pretty inexperienced', she could make things happen.

From General Management to HR

For Graham White, a move into personnel was not deliberate. He went in to general management initially and realised that the reason that he was succeeding wasn't that he knew anything about the function that he was managing, but rather because of the relationship and the engagement he was having with his staff. And that's why in Graham's own words: '*I managed to con an organisation to make me their Financial Director for two years. I had such a powerful relationship with my team that that was far more important than the critical knowledge that was within the team. My role was very different. But I found the clutter of the day job getting in the way of the real value, which was discovering just how much an organisation could succeed or fail based on its relationship with its workforce.*

So when Graham got the opportunity to go back into a more purist role, again in a large textile organisation he took it. '*At the time the organisation was in very real difficulties, suffering financial and marketing problems and we could not afford to recruit new people or buy new machines so they wanted to see if they could do anything with the workforce. I went in there for four years and had a marvellous time. We turned the organisation from a loss making organisation into a profit making organisation. And we didn't change anything – we just built a new relationship with the staff. I did a lot more learning, training, communicating, engaging, empowering, acknowledging, rewarding, recognising, all the things that 20 years later we are not still doing very well at. So I realised that was a very powerful place to be in an organisation. I realised that if you really did want to make a difference that was the place to do it.*'

DEVELOPMENTAL LOGIC

It's not only a desire for success at work that characterises our interviewees; they are all very driven and want to succeed in every area of their lives. They naturally pursue their careers in very different ways. The seven developmental action logics identified by Rooke et al. (2000) can be helpful in understanding the various ways our leaders pursue their development. These are:

- Opportunists – who are out for themselves;
- Diplomats – avoid conflict and obey the norms;

- Experts – rule by logic and expertise;
- Achievers – achieve strategic goals through teams;
- Individualists – interweave competing personal and company action logics;
- Strategists – generate organisational and personal transformations; and
- Alchemists – generate social transformations.

Rooke et al. (2000) suggest that leaders can move from one action logic to another. Triggers can be external events, changes to work practices and environment, and planned and structured interventions. Moreover, teams and organisations can be classified using the same constructs. These authors acknowledge that the leader's voyage of development is not an easy one, and this is echoed in the experiences of many of the HR leaders interviewed for this book.

FORMATIVE EXPERIENCES

It seems that early exposure to challenging situations acts as preparation for later senior responsibilities, but dealing with them can make or break would-be HR leaders. Mostly, our leaders have learned significantly through having tough challenges to deal with earlier in their career. These experiences have helped shape their philosophy and vision for how things could be, as well as expand their skill sets. The way our HR leaders have navigated various setbacks and challenges marks them out as 'achievers' according to the Rooke et al. developmental logics. As David Smith comments, 'if something comes at you it will develop you, as long as you've got what it takes'.

Most of our HR leaders can describe such incidents, some of which were traumatic for those involved. Graham, Anne and Liane in particular appeared to have thrived in these challenging situations and have subsequently taken on an 'HR troubleshooter' career characteristic. For instance, Liane Hornsey describes her early experience working for NTL, a firm that went into Chapter 11 just after she had started working for them:

> 'I remember day two, my boss called me into the room and said, 'Look Liane, we've got to shed about several thousand people', and I went, 'mm okay. When?' It was November, and he said 'December,' and I said, 'Oh that's fine— we've got 13 months.' And he said 'No - this December!' So I was thrown into massive reorganisation, losing 5000 people in about four or five weeks, and then taking the company through Chapter 11. Huge, huge learning, fantastic learning, because no-one else could tell me what to do. I'd never had a mentor in my life, I just had to get on and do it and I loved the guy I was working for. So that was a hideous set of circumstances, having to let people go and refinance the business and stuff, but hugely developmental and the one thing that I would say had characterised my whole career has definitely been learning. Every single role I've gone into I've had to just get off the fence and learn very fast, because I've always been put into different situations.

Subsequently, Liane deliberately moved on to a number of troubled departments and turned them round.

Learning From Mistakes

Some challenges can be self-inflicted. Liane Hornsey recognised she had a lot to learn when she first started at Google. She'd worked for an American company before, so she thought she knew how to work in an American environment. When she first came in she was overly business-like and critical and made some strong observations, such as 'this is very daft, this needs to change'. After about six weeks, Liane realised that there were more positives than she'd realised. She had not spent enough time building really solid networks and relationships with the other functional people in HR, a situation she soon rectified.

Industrial Relations (IR)

David Smith's experience of the miners' strikes of the 1980s helped shape him as a young executive. Early responsibility and trauma provided that opportunity. During that time he saw things that made him realise the way that the world really worked, citing the BBC's biased, savage coverage of the strikes. The work he did on restructuring post-strike helped to hone his people skills, as he was dealing with people face to face, in very difficult circumstances. There were a number of executives early on in his career who were real change agents, all of whom influenced the person he became in different ways.

Geoff Armstrong too has a very strong IR background and led the creation of new working relations with trades unions in the automotive industry during the 1970s. Geoff's experiences will be described more fully in Chapter 7.

Downsizing and Turnarounds

Managing downsizing is a common element to several of the careers of our HR leaders. For Graham White the turning point in his working life was taking on the role of Personnel and Training Manager and four weeks after joining being informed that the organisation was £10 million in debt and was very likely to close down. It taught him many lessons that are still useful to him today about dealing with people and building relationships. He actively recommends this type of experience to new HR professionals to help them quickly develop their skills.

While working in the steel industry Jackie Orme managed a small group of people development managers. She became Institute of Personnel Management (IPM) qualified and mastered labour relations and change management as part of delivering downsizing in the company's quest to become the lowest cost producer.

This experience stood her in good stead when she moved to Walkers in Swansea, a fast moving consumer goods (FMCG) company manufacturing company, which is part of PepsiCo. PepsiCo is known as an 'Academy Co' which is good at individual development as well as being a stable for high-calibre

HR professionals. HR is therefore a strong driver group within PepsiCo and has never had to 'bang on the (boardroom) door'. Jackie took on various roles, supply chain, organisation and management development (OMD), before moving on to broader HR. Her last role in PepsiCo before moving to the The Chartered Institute of Personnel and Development, (CIPD, previously IPM) as CEO was as Vice-President HR (the role is now Chief Personnel Officer).

Challenging Tasks

Early in his career David Fairhurst led an HR team on a major acquisition of Farley Healthcare from Boots, a £200 million deal. Bringing people together in such circumstances taught David a lot about people and their behaviours/reactions. Having to understand the commercial aspects of the merger helped him manage the people issues surrounding it. David learned that people can make or break any key strategic organisational change, i.e. merger, acquisition, office move, product launches, etc. He also recognised that the finest strategy is worthless without effective execution.

Jon Sparkes' career choices have mostly been in pursuit of his personal mission around social change. Early in his career he worked as HRD for the Training and Enterprise Council (TEC) in Derby. The TEC had influence outside pure training – it provided funding for Further Education colleges as well as supporting local economic development, education–business partnerships and labour market research. Jon's horizons were beyond the organisation and the City of Derby which was going through economic restructuring – 40% unemployment. This was the first social enterprise to get people into employment, employing 100 people who had been unemployed in the previous two years. They were given job skills training for 18 months until they were ready to move on.

Angela O'Connor moved to Hackney to progress her career. Such is her work ethic that she took only one week off from night school when she had her baby daughter. She returned to work as a job sharer for a year (as did her husband, an architect in the private sector). At Hackney she had her most meaningful career experience since the start of her career. It was roller coaster of political in-fighting. People worked all day and often until the early hours of the morning. There were major policy changes weekly, resulting in chaos. At the time the Inner London Education Authority (ILEA) was being disbanded and its responsibilities were being transferred to local authorities across London.

Angela managed the transfer of staff from ILEA to Hackney, from a strategic and tactical standpoint – at one point going to Woolworths to purchase cleaning materials for the offices of the education department. At that point staff had no faith in Hackney and 400 education workers were protesting as the payroll failed. The teachers' pay issue was major learning experience. Angela employed a county hall official, as she needed this person to come and work in

Hackney Education with her. Angela wrote her a contract on a serviette in a local cafe due to the need to close the deal quickly before the employee was offered another job. She led the negotiations with the Teachers' Unions, sitting with the teachers in the classrooms, getting to understand their point of view. For Angela this was a very formative period, and everything was being developed on the hoof. Flexibility in approach was key.

Influential Others

Many of our HR leaders recognise the influence of significant others in helping them develop their careers and learning. David Smith cites theory, experience and people as the three most important factors in shaping young high potentials. While he does not recommend shaping yourself around other people, he's drawn from a number of people that he worked with whom he considered to be real change agents.

Spotlight: Mike Campbell – From Training to HR

Mike Campbell, now People HRD at easyJet, illustrates many of the career characteristics described above in the early phase of his career. Here he describes how he moved into HR from his first role in training and change at International Computers Limited (ICL) (now Fujitsu).

Training and change at ICL

'I designed and delivered courses at ICL on products and engineers repair techniques, e.g. break-fix on linewriter band printers, distributed systems, PCs and even early excel spreadsheets. Early days, I was just standard delivery of repetitive training packages to in-house staff and customers. I got bored, learned some new techniques and then saw an internal advert for a Training Officer role. I was interviewed, got the job and ended up at the leading edge of some really interesting change programmes e.g. harmonisation of Terms and Condition within a unionised environment, European graduate recruitment, performance management etc.

I became interested in how you can drive culture change in the manufacturing environment from a people point of view (autonomous work teams, kanban, flexible manufacturing systems, KRAs, etc.). Any change is brought about by behaviour change. Amongst other things I ran graduate recruitment too. I was introduced to assessment centre methodologies, competency-based interviewing, high-potential career planning, etc.; found it interesting and effective-particularly in terms of engaging line management with objective measurements around recruitment and performance. There was a huge exposure to the OD delivery sides of contract change when the business was both down- and upsizing.

HR in ICL

Then I had a chance to get exposed to HR. Training is mostly about things people want to do – in general people are mostly up for learning and typically you are

Spotlight: Mike Campbell – From Training to HR—cont'd

a provider. HR is more 'hard-nosed' and can seem more about preventing things than enabling. I wanted to balance out my experience. I was lucky - I was in the right place at the right time. And as a personnel officer at ICL's unionised manufacturing sites, you had to be able to explain how what you were doing helped the business. You had to be able to articulate in ways people can understand, talk the same language. If people ask you why something needs to change, you can talk about the competition, how we are doing and relate that to what's in it for them, even if it means if we don't change then 'we'll all be out of a job' – they might not like it, but atleast they understand.

At that time there was massive transformation across ICL, including manufacturing and supply. To manage the change successfully involved understanding the future of manufacturing hardware and deciding what to do. We turned the model on its head. We went from being an in-house manufacturer to an outsourced one. I ended up in a small team of four setting up a wholly owned subsidiary in effect offering our manufacturing services (design, manufacture, test and distribution of printed circuit boards and finished products-computers) to third party companies including Sun Microsystems, Dell – as well as to ICL. We grew from 0 to £200m contract business in 18 months, and then continued to grow. To get a streamlined operation it was essential to understand the drivers of change in manufacturing sales – such as activity-based costing, unsocial hours 'policies, annualised hours etc. During that period our factories won the British Quality Award twice and the EFQM award (European Foundation for Quality Management).'

These early experiences helped prepare Mike for his later HR and business leadership roles.

WHAT DO THESE HR LEADERS HAVE IN COMMON?

Few of our HR leaders would claim to be good at detail, but they do have the ability to put a process around situations to move things forward. All have the ability to create teams which complement them and many have grown their abilities as a result of early exposure to the twin challenges of reward and industrial or employee relations.

High Achievement Drive

All our HR leaders appear to have a very high achievement drive. For instance of Graham White's various careers – as a Christian Minister, a Finance Director, General Manager and HRD – HR has provided him with the greatest opportunities to experience the thrill of achievement.

When Liane Hornsey realised that she couldn't achieve the things she wanted to in her teaching role, she quickly changed career direction. During the three years she spent in her new career in sales for BT she was top sales person in the UK all three years. By the age of 27 she was the most senior person on her grade and at her age in BT and had 60 or 70 people under her.

For Jackie Orme the move to be CEO at CIPD was not only an opportunity to do something different, but was also 'a legacy job' on a big playing field. She considers the CIPD uniquely positioned to have voice about people, leadership and performance, and relishes the chance to influence public policy and practice in organisations as well as help shape the future of the HR profession.

Hunger for Development (See Also Chapter 9)

All our interviewees share a thirst for knowledge and a hunger for learning. They come from a huge range of educational backgrounds, but whatever their academic background, they have all deliberately continued to develop themselves throughout their careers. Several of them continued to study while they were working and they all share a desire to keep on learning. For instance David Fairhurst was a graduate trainee specialising in HR in Lucas Industries where he built an HR department from scratch for the Transport Development Group. While there he studied for a Masters in Strategic HR at Manchester Metropolitan University.

David Smith loves all things academic. He did an MBA at Henley by distance learning over four years, during which time he had small children and a new job. David thinks that good HR professionals need an academic foundation, as you need to hang things on a theoretical underpinning, then early responsibility and even trauma, which can provide development opportunities and, finally, contact with influential others.

While at Reed Employment, Angela O'Connor decided to do something to improve her own prospects and went to night school to complete her education. She took a Post-Graduate Diploma in Labour Studies as a mature student in London, covering law, IR and gaining exemptions from the CIPD qualification. Angela found that she loved studying and was horrified about the lack of rigour amongst many young students. For her, studying had been inspirational, opening the door to how organisations work and how things come together. She wanted to explore what HR/Personnel could really mean – how HR could make a difference. She subsequently achieved an MA in Human Resource Management whilst pregnant with her second child taking her final examinations a week before giving birth.

Although Martin Ferber describes himself as not particularly academic, he completed a PhD. After working in the Civil Service for two years, Graham White realised that he had a religious vocation and went off to theological college. Liane Hornsey said that the one thing that has characterised her whole career has definitely been learning.

They all read a lot too. David Smith reads any book that comes out. Anne Minto loved reading as a child, and her parents really encouraged her to read from a young age. She also said that it's a sad week if you come to the end of a Friday and you haven't learned something new. And she thinks if that happens, then you should ask yourself if you ought to be in this job.

THE MARK OF A GREAT HR LEADER

What is a great HR leader? Ulrich and Brockbank (2008) suggest that the HR profession as a whole is quickly moving to add greater value through a more strategic focus. As talent and organisational issues grow in business importance, HR must take on a variety of shaping roles – architects, designers, facilitators. Above all, they argue, general managers expect HR professionals to provide intellectual and process leadership for people and organisational issues. This includes having good judgement, knowing when an organisation's success depends on individual abilities and organisational capabilities – or not – and pushing for alignment, as appropriate.

For instance, in a highly creative company like Google, where innovative product development depends on the abilities of its people, it is crucially important to provide an environment and work climate conducive to both the task and the people. HR leadership is about contributing to business success by having both the insight into what is required and the ability to bring that into reality. As Liane Hornsey points out: "HR here at Google is genuinely different from anywhere else. I have worked in some young and funky environments, in dot-com, and in the music industry. It's all about creativity and innovation here. It's about trying to do stuff that's different for our people, so we hire people from an HR point of view who we think can be innovative".

Hornsey likes to compare the atmosphere at Google to campus life. "What you have to understand about our founders is that they went to university, they were PhD students and then founded Google. That is really what we are trying to build here. It's not necessarily about youth, but it is about vibrancy".

But Liane insists that the funky exterior the company projects comes with a purpose. "You can cut it in two ways. You can look at what I call the fluff – the games room, the table football, Hershey bars, the orange juice and all that nice stuff. And then there are the more fundamental policy issues. One of the things this organisation does very differently from others is that we put a lot of energy into the front end. Many of our managers – at all levels – spend a significant amount of time hiring. We hire by consensus, and the reason for this is that if we hire somebody, we want to keep them. We do make sure our managers are approachable, we do run dress-down days, and make it informal. So there is the stuff you see and the underpinning stuff you don't see that is in the fabric," she says.

Conversely, there may be occasional cases where an organisation's success does not depend on individual abilities or organisational capabilities. As Ulrich and Brockbank (2008) point out, a company with a monopoly for instance may be protected from competitive pressures. They argue that in such circumstances, HR professionals pushing for alignment, integration and innovation in talent management would be less likely to contribute to business success.

Given that 'providing direction' is a key function of leadership, how do our leaders seek to do this? The different visions of these HR leaders shape their priorities and general approach. David Fairhurst suggests that a great HR leader:

1. Has a vision of where you want to get to;
2. Is able to get people to want to follow you towards that vision; and
3. Is able to create the environment in which you can all succeed.

For Martin Ferber a great HR leader is about being a partner. Martin had the opportunity to be a business partner years ago because he was reporting directly to the Chief Executive of a laboratory and he has supported five successive heads of operation.

For Anne Minto the mark of a good HR leader is integrity; 'An HRD must have a higher standard of ethics to do this job. If you are not seen as somebody who can be trusted and as somebody who doesn't change with the winds, I don't think you can be credible in this job'. Anne was paid a huge compliment by a senior manager who retired from the company after 30 years service. He said that she was a person of consistency and high ethics and one didn't see her constantly changing, sailing with the wind in one direction one day and saying something else the next day. Since Anne's word is her bond, what he said was terribly important to her.

For Graham White the mark of a great HR leader is the quality of their team, the relationship the team has with its leader and the overall organisation's impression of HR. The most critical thing out of all of them is the relationship with the HR team. For Graham, the Surrey HR team is one of the finest HR teams he has ever worked with. For David Smith the mark of a great HR leader is 'being as un-HR like as possible'!

CONCLUSION

So how these leaders provide leadership will be explored in later chapters, but it is clear that no one size fits all when it comes to HR leadership. These people took different career routes, are of different generations and have been exposed to many different experiences. However they all share a strong achievement drive and are driven by clear values. They all took opportunities when they arose or made them when necessary. They all want to make a difference and to carry on doing so, wherever their career takes them. Most are clearly strategists and some are alchemists as we shall see later in the book. They are all clear that HR leadership is about people and organisation, and providing the basis for both to succeed. In the next chapter, we shall consider how HR leaders win the platform to make things happen, through their relationships with other key stakeholders.

Chapter 3

Exercising HR Leadership

What is an absolute truism is that an effective HRD must achieve power and influence within their organisations if they are to play a meaningful role. With that power and influence HR can lead rather than simply follow. Without power and influence HR executives are merely implementing policies and strategies for the organisation that have been determined by others.

Hesketh and Hird (2008)

In this chapter we shall consider what it means to exercise strategic HR leadership. We shall look at how HR's purpose is evolving, causing the scope of the role and the capabilities required to do it to stretch. In particular we shall examine how HR leaders exert influence in ways which provide their 'licence to operate'.

THE PURPOSE OF HR

The Chartered Institute of Personnel and Development (CIPD) has been getting to grips with the changing role of HR by carrying out research amongst HR practitioners and executives to establish the purpose of HR today. Consistent themes emerged, with consensus that HR's ultimate purpose is to deliver sustainable high performance through people.

This purpose extends HR beyond its traditional heartland since HR's role becomes:

- About both the *individual* and the *organisation;*
- To lead the way;
- To facilitate the way;
- Focusing on both the short term and the long term
- Impacting on the business.

HR must therefore not only deliver great people strategies, but also great organisational strategies. This is about people and performance, the individual and the organisation, addressing internal and external drivers.

This twin focus places a different emphasis from in the past on the HR role, and the skills needed to do it effectively. Of course, HR leaders remain accountable for the operational effectiveness of HR delivery, as we saw in Chapter 1, but they must also be effective strategically. To deliver this purpose HR leaders must continue to focus on the traditional HR drivers – such as attracting and retaining employees, cementing good employee relations, etc. – but they must also take responsibility for developing the organisation, deliberately aiming to build high-performance cultures.

This purpose requires HR leaders to be strategic in their approach, taking a whole systems view of their organisations – understanding what happens and why, internally and externally. It requires taking the needs of a wider range of stakeholders into account. Given their influence on the culture and performance of the organisation, the calibre and practice of senior leaders becomes a key focus of HR leader attention. HR leaders need a view about what their organisation will require from its leaders in future, and must take a shaping role in building the kinds of management and leadership practice that will be fit for today's and tomorrow's challenges.

Given the volatile context, HR leaders must ensure that their organisations are change-ready. They must lead the building of organisational cultures which are agile and supportive of innovation. They must exercise a balanced approach to risk management, using HR's traditional compliance role as an opportunity to create better governance. They must build authentic, transparent processes and cement employee relations on the basis of mutual trust and fair employee value propositions. They must act as chief integrity officers – willing and able to run a commentary on their organisation's health and effectiveness, and be a provocateur of better organisational practice.

Legacy Issues

This strategic intent must drive short-term delivery. Yet stereotypically HR is rarely accused of being strategic; more often the words process, *administration*, *operations* and *policies* are used to describe HR's preoccupations. And sadly these perceptions and implicit limitations are often correct. According to Truss (2008): '*The consensus within the prescriptive literature is that a move towards a more strategic role is desirable if not essential for the future of the HR function.... However the conclusion from the empirical literature is that the role played by HR functions in most organisations remains primarily administrative or reactive.*'

This may be partly because people who have conventionally been attracted into the HR profession are interested first and foremost in people, rather than in people in the business context. Indeed in the past, given the function's relatively slow evolution from its welfare origins through personnel to the HR profession and now human capital, it has been perfectly possible for some HR practitioners to pass through their entire careers unable to articulate some of the core drivers for their business, or to be able to read a balance sheet or even make a business case for investment. As a result, lacking business acumen and being commercially naive, many practitioners have lacked the confidence to contribute to business debates beyond their own functional comfort zone.

And this has left question marks about the capability of some HR professionals to make the shift to a more strategic role.

This legacy has left a long trace and even though people issues have now become the key business driver in knowledge and service intensive firms in particular, HR is still fighting to exert influence at the highest level. A survey of 50 Chief Executive Officers (CEOs) and business leaders by Hewitt (Sforza, 2009) found that HR was generally less influential than other business leaders: *'While 98% of HR leaders surveyed consider themselves part of senior management, 42% believe they have less influence than other members of that team. Approximately 42% of European HR leaders believe that they have the same level of influence as other members of the senior team, compared with just 25% in North America.'*

This context of low and conservative expectations of HR means that in many organisations HR is still positioned as a support function that delivers some specialist services, and increasingly some of these services can be delivered through different means.

The way the HR function (HRF) organises itself can also contribute to the problem. The more that potentially strategic elements of the function, such as business partnering, become so embedded in the business that their potential corporate impact is spread thin, the more that HR thinking and practice can lack strategic strength. Opportunities to act as an enabling force for corporate knowledge sharing or integration of good practice are dissipated. Moreover, HR often lacks and fails to speak the language of business, making it difficult to explain business and people linkages in terms which make sense to other colleagues. Where functional experts are grouped into a small central core, the more jargon-laden and 'ivory tower' HR professionals can sometimes appear. Anne Minto, for instance, suggests that many HRFs tend not to be very good at articulating employee propositions and don't make them part of the business agenda.

Another perceptual challenge, according to one Human Resources Division (HRD) focus group participant, is that HR generally lacks confidence to push things forward: 'I think that sometimes HR want it to happen, but don't put themselves forward'. After all, HR was generally silent when it came to challenging reward practices which contributed to the problems in the financial services sector. As a result HR can come across to others as operating in an irrelevant 'do good' category, and isolated from business priorities especially if there is no quantification of HR's value. Conversely, the HRF can become overly obsessed with measuring every activity in order to justify its existence.

HR can sometimes be its own worst enemy. Innovation, for instance, is clearly a key factor in organisational and business performance, yet as the profession struggles to define itself as a strategic partner with a strong business sense, some HR executives have become even more conservative and cautious – and less open to ideas – than the line managers they support, according to Rosabeth Moss Kanter (Harvard Business School) who has studied innovation for 25 years. Similarly, Jeffrey Pfeffer (a professor of organisational behaviour at Stanford University's Graduate School of Business) says: 'Most of what HR does kills innovation'.

When this happens, a vicious circle gets under way. HR's perceived lack of business relevance reduces the value of the function in the eyes of internal stakeholders, making it harder for HR to contribute strategically, and results in HR being seen as a costly overhead. Then HR is driven to cut costs and improve efficiencies. Cost cutting gets enacted in two ways. First, the function itself is challenged to improve its cost:benefit ratios. There can be something of a 'macho' element about this. For instance HR professionals taking part in an HR Director's networking meeting were heard to boast about their HR:line ratios being anything from 1:700 and upwards. Second, HR gets drawn into assisting in headcount reduction across the business, whether or not the organisation actually needs the heads which are being cut. If HR is merely executing the plan, rather than part of the decision-making process, the purpose of building sustainable performance may be severely undermined. And as we know, cost cutting can only go so far before it becomes counterproductive to the longer-term viability of the organisation.

Establishing the Value of HR

Over the past two decades there has been widespread debate on both sides of the Atlantic about leadership in general and the HRF in particular. The debate has largely centred on the ability of the HRF – or lack of it – to make a substantial contribution to business success. One aspect of the debate centres on the measurement of value. In the 1990s, researchers on both sides of the Atlantic worked to establish a 'science' around the impact of HR practice on organisational performance. Huselid (1995) and others attempted to establish cause and effect links between HR practice and top-level financial returns, and although this work was influential, empirical evidence still remains relatively slight.

The UK and Ireland's professional body for HR – the CIPD – under the leadership of Geoff Armstrong, was instrumental in commissioning various research studies into the links between people and organisational performance. Part of the driver for this research was to establish once and for all how HR contributes to business success. One major study led by John Purcell at Bath University (Purcell et al. (2009)) looked into the 'Black Box' links between people and performance, while David Guest at Kings College, London identified a wide range of variables (or 'bundles' of HR practices) which appear important to the achievement of high performance. On the whole though, the 'science' underpinning the financial contribution of HR is still at a formative stage.

Similarly, in the late 1990s, the human capital movement in the UK aimed to establish the value of HR as a business contributor in its own right. The goal was to establish a formula for calculating a causal link with business results and a financial rate of return on investment in people which could then be used in valuing companies. It was assumed that as a result of establishing the business case, the boardroom door would open to HR and in some cases this happened. However, interest in the human capital movement appeared to dwindle when the then Chancellor of the Exchequer, Gordon Brown, did not include the formula as part of the Operating Financial Review (OFR).

John Boudreau (2007) and others continue in the quest to produce a 'decision science' which can inform business decision-making about HR issues, processes and their impact. 'Evidence-based HR' is the current manifestation of the trend to use data to pinpoint where and how value can be created and also t measure progress.

A Seat at the Table?

A related debate in the 1990s was about whether or not HR leaders should be members of the board. This 'seat at the table' discussion was seen as a benchmark measure of the HR profession's progress towards being seen as a business relevant function. In practice, board presence tends to be more reflective of the erratic power and influence of HR, where presence on the board is often almost an accident of history. In some organisations there is a legacy of board level HR participation. In many others there is not. In others still, the presence of a highly effective HR Director on the board is no guarantee that their successor will occupy the same position.

Many HR executives are still excluded from the boardroom. Does this matter? Various HR leaders we have interviewed for this book consider the 'seat at the table' issue irrelevant to HR leaders' ability to deliver. According to Hesketh and Hird (2008): *'The reality… is much more complex than the mere symbolic presence of HR in the boardroom. It is our contention that this "presence" is far more complex than mere access to the formal decision-making structures in an organisation. Access to the boardroom is in fact a chimera to the role played by HR inside organisations. It distorts and relegates the debate over the importance of people in strategy development and deployment and organisational design to the mere symbolic status of a seat at the table.'*

David Smith and Anne Minto in particular consider the board membership question as a 1990s issue and very much a red herring. Generally there are fewer people on main boards now; for instance, Rio Tinto has only two people on its board, the Chief Executive and the Finance Director. It's the Executive of the Company that is running the company on a day-to-day basis. The more serious issue is whether or not HR issues are treated as priorities by boards, which increasingly they are. Anne Minto expects that when she leaves Centrica, she won't be judged on where she sat but on what she delivered. And David Smith puts the point more forcefully: *'I suppose in terms of the balance of power it's time the profession generally got off its bottom and began to make a difference rather than just talking about how life could be so much better if they had a seat around the table'*.

REPOSITIONING THE FUNCTION

In the past decade or more, the HRF has worked hard to align itself more closely with business. This is evident not only in the changing nature of HR roles and structures but also by the determined effort made by HR teams to align people and business strategies. Anne Minto for one realised early on that 'HR can't be kept in an isolated box. People are integral to a business and everything you do with respect to your people has to be integrated with your business strategy and goals'. Ironically, when the business is operating to a very short-term agenda, aligning people strategies to this can reduce HR to the role of (junior) business partner who reacts to the demands of the business, rather than providing a proactive leadership contribution. After all, many people challenges, such as building leadership pipelines, take time to deliver.

The debate over the strategic contribution made by people has now broadened out into the related field of talent and its management. Ironically, since talent is now widely recognised as crucial to business success, the talent agenda is increasingly owned by CEOs – with the risk that in the future, HR could be sidelined or relegated once again to back office status. And the more reactive HR is, the more likely it is that the function will be driven down a cost-cutting route which adds little value other than in the immediate short term.

To break the vicious circle means stepping up in terms of HR thinking and contribution. As Hagler (2008) suggests, *'There are clearly a number of issues to focus HR efforts in the coming years. HR leaders now operate at the highest level of global companies, but they recognise the need to continue to contribute to "higher" level corporate objectives for their influence to expand'*.

And unless HR exercises leadership, others will. Emerging from a period of economic crisis is precisely the time to redefine the profession, give people confidence and move forward with a new level and type of contribution.

Building HR Credibility

HR needs to step up to lead the talent and performance debates more by *walking* than *talking*. So HR leaders need both to create operational excellence, and also have the capacity for organisational insight and influence in order to run a commentary on the organisation which produces positive change. They need to act as conscience and guardian of the organisation, have the courage to challenge and the judgement to know when to act. They need to be people that others are keen to listen to.

A credible HR leader is able to influence the thinking and practice of others. To be credible the HR leader/function needs to understand the business and its needs and use that understanding insightfully. Anne Minto thinks that business understanding is the basis for HR's credibility. She herself took on an HR role having acquired diverse experience in other roles and businesses: *'I think you should have worked somewhere else in your career as well as having worked in*

HR and it does not have to be years, but it is a good idea to have had some experience of running something other than an HRF because it gives you a different dimension on life – you have been there in the trenches yourself doing it and you have perhaps a bit more empathy with line managers'. If not, non-HR people tend to be brought into HR leadership roles. They tend to succeed in senior HR roles because they trust their business instincts.

Who Are HR's Stakeholders?

Ulrich has urged HR to remember that perceptions count. Value is not what HR thinks they are delivering but 'Value in this light is defined by the receiver more than the giver. HR professionals add value when their work helps someone reach their goals. It is not the design of a program or declaration of policy that matters most, but what recipients gain from these actions'. Ulrich urged HR to think about its activities less as 'do-ables' but rather as 'deliverables', i.e. the value being delivered to someone by the focused application of HR effort.

Previously HR's principal stakeholders have been considered internal to the organisation. As Ulrich and Brockbank (2005) point out: *'HR professionals have been coached to spend time with general managers and with their counterparts in sales, marketing, and manufacturing to ensure that HR work helps deliver business results …(they) built staffing, compensation, training, and other programs and policies that focused on employees and kept companies legally compliant'.*

So who are HR's stakeholders now? The stakeholder landscape is widening. More recently, Dave Ulrich in particular has urged HR practitioners to focus their efforts on meeting the needs of a broader group of stakeholders. For Ulrich and Brockbank, 'The HR value proposition means that HR practices, departments, and professionals produce positive outcomes for key stakeholders, employees, line managers, customers, and investors'. This involves working back from the needs of the end-user (the customer) and the beneficiary (the shareholder or equivalent), identifying what employees and managers will need to be able to deliver what the customer requires and defining the HR value proposition to meet these needs.

Towards a More Shaping Role

Exercising leadership involves not only deducing what is needed, but also proactively seeking to create value. This means that HR leaders need to adopt a shaping role, which Ulrich describes as that of a 'credible activist'. This is someone who does 'HR with attitude', delivers results, acts with integrity, shares information and builds relationships of trust. Going back to the leadership functions described in the first chapter, HR leaders who really want to create value need to be able to create a shared sense of direction, lead with courage, influence others and champion change if necessary.

AN HR LEADERSHIP PERSPECTIVE

To inform this more shaping role, HR leaders need to develop a perspective which can fashion the contribution of the function to business success both now and tomorrow. For Jackie Orme, there are two main ways of adding value as an HR leader:

(1) By developing depth of expertise in specialist functions, such as professional talent management, supporting change readiness of the whole or part of the organisation, and hence shaping the organisational agenda by having a strong viewpoint – for instance on helping the organisation to find new solutions to a pension deficit challenge and having the expertise to back it up.

(2) By trading on HR's insight into people and organisation – HR provides leadership for the organisation through trading on its insight by virtue of its close proximity to the organisation and its people. Through numerous conversations with leaders, challenges to conventional thinking and many types of 'mirror holding' activities, HR leaders help organisations see themselves in a different light, which in their own way will be as significant as marketing having a breakthrough customer insight. And this means having such credibility that senior colleagues want to have your viewpoint on complex issues.

An active perspective equips HR to be interventionist, rather than just a facilitative observer. Mike Campbell thinks that HR practitioners rely too much on their facilitative skills and miss the opportunity to express a view. He offers this note of warning: *'Don't be seduced by the siren call of facilitation. In most businesses leaders have limited time. Sometimes we in HR need to be leading the business not just following or supporting. Of all the functions we're probably perceived as the most "soft and fluffy" as far as other business leaders are concerned. We're probably doing too much facilitation in challenging times – that's the last thing you need. If you're the right person you need to tell people how to get off a burning platform.'*

Customer Focused

An HR perspective that is both unique and powerful is one that establishes the linkages between employee commitment, customer attitudes and investor returns, and then leads to effective delivery. As Ulrich says, HR value for customers will require that HR professionals answer the question 'How do customers and other key stakeholders – investors, managers, and employees – benefit if they spend time with HR professionals or adapt innovative HR practices?'

According to Brockbank (1997), strong customer focus will drive HR's strategic agenda and therefore the next step for HR is to connect with those outside the firm and understand what customers need from the organisation – what kinds of service, product or brand promise they want delivered – and then work out what will be needed in terms of people and organisation to deliver that.

Future Focused

Typically an overemphasis on alignment with business strategy can lead to HR developing systems to improve performance only in the short term. Particularly in turbulent times like these, taking an exclusively short-term focus runs the risk that organisations will miss out on the opportunity to prepare for the recovery and lack the capabilities they need when growth returns.

The HR leader perspective needs to be both short and long terms. For Brockbank (1997), a strategic agenda for HR will include building organisational capabilities for the long term which make the organisation 'capable of leap-frogging the competition through continual and radical innovation'. The key capabilities include talent, change, leadership and administrative efficiency. For Brockbank, organisational culture is essentially bundles of organisational capabilities required to deliver current and future business strategies. For Ulrich, these include speed, shared mindset, learning, collaboration, accountability, leadership, strategic clarity, efficiency and customer service as well as innovation.

Of course all HR activities can be both short- and long-term in their effects on organisational capability. Recruiting, developing and retaining people are critical activities when organisational success and competitive advantage depend on intellectual capital and organisational capabilities. Working on incentive pay plans and improving recruitment systems are also important. But short-term alignment activities are inherently reactive unless they are underpinned by a future focus and take longer-term implications into account. What distinguishes how these activities are used – reactively versus in shaping mode – is the focus on longer-term capability growth.

For Jackie Orme, a long-term perspective is not an optional extra if you want to unlock competitive capability: '*Naturally you have to hit your near-term targets, e.g. cost drivers, revenue per headcount etc., but if that is all you do, you will have failed*'. The guiding principle is both supporting and challenging the organisation to deliver today's agenda and laying the right foundations for tomorrow.

The longer-term perspective involves taking into account how the business context is changing and the external business realities that influence how HR practices are best applied. Therefore HR leadership involves understanding where your organisation's growth plan is heading and the implications of current and future external business/global contexts on this. Technology, economic and regulatory turbulence, globalisation and demographic changes are identified as the four particularly key external factors for HR to understand so they can make strategic contribution, according to Ulrich and Brockbank (2008).

Then HR leaders work out the implications for people strategy, together with a realistic sense of time frame. Building leadership talent has a long lead time, so too does building high-performance capabilities. These include shared mindset and employee engagement; talent and leadership; strategic clarity and speed; the ability to work effectively across boundaries and learning; collaboration and speed; customer responsiveness and accountability. All aspects of culture change take longer, and there are classic risks of overestimating what can be achieved even in five years. However, all aspects of culture change are happening naturally in the moment, so leaders must work out the nature of changes required and positive influence the culture and talent building processes with the longer-term in mind. This is what Ulrich and Brockbank term the skill of the 'Culture and Change Steward': HR professionals recognizing, articulating, and helping shape a company's culture.

Strategic anticipation

By studying how the context is changing, HR leaders gain invaluable insight which enables them to strategically anticipate key issues which will affect their business down the line. As 'Business Allies' HR professionals know how the business makes money - who their customers are, and why they buy the company's products or services. And they have a basic understanding of the functions of various corporate departments such as finance, marketing, R&D, and engineering, so they can help the business make money". This enables them to take both a short- and long-term view of what needs to be done to help their organisations survive and thrive. And the economic crisis adds extra impetus to this argument. Given the pace of change, even faster responses still are needed just to stay put, let alone get ahead of the next wave of change. A lack of sensitivity to changing events can trip up even the most brilliant of executives, as Mayo and Nohria (2009) found. Without the ability to read and adapt to changing business conditions, a leader's personality and skill are but temporal strengths. After all, the seeds for the economic crisis were sown before 2008–2009 and those organisations which are well placed now have generally had leaders who read the zeitgeist well.

Strategic anticipation is a key element of what Mayo and Nohria call 'Zeitgeist Leadership'. They coined the term to describe the ability to understand and pursue the unique opportunities the zeitgeist presents for each company. From their study of 1000 US business leaders, entrepreneurs and managers, these authors found that what separates the truly great leaders from the merely competent is their understanding of the main contextual factors. These included government intervention, global events, demographics, social mores, technology and labour, and making strategic choices accordingly. Moreover these authors found that some CEOs and founders played an important role in defining and shaping the context in which they lived and worked.

Schein (1992) introduced the notion of leader as agent of change. He argued that 'leadership… is the ability to step outside the culture… to start evolutionary change processes that are more adaptive. This requires one to look beyond the status quo and ask…what if?' Boston Consulting Group (Strack et al., 2008, 2009) carried out two phases of research on behalf of the European Association of Personnel Management (EAPM). The research was carried out with business leaders and HR executives to understand how organisations can create people advantage during these times of economic crisis. There was consensus that the crisis has reinforced the need for HR to be able to anticipate change by managing demographics, globalisation and change in ways which equip organisations to thrive.

And since it is now clear that some of the rules by which business will be conducted may be changing, and that economies and labour markets are changing too, big ticket items for HR, such as talent, will be transformed – that much is clear. How can HR change the economics of the business? HR professionals must take a view about what needs to be done, and get into a position where their words carry weight. After all, HR leaders cannot sit around complaining about being excluded. HR leaders need to work out for instance into how companies can keep focused on their customers and markets while struggling to find the means of production.

Strack et al. recommend the following practices:

- *Strategic Workforce Planning.* Companies should build scenarios based on a precise understanding of their supply (influenced by retirement and other attrition rates) and demand (influenced by business strategy and productivity) needs. In this way, they can better redeploy their staff – rather than simply sacking them – and anticipate any future shortages of skilled workers.
- *Performance Management.* Companies should overhaul their performance management and rewards systems so that these better reflect long-term business goals and reinforce the company's values.
- *Employee Engagement.* Companies should engage with employees in an honest, direct and empathetic way and create excitement around the opportunities at a time when traditional motivators, such as pay increases and promotion, are not an option.
- *Leadership Capabilities.* Companies should equip their leaders with the very different set of skills needed to run a company struggling with cutbacks rather than growth opportunities.

Moreover, since change is likely to be ongoing, companies should ensure that when introducing change they have a clear change agenda and sustained and rigorous programme management in place. In particular HR should ensure that employee communication is more personal, more frequent and more likely to build trust.

Armed with this future focus, and their organisation's growth plan to understand where their organisation is really trying to go, HR leaders must anticipate the main areas of potential growth opportunities, organisational strengths and weaknesses, as well as risk areas which must be acted on. They know that some are longer-term deliverables and they may have to work hard to achieve sustained commitment from key stakeholders. But as Angela Smith of Virgin Atlantic, who took part in Personnel Today's focus group suggests, you have to be able to put the business case across convincingly: '*HR is a business operation. If you are not talking in the same language then you are going to isolate yourself. Virgin works really hard to create its culture, and work with its employees and create empowerment, but it is a business. If I just rock up to my group CEO's office and offer a fluffy reason why we should do something, then he is simply not going to listen. It's about the output, return on investment and sound commercial reasons why* (Williams, 2009).'

Willingness to seize the moment and promote a strong business case is required, especially during the economic crisis when speed may make the difference between organisational success or failure. But results speak louder than words and HR leaders must strengthen the tie between activity and value, increasing the capacity for sustainability. Angela Smith argues that HR is sometimes too diffident: '*An HR leader should be seen as that go-to person and true strategic partner. I think that sometimes HR want it to happen, but don't put themselves forward.*' And Anne Minto agrees: '*You need to have the courage of your own convictions; that if it is something you believe is right, then you have to stand up and be counted for that. That way you can get people to understand that what you are pushing forward is for the benefit of the business.*'

Management Innovation

Another area where HR can demonstrate organisational insight is through management innovation, i.e. a marked departure from traditional management principles. Hamel and Breen (2007) declared that 'management is out of date'. The changing workforce, and the changing nature of work suggest that conventional management styles which were suitable for co-located homogeneous workforces may no longer be most effective at getting the best out of people. But what is?

HR leaders need a perspective on what management and leadership are needed for their organisations – now and tomorrow – taking into account the needs of the changing workforce. For instance teams are often now transitory, and virtual. Work is complex and requires collaboration. HR will need to develop strategies that reflect/anticipate these changing needs, even if the task may be challenging. As Gratton (2007) points out, senior leaders must provide role models of collaboration even if they were not brought up in this context.

High-Performance Principles

An HR leadership perspective should be underpinned by sound principles. I believe that HR's greatest contribution is building an organisation which is capable of sustainable performance. That is about unlocking competitive capability and requires a focus on organisational culture as much as on talent. Effective HR professionals not only work with business leaders to draft strategies, they also collaborate on how to implement strategies. I consider the following principles are as relevant to HR as they are to high-performing government organisations from which they were deduced. The following key principles guide how work is done (Accenture study reported in Linder and Brooks, 2004). High performing government organisations are:

- *Client-centred* and 'define their mission in terms of the needs, expectations and perceptions of their constituents' – Similarly HR needs to be able to help build client-centred business models which are robust yet flexible. Therefore HR leaders really need a view on how best to improve employee commitment in such a way that it leads to improved customer service, product innovation, etc.
- *Outcome oriented* and their performance measures reflect their strategic objectives – For high performing HR teams the strategic agenda will set the criteria and framework for flexible HR practices in the short term which can be adjusted as conditions change. Outcomes will include improved organisational effectiveness, achieved by anticipating and proactively seeking to address aspects of culture and management styles that help or hinder business performance.
- *Accountable*, making their accounts visible as well as the way they spend their money – in HR's case, using appropriate metrics to identify progress to key outcomes.
- *Innovative and flexible* and, 'actively seek new opportunities and respond creatively to new challenges' – HR leaders must be willing to lead and differentiate their HR practices to give their organisation competitive advantage. They need to consider delivering talent development and planning in new ways, for instance via supply chain management techniques. They also need to be innovative, not only in HR's own functional practices, but also in seeing and making opportunities for the business as a whole.
- *Open and collaborative,* developing relationships with stakeholders and other agencies – HR leaders and teams must also role model the high-performance capabilities required as a foundation for organisational performance.

To these principles I would add 'speedy': HR needs to act with pace to move a leadership agenda forward. And HR has to be extremely influential, and capable of building powerful collaborative relationships if it is to deliver an agenda whose outcomes are valued by stakeholders. The most talented HR leaders tend to work 'in pockets within a business'. They have a relationship with their client executives, and are able to have a dialogue and push back as appropriate (Cappelli, 2005). The challenge here is that these relationships can depend on individual leaders rather than the wider HR function, and can therefore also be a source of vulnerability if something changes between the key participants in the relationship.

Ability to Convert Perspective Into Insight and Action

But a perspective alone is unlikely to be of use if HR leaders are unable to create insights and then apply insights to practice. According to Jackie Orme, *'You need to know what separates the mediocre from the good, and the great. You need the strong ability to understand what drives performance and what gets in the way. Then you need to be able to turn that understanding into insight and action. You need to plan for both today and tomorrow'*. HR leaders should be able to articulate and shape the underpinning strategies and business models across other parts of business, together with co-progenitors from other functions. And while Schein (1988) argues that leaders must introduce change effectively so the organisation does not become archaic or self-destructive, HR leaders need to be able to orchestrate the change process.

BUILDING IMPACTFUL STRATEGY

So as strategic partners – whether they are integrated within lines of business or working with executive teams to create overall people strategies that deliver tangible results. This is the competency of 'Strategy Architect' according to Ulrich et al. (2008): HR professionals need to have a vision for how the organization can win in the future, and play an active part in the establishment of the overall strategy to deliver this vision. Having studied the market environment, HR leaders need to address the following questions:

- Where is business going?
- What are the organisational capabilities that we must have to create products and services that result in our customers' favouring us ahead of our competitors?
- What are our measures of success, i.e. business drivers?
- How well is the business performing on these success measures?
- What are some of key challenges faced in achieving success? In times of economic crisis, these are likely to include how to develop resilient strategy, how to keep innovating so that you become a first mover in the recovery. Maintaining quality of product and proposition will be the key, as well as improving your ability to move with speed so that you can quickly move to recovery.

Then the work as Business Partners should be framed as follows:

- What is the business strategy that sets an agenda for how HR will help our company succeed? What are the business issues which require partnership from HR? (i.e. the people implications of business strategy.)
- What employee abilities do our people need so that they can understand and respond to short- and long-term market demands?
- How do we invest in HR practices that deliver business results?
- How do we organise HR activities to deliver maximum value?
- What are the skills needed? Specifically, how do you do it? How do we ensure that HR professionals will know what to do and have the skills to do it?
- How do you measure the impact of the HR strategy on the business success measures?
- How will the strategy be executed?

(Based on Ulrich (1997) and SHRM (2004)

HR leaders must also forecast potential obstacles to success, and facilitate the process of gaining strategic clarity. To be perceived as relevant, HR must be able to execute strategies which deliver value to customers, investors, managers and employees. To make things happen as an HR leader, Tybura advocates a processual approach to strategy making and the management of change, in which an HR leader needs skills of critical analysis, the ability to identify and manage connections and to influence key decision makers who may take a more analytical approach than HR stereotypically does. Of course good execution requires great team working, project management and organisational skills within the HR team, and the ability to partner key stakeholders along the way.

But even a strong set of insights and good execution are only part of what HR leaders need if they are to be successful. By far the most important skill in partnering is that of relationship management and, by extension, the ability to influence others. Influence is the enabling mechanism of change, as Katz and Kahn (1978) point out: 'Leadership is the influential increment over and above mechanical compliance with the routine directives of the organization.'

THE ABILITY TO INFLUENCE

Effective HRDs are 'clearly leading HR and people strategies on behalf of the board', according to Hesketh and Hird (2008). They are what Ulrich and Brockbank (2008) describe as "credible activists" - who perform "human resources with an attitude." However, the position HR occupies in terms of its power and influence within organisations is highly contested both within and without organisations, as we have discussed earlier in this chapter. Individuals and organisations are political systems in which individuals enact a strategy, or not, according to how politically powerful they are in the organisation and the level and type of conflict inherent in the organisation at the time. Organisations are 'shifting coalitions of individuals and groups with different interests, imperfect knowledge and short attention spans.' Within such political contexts, the skill of influencing is key to shifting perceptions, gaining agreement and making things happen.

HR Positioning

How much HR is able to exercise influence very much depends on how HR is positioned in the system. Julia Tybura points out that other people's perception is the key to an HR leader's success. That perception will determine or reflect an HR leader's personal power base. And as Andy Egginton, one of the HRDs taking part in Personnel Today's focus group suggests: 'If HR is seen as a strategic partner with the business, then it works really well. If HR is seen simply as the provider of HR services and products, then the ability to be able to shape the "what now?", even if we do know where the business is going, is severely limited. If HR can get itself into that position, we have the best chance of influencing and using the added value we can bring.' As Ulrich et al. (2008) point out: "HR professionals who are credible, but not activists, are admired, but do not have much impact. Those who are activists, but not credible, may have ideas, but will not be listened to." Moreover, no matter how effective an HR leader might be as an individual, without great execution from the HR team an HR leader's credibility is shot. Similarly, HR's impact on the business may vary according to the business context. Ulrich and Brockbank (2008) argue that HR is most closely associated with business performance under conditions of significant change and has substantially less influence under conditions of little change.

Building a powerful position is therefore essential if the HR leader is to really deliver an effective people and organisation agenda. And with a political system, achieving that degree of influence can be a murky process which challenges a leader's value set. According to Clark (2000), executives use personal strategies which involve them in power struggles over limited resources and the deployment of material, symbolic and ideological powers to secure distributional advantages for themselves and the functions they represent. Clark argues that the importance of these (power) networks in constructing, shaping and ultimately determining the outcome of material resources is generally under-estimated. Being able to work with these informal and relational aspects of an HR leader's role is arguably as important to an HR leader's success as their intellectual calibre, their 'hip-pocket' HR skills (to quote Jackie Orme) or their team's effectiveness.

Totally Integrated

In most cases described by our contributors, the HRF is completely integrated as a business function in their organisations. For instance in the case of the HR team at Centrica, HR is structurally completely integrated as a business function as Anne Minto describes: '*I sit on the Centrica executive. All of my HR*

directors sit on the management teams for each of the business units and they
have dual reporting relationships into the managing director of that business
and also to me. I also have a HR Leadership team (HRLT) which comprises all
the HRD's of the main business units plus the directors of reward, pensions,
people development and the SMO which is our shared management organi-
sation. The Centrica People Agenda is comprehensive and integrated into the
business strategy for Centrica. The people agenda is integrated fully into each
Business Unit to ensure consistency and fairness across the group.'

A close working relationship

Where HR is positioned in the system depends to a very large extent on the HR
leader's relationship with executives at the highest level and his/her skill as
a critical influencer. HR leaders must be politically able, capable of immediate
impact and a strategic contribution, good at team working and worthy of
respect. If their own team does not operate at a high level, it undermines the HR
leaders' credibility and they lose the respect of their colleagues. Therefore all of
our contributors place great emphasis on building their own team's effectiveness. When the HR leader has a close personal working relationship with the
most senior business leaders, especially the CEO and the Chief Financial
Officer (CFO), HR's power and influence is at its highest. Then HR performance tends to be judged less on quantifiable measures than on quality. Again –
perception is the key.

So important is having a close working relationship with the CEO that Liane
Hornsey, for instance, wouldn't go to work in an organisation if she didn't think
that she'd be able to build a good relationship with the CEO: *'If at interview*
I've not felt that I could work with this guy, and this guy would be totally open
with me and I'd be his confidante and part of his kitchen cabinet, I wouldn't
want to work at the company.' Previous career choices, such as going to work at
NTL and lastminute.com were because she knew and liked the CEOs there.
Indeed all of the HR leaders interviewed for this book had strong relationships
with their organisations' top teams.

This close relationship has been termed 'the Golden Triangle' by Hesketh
and Hird (2008) to describe the informal, tacit or intangible network of executive relationships and conversations – typically but not exclusively operating
between the CEO, finance director and their director or vice president of human
resources. I term this 'the charmed circle' which can also act as a 'closet
cabinet'. When it works positively, this tight alliance ensures that the centrality
of people issues is recognised and therefore helps the HR leader role grow in
scope and influence. This is also echoed by the SHRM report (2002) on the
Future of HR: 'The partnership between leaders who are committed to their
workforce and HR professionals who understand the drivers of the business is
incredibly powerful.'

Hesketh and Hird identify a number of structural influences which tend to lead to the formation of a 'golden triangle'. They found that these relationships are more typical of large organisations and those with high labour costs, where the key metric used is not costs of HR per FTE ($1000 in US) or value added per employee (£56,700 in top EU 750 in 2007) but the extent to which investment in people and equipment is leveraged through people. In such contexts HRDs understand the high correlation between changes in Market Capitalisation and people leverage and keep this relationship under constant review.

Another important structural factor is the presence of powerful Trade Unions – which tend to make CEOs nervous. As will be evident from the backgrounds of some of our HR leaders, employee relations have conventionally provided a strong power base for HR Directors who have successfully managed union relationships, especially during periods of industrial tension, where HR becomes the ultimate negotiator. Hesketh and Hird point out that no news can be bad news for HR: when employee relationships are less adversarial, HR's power base can erode. In scientific and technical contexts, where managers have little preparation for managing people, HR becomes powerful as a source of support on labour relations, development, employee engagement, etc. Conversely, when a CEO is 'bottom line only' – driven by financial returns for shareholders – she/he is likely to undervalue the contribution of effective people strategies and HR leadership, and a 'golden triangle' is unlikely to form in the first place. Similarly, in a global organisation where HR tends to be limited to in-country activity and global programmes of delivery, HR locally may lack power and influence within the corporate whole.

However crucial they may be to HR leadership effectiveness, these partnerships are essentially fragile and can change in an instant since they reflect individual personalities, responses to external pressures and group 'politics'. Moreover, senior colleagues who are not part of this charmed circle may resent HR's place in it.

Active Engagement is the Only Option

But given the growing recognition of the importance of human capital to business success, gaining the support of executive colleagues for effective people strategy becomes paramount. Membership of this charmed circle therefore becomes a necessity, rather than an option, especially when an HR leader lacks a formal boardroom place. The HR leader has to be willing to find themselves in the middle of the political power games of executive networks, whether or not these are to their taste. If not, they can be forced out. Then HR is forced instead to focus upon the longer-term policy of strong HR advocacy, and delivery which is tightly focused on business success and measured by performance criteria.

Supporting the CEO

The centrality of these close working relationships to the effectiveness of HR leaders at the top is evident to all our contributors. In Google, HR is very much at the top table. Liane Hornsey said that she could not work any other way: *'The most important job I do is supporting the most senior person that I work with, no question. And one thing that I've learnt over time is you have to be a very different sort of person to be able to do that. You have to be willing to get a kick out of hearing a CEO using your words, and not tell anyone they're yours. You have to genially think that's really cool, and I do. Of the time I spend with the senior team, I would say the vast majority of it I spend with the very senior team and that's where I get my kicks and that's what I love doing. And I would just leave my job if I didn't have that relationship with the CEO – I just wouldn't stay.'*

David Smith views his role as the conscience of the organisation, and therefore feels that it's important to spend time with the CEO talking about where things are going and giving feedback behind closed doors. In his role it's important to interact equally with members of the executive team, with whom you need to be influential.

A Key Member of the Senior Team

The HR executive must also have strong influencing and leadership skills across their executive cadre, be clearly perceived as a key member of senior team and be known for participating effectively in strategic discussions. Typically, the pattern of such close working relationships amongst executives is that members meet frequently, often in an informal and relaxed manner, in a culture of mutual trust and respect.

Anne Minto for instance has a very close working relationship with her colleagues on the Centrica Executive Committee. For Anne this close working relationship ensures that the voice of the People Agenda and the role of HR is articulated around the table on the macro strategic people issues. The Centrica executive Team, under the leadership of Chief Executive Sam Laidlaw, are fully involved in the major people decision making particularly around talent management and organisational change.

It is important for Anne to get her executive colleagues on board with the people agenda, and to make sure that the people agenda is reflective of the needs of the business. Ensuring that HR is at the heart of major decision making is vital as nine times out of ten there will be a significant people element to be addressed. The constraints are around how quickly initiatives can proceed because they need a time frame and financial commitment and they may sometimes be vying for position with other projects.

Confidante of CEO

Anne Minto acts as confidante to her CEO: '*I probably am the main confidante of not just the Chief Executive, but also with my colleagues on the executive. That is an extremely important role for an HRD to do well and one which I personally take very seriously. I think I am in a hugely privileged position that I will often be the conduit and the Chief Executive. That's a role that if you play it well is extremely valuable for the organisation.*'

Anne believes that having good listening skills is very important. The CEO needs somebody that they can trust to talk about the issues that he or she may have in respect of certain members of the senior team. When issues arise a CEO will want to discuss in confidence and seek advice and this is a phenomenally important role for an HRD. Anne believes that if you can't be that person, and keep things very confidential, then it would be very difficult, if not impossible to do the job.

But however valuable, this role is not without its risks, not least to the HRD's integrity, and Anne points out the dangers: 'Play it incorrectly and your trust and ethics just disappear. So you have to be quite skilled to play this role as you also have to be able to articulate on issues which may have been brought to your attention or require resolution and help avoid conflicts arising.'

Development of the Senior Team

Anne works very closely with her CEO, especially with respect to senior leadership development. This partnership works as follows: overall the CEO of Centrica is responsible for people leadership. He gets; very involved with, and takes a great interest in the development of those senior managers Anne's job is about unlocking the capacity of people for competitive advantage. Anne spends a great deal of her time with Centrica's Executive Committee and also with the top fifty managers in Centrica, working on their development. Each of them has a development plan that is regularly discussed, updated and acted upon. Anne also plays a key role in how the Executive Team itself can function better: "It is important in any Executive Team that no one person's opinion dominates and that open discussion is encouraged. The HRD can play a very important role in coaching the development of the senior team to work as effectively as it possibly can and where everyone's contribution is valued."

Anne manages the processes to understand talent and organisational capability requirements: what's working well, what needs to be changed and how the organisation can develop. Succession planning for senior and middle managers occupies a lot of Anne's time: '*We regularly review our talent – where we are planning to place people, who is ready for a move, who's coming on up the organisation, making sure that we are nurturing, developing and mentoring those people with potential. I am passionate about developing people at all levels from Graduates through to the Board.*'

Strategy Formulation and Implementation

So while membership of the charmed circle provides legitimacy for an HR leader, to become part of the circle and remain there requires considerable political acumen. Being part of the circle enables HR to gain support for their role of strategy architect (as Ulrich describes it) or strategic progenitor (as Hesketh and Hird call it). To be successful strategic progenitors, HR leaders should not restrict themselves to commentary about their own function. As Ulrich and Brockbank insist, '*HR professionals need a perspective that is compatible with, and distinct from, other business perspectives. That is, they must be able to understand and value the finance and sales perspectives, but they must also add their own point of view. Without such a unique and powerful perspective, they are redundant and fail in their aspirations as full business contributors.*' Rather, HR leaders should exercise their business leadership skills more widely, be able to originate and add value to any discussion with respect to different functions or business operations beyond the HRF.

Inside the 'charmed circle', HR executives need to be in vanguard of strategy formulation – thinking first about the business and then the related people issues. They need to play a strong role in articulating and shaping the underpinning strategies of new and evolving business models – which are usually well beyond the HR comfort zone of HR administration – and be able to operate fluently in more complex service delivery and financial models.

Spotlight Example: Mike Campbell at ICL/Fujitsu

Mike Campbell (now People Director at easyJet) describes his early career experience working for International Computers Limited (ICL) (now Fujitsu). In this example Mike's own membership of the the 'charmed circle' is a vital element of delivering business success. So too is Mike's leadership emphasis – business first, people second:

'I became Personnel Director for ICL's International businesses and went to work in the business outside Western Europe – I was part of a triumvirate of MD, CFO and me. My role was to leverage competence to help growth. We operated in over 20 different countries often in difficult parts of the world – Zimbabwe, India, Kenya, Malawi, Poland, Hungary, Czech Republic, Russia, Croatia, Egypt, United Arab Emirates, Malaysia, Singapore, Hong Kong, etc. These all operated as separate businesses with their own Profit and Loss Accounts (P&L). This was the time when the USSR was ending and things were freeing up after the fall of communism.

We three acted as advisers to these different businesses at different stages of their life-cycle. With such fast change we needed to attract, recruit and develop good quality people and there was risk of losing key people – we were one of the few western companies in communist Eastern Europe, so as the economies freed up we became a clear target for inbound western companies seeking good local business

Continued

Spotlight Example: Mike Campbell at ICL/Fujitsu—cont'd

managers. One approach would not work across them all. It forced you to think about business dynamics and working closely with the finance guy and MD helped.

ICL then started to separate out its hardware business – we were demerging it into Fujitsu. The volume products business (PCs, notebooks, servers) consisted of all the design, manufacturing, sales and supply aspects from the hardware business that ICL had together with those that had been acquired with cultures around Europe that were ex-Nokia, Eriksson, Data Saab, Regnecentralen, ASi, etc. The backgrounds and cultures were very different, but we wanted to create one blended product based solutions business behind one brand sourced with development experience in the UK, Sweden and Finland – and leveraging that which was based in Japan. We had lots of separate businesses working in Western Europe and a strategic focus was needed – We changed the business model from a transfer price to a transfer cost model as part of a major change program including shifting the incentive programme and what we would now describe as talent management to align with business objectives and then sold the ideas back into the Japanese head office. It was great experience of understanding and being successful within other cultures.

With a transfer price model it was easier for salesmen in the field to agree a reduction in internal price with one or other of the factories, (who were looking for volume to recover against overheads), than it was to drive for better price and company margin from the customer. This shift in model focused the sales force on the commercial success in their area of operation thus generating better overall company margin – there was a risk in the short term that salesmen may turn down low margin high volume business which helped in the factories, but a strong education and incentive system based on absolute margin as opposed to percentage margin ensured the right behaviours and results. We went from losing £65 m pa to making gross £20 m in 18 months and grew the revenue over the same period. (We were awarded the Fujitsu Presidents Award for our success). So I was exposed to European management and the development of people at all levels, and to the disciplines of not only P&L but also to cash and valuation management.

Fujitsu (with 1500 employees and £ 2 bn turnover) and Siemens (with 7000 employees and £ 5 bn turnover) then agreed a 50:50 joint venture resulting in the new entity Fujitsu Siemens Computers – both separate businesses valued equally. I was involved in the due diligence and ran the integration program and had to make good choices – for instance you have two country managers, how do you choose the best? Out of four factories in Europe which do you keep going? How do you keep business as usual running while making massive changes? What do you know about what the competitors are up to? How do you deal with Works Councils in Germany?' Understanding the strategic drivers and business dynamics and being able to leverage competitive advantage through people are powerful HR leadership credentials. They are characteristic of Mike Campbell's career approach as we shall explore further.

Vulnerabilities of Special Relationships

And while the success of HR leaders is intimately linked to their relationships with their executive colleagues, their enduring credibility and influence are also directly linked to the effectiveness of their own teams. Without a credible HR team delivering effectively, how can HRD expect to have their advice on any aspect of HR delivery be respected?

Even with good delivery, HR's reputation can be vulnerable to fast-changing perceptions. In Graham White's view, HR's relationship with the organisation is only as good as their last delivery. He thinks that people have short memories when it comes to services like HR or Information Technology (IT). When they're doing a great job in terms of delivery, they're the best thing since sliced bread, but the first time something goes wrong then HR is the cause of their dilemma.

Moreover, even membership of the charmed circle is no guarantee of continuing power. For Graham, building individual personal relationships with key players is the best insurance against this. Graham has very strong personal relationships with the CEO and the Finance Director and his business partners have strong personal relationships with service heads. Graham's philosophy is that it's much harder to fall out with a friend than a stranger.

For all their benefits, these close relationships can have major downsides. They tend not to last – and are contingent on the context and externalities of the relationship between the main players such as when one of them moves on, or when the organisation is involved in a merger or acquisition and other senior players come to the fore. The continuation of the alliance also depends on the competence of the HR executive – she/he must be credible and the capable. And HR leader's own skills can increase the focus on people strategies. Without a close working relationship with the CEO and CFO, n HR leader's power base is limited. However, as Hesketh and Hird point out, the increasing centrality of people to the execution of organisational strategy means that a people-oriented CEO can compensate for excluding the HR leader from the 'charmed circle'.

But if this close relationship is so important to an HR leader's power base, how easy is it to be an internal challenger without putting at risk the close relationship? Time and again in our interviews, HR leaders emphasise the importance of courage, of being prepared to state your case and provide challenge.

Of course it helps if you have good emotional intelligence and know how to communicate with your close senior colleagues in ways they prefer. As Mike Campbell says of his current MD, '*I know what makes him tick, what he is looking for. I had a long discussion with him about the impact of change on the key people we depend on for our success. You have to try and influence, be prepared to stick to your ideas but be pragmatic.*' And when things get really tough it's about helping senior colleagues to function effectively under pressure: '*With other Management Team members, it's about helping keep people steady when they may be working under trying circumstances'.* And as for who watches out for the HR Director? This may be a case of cobblers' children: *'It is important to get things into perspective. We're an important business, worse things happen at sea. If you don't have an outside life you'll struggle. For me, my family, friends are important. I enjoy football, I try to keep fit and I really try to retain a sense of humour.'*

CONCLUSION

The presence of these close executive relationships ensures that HR does not exist in a separate, isolated world, but is integral to business success. But in themselves these relationships are fragile, temporary and need working at. HR leaders need to be skilful at managing these relationships and developing their executive team colleagues. They need discretion, judgement and courage to challenge when needed.

HR's core role is to understand people – to think about how to recruit, nurture and develop people. But given the changing world we work in, HR must learn to master and play new roles and develop new skills. And as HR takes on these new roles we must invest in the next generation of HR professionalism to grow HR professionals both within the profession and within firms. An HR leader's credibility depends on their strategic insight, authenticity and political skills. This then equips them to carry out HR's strategic mandate – to deliver a people and organisational agenda which will create sustainable value. In the next chapter we shall consider how HR leaders are transforming their operations to better deliver that agenda.

Chapter 4

Leading for Strategic and Operational Excellence

'Previously success in HR meant either a valued coaching relationship with senior leadership or a strong administrative function. By leveraging technology in new ways there is the potential to marry these functions and create an HR function that effectively services both the administrative and strategic needs of the organisation.'

Society of Human Resource Management (SHRM), 2002

In companies that create competitive advantage through people the HR leader's agenda is about building their organisation's capability to survive and thrive in fast-changing contexts. This is about understanding what the organisation needs in terms of capabilities, both now and in the future, and then developing and implementing plans to build or strengthen these. As we saw in Chapter 3, the key organisational capabilities which HR needs to drive for the future are talent, change, leadership and administrative efficiency. In this and later chapters we shall examine these capabilities in more detail.

Leading for strategic and operational excellence must reflect the changing context, including the changing labour market. Organisations are increasingly becoming global in their operations, creating a more complex HR environment, particularly with respect to integrating diverse cultures. Just some of the elements of complexity include the pace of change required to deliver to mass markets, the speed of communications, economic migration and more rigorous public sector accountability. To survive and thrive in this sort of environment organisations must become agile, ruthlessly decisive and focused intensely on their customers. In times of downturn, HR professionals should help their organisations to prepare for the recovery by becoming more nimble in adapting to change. What they do today will position their organisations to look smart as business conditions improve, or, if they do nothing, they may end up playing catch-up with their more agile competitors.

But the organisational and talent development agenda can be undermined if HR's own delivery capability is underpowered, perhaps because HR is structured in ways which underutilise the talents of HR, or because HR professionals lack the skills to deliver what is required. Then it is HR leadership which must be held accountable if HR fails to add value. The basic HR operations must be done well, but there is a growing argument that these do not add value in their own right and can be delivered in other ways. HR leaders are generally very clear that HR transformation is needed if they are to free up capacity for more value-adding activities. In challenging times like these, HR technology investments, shared services and outsourcing tend to accelerate, as does a focus on finding cost-savings.

In this chapter we consider what is required to both build organisational capability and achieve operational excellence. More specifically we shall look at what HR leaders are doing to transform their functions to achieve greater administrative efficiency, and at the nature of the strategic agenda made possible through a more effective HR organisation.

WAVES OF TRANSFORMATION

But first by way of context, David Fairhurst, Senior Vice-President (People) at McDonalds, provides his perspective on how organisations have been transforming themselves in the past, together with his prediction about what the next wave of transformation might look like:

> 'Workplaces are about getting things done as efficiently and effectively as possible – a truth that applies as much to a public service organisation or a charity as it does to a commercial firm. And over the past 300 years the transformation in organisational efficiency and effectiveness has been dramatic.

> The First Wave of transformation came from machines. But as machines became ever more sophisticated, step-change improvements became harder to find, so the Second Wave of performance enhancement emerged – the management of processes exemplified by Henry Ford with his moving assembly line. But before too long processes were in pretty good shape and once again organisations were looking for the source of the next step-change. And the Third Wave of transformation, the Information Revolution, was enabled by developments in computing and communication technologies. But the capacity of these technologies to deliver step-change performance improvements is already coming to an end.

> So, where will the Fourth Wave be found? Well, with surveys consistently finding levels of employee engagement in the UK at between 20% and 35%. It isn't hard to imagine the performance improvements organisations would enjoy if they could get this resource working at optimum levels. And this is why I firmly believe that improving the way organisations manage their people will deliver the Fourth Wave of transformation. And the potential role of HR in achieving that transformation is clear'.

I agree with David's assessment. This level of workplace transformation requires an HR function which can lead developments, not just follow them. Therefore one aspect of the wider debate about HR's value centres on the design and delivery of HR functions and their contribution to the top-line of organisations. In recent years, the first phase of HR transformation has focused on making HR operations more efficient and effective through process stand-ardisation and technology. The idea is to find new ways to provide HR administration with due attention to cost, quality, efficiency and effectiveness. By so doing, the theory goes, HR is freed up to be more strategic and build the organisation's capabilities.

And there is some urgency to this argument: HR's own capability to be more strategic depends to some extent on how HR is organised. And unless HR is in a position to contribute strategically, HR departments might become a thing of the past, according to Martin Tiplady (2007), HR Director for London's Metropolitan Police Force. And Martin points out, if HR remains exclusively focused on administration that is the road to obsolescence: 'Put simply, there are cheaper – and probably more effective – ways of handling personnel matters. It is called clerking and doesn't, in all cases, require qualified HR professionals.' Martin points out the need for urgency in managing this transformation: 'That is, unless we refocus. And we need to do so pretty darn quickly. Far too long, we have navel-gazed about what HR is, and worried far too much about processing'.

For Ulrich (2008) carrying out the operational aspects of managing people and organizations, is the 'Operational Executor' competency: HR professionals drafting, adapting, and implementing policies ensuring that employees' basic needs - including being paid, relocated, hired, and trained - are efficiently delivered through technology, shared services, and/or outsourcing. Deloitte (2006) suggests that the next phase of HR transformation is more tightly linked to corporate strategy and to creating business value through HR services that address a company's most pressing strategic challenges. That means anticipating critical workforce trends, shaping and executing business strategy, identifying and addressing people-related risks and regulations, enhancing workforce performance and productivity, and offering new HR services to help a company improve and grow. However, many HR leaders are still pursuing in first phase HR organisation on the assumption that improving the design and delivery of HR itself will lead to causal improvement in the performance of the organisation (Ulrich et al., 2008).

TRANSFORMING HR

Deloitte suggests that the focus of First Generation HR Transformation was inward-looking: finding ways to manage and deliver existing HR services more efficiently. HR leaders need to ensure that their internal operations are effective and that they are optimising the HR delivery model. Dave Ulrich (1997) in particular has led thinking on how HR functions can be reoriented to provide value. In the UK, approximately one-third of large organisations have adopted some form of 'Ulrich model', i.e. outsourced or technology-enabled HR transactions, business partners and centres of excellence (or expertise). At the heart of this 'three legged stool' sits a small corporate centre. Unfortunately though, in many cases the process of HR transformation can prove all-consuming, becoming the end in itself rather than the means to greater effectiveness and value creation. Martin Tiplady continues: 'And I know – from personal experience – that the journey to a different structure is pretty painful. But it is an essential one, as the alternative is death by a thousand cuts.'

However, the benefits should outweigh the effort. Technology is repeatedly identified as the key enabler in a range of HR-related operations or services such as e-learning, outsourcing, offshoring and the use of Web 2.0 for recruitment purposes. Automating processes where possible is one of the seven factors the Towers Perrin survey (2008) identified as associated with global merger and acquisition (M&A) success. This is about improving HR service delivery through harnessing technology and ensuring basic HR services are not disrupted (the other six were also linked with HR, for example culture, leadership, rewards, organisation design, staffing and governance). Automation should also improve the consistency of HR processes across operations.

The next generation of HR transformation, according to Deloitte, looks outside the function to help companies achieve their desired results and growth in an environment where competition is global and talent is scarce. This next phase of transformation will require a significant change of focus, 'from today's on HR operations – which are typically budgeted at 0.5% to 0.7% of revenue – to tomorrow's focus on building strategic business services that can help drive share price', such as increasing revenue through new market entry or mergers and acquisitions. HR will need to build services in new or non-traditional areas, such as workforce planning, talent management, mergers and acquisitions, global workforce security, change management and global mobility. As the report's authors comment: 'The next decade will provide HR with significant opportunities to help make a difference to the company; it will be interesting to see how HR steps up to the challenge.'

To maximise the benefits of transformation, HR leaders must address their own capacity issues: both with respect to their own team's capability, and with respect to technology. HR executives are line managers of their own functions. One of the essential steps in getting their own house is staffing the HR organisation with high performers who understand the business, its issues and their implications. Then HR leaders need to review and improve the efficiency and effectiveness of internal operations, and develop their own and line managers' skill sets to equip them for the tasks ahead.

Technology enables employee self-service through Web-based portals and sophisticated call-centres, freeing up HR from administration; these are also a vehicle to leverage information about the workforce, in the way that supermarkets can segment their offering to meet the needs of different groups of consumers. The potential utility of technology in understanding employee needs should not be underestimated. By refocusing HR's efforts on real employee needs, bonds with employees can be reinforced. With hard data, evidence-based HR can know more, do more and be better business advisers.

Outsourcing and Shared Services

The main alternative means of delivering HR administration are by outsourcing or by bundling HR functions together in shared service centres. These arrangements should allow operational aspects of HR to be handled effectively in order to allow HR to focus on value-adding activities. Shared services are increasingly common, particularly in large organisations, but are far less common as joint ventures between organisations. For instance, there has been much discussion about providing HR-shared services across UK Central Government departments but this is only slowly starting to happen as public sector cuts start to bite. Martin Tiplady comments: 'Many of us have developed, or are developing, service centre-type structures. It is the only model in town and we have to make it work. What I have seen so far impresses me, but the longevity of this approach will be the real test. I don't know another model that is affordable.'

Two consultancy-led research papers from Towers Perrin (2007) and the Corporate Research Forum (CRF)/Accenture Lambert (2009) suggest that the use of outsourcing has advanced and expanded in the last 10 years and that HR outsourcing is now established as a popular and viable service delivery strategy for a growing number of organisations (according to another Towers Perrin survey, 2008). They argue that business and service demands are increasingly complex and that these require a re-think of the support systems required for HR.

However, other research by the CIPD suggests that total outsourcing in particular may be less well established than providers might claim. Indeed there are relatively low levels of HR process outsourcing. In their global HR survey Resources Global Professionals (2008) found that reducing administrative costs and simplifying processes are high priorities for companies, but the preferred route is through the creation of shared service centres (providing back office optimisation of process and support activities) rather than outsourcing.

The Challenges of Outsourcing

One of the challenges with HR outsourcing is that people are often not clear what they want to achieve by it. HR outsourcing means different things and is undertaken for different reasons in different organisations. Examples of what outsourcing might mean include:

- Being able to replace time and money on technology;
- Ability to scale up and down more efficiently (risk moves to outsourcer);
- Ability to gain access to best practices;
- Operate multiple processes from a single platform (more efficient); and
- Improve performance (Ephor Group, 2008).

So its purpose is both to achieve cost reductions and also to achieve HR transformation. But what does HR transformation mean – standardisation and control; commercial consciousness or enhanced capability – or all of these? In theory, since day-to-day advice for managers and employees is available from a supplier, outsourcing means that the HR department can be leaner and can focus on strategy, shaping policy and influencing leadership.

However, achieving operational excellence through outsourcing is no mean feat. The road is laid with many bear traps. Towers Perrin points out that outsourcing can fail to deliver its promised benefits. They report that many organisations found no significant decrease in the amount of time spent on administrative tasks post-outsourcing. Furthermore, retained staff felt they continued to spend significant time on transition and change, as well as managing the HR outsourcing arrangement, and less time than expected on business strategy and related tasks. Similarly, quality improvement targets post-outsourcing are also largely unmet. Cost savings are also proving elusive - few always operations managers do see a reduction in the cost of providing HR services for the line business after outsourcing.

New competencies are required to allow the retained HR people to leverage the value of the outsourcing model but acquiring these competencies has been a slow process. While he was at Westminster Council, Jonathan Evans learned a lot both about how local government works and also about the challenges of operating with outsourced HR. As he says: 'It's tougher than you think.' Jonathan argues that since outsourcing is sold on price, if the providers can't deliver on price, relationships become acrimonious. He recommends caution about what you're getting versus what you've contracted for. Jonathan comments that HR tends to be a bit naive when it comes to the contracting business. And while HR people have recognised that to achieve service improvement requires the introduction and application of new technology, this is not an area of interest for many HR professionals. More generally, this lack of competence is being addressed through retraining or bringing in external people.

The Benefits of Outsourcing

In contrast, some organisations are convinced of the benefits of outsourcing, especially with respect to transforming HR's role. For instance BT signed a 10-year global agreement with Accenture in 2005 and Alex Wilson, BT's HR leader stated that by so doing, 'BT is ahead of the game.' He identified three main reasons for renewing the contract with Accenture; 'Accenture has improved the reputation of the function; they've improved service levels and taken out cost; it has freed the business partners to have different types of conversations and interactions with the line.' (Thomas, 2005).

Integral to the People Strategy

The key to using alternative delivery vehicles such as outsourcing successfully is that they are part of the overall people strategy (SHRM, 2002). The best HR strategies derive from the company's business objectives and focus on a few strategic priorities. In this example, David Fairhurst describes the strategic framework for HR activities in McDonalds as follows:

> 'We have identified three "pillars" of activity which provide a focus for our People initiatives: Operational Excellence – ensuring we run a really effective business through People; Education – a broad agenda around capability, skills, training and education; and Modernity – ensuring we are progressive. These are not discrete. They naturally overlap and many initiatives sit in two areas or, indeed, all three. These three pillars are essential to prioritising our efforts. In fact, if an initiative does not contribute to at least one of these areas we will not pursue it.
>
> Furthermore, because the pillars apply equally to all of the disciplines within the team, they provide a framework which enables us to share ideas and work together in an integrated way. Our approach to developing initiatives within the pillars has been threefold. Firstly: to get the *basics right*. These are the crown jewels and the foundation of all our work. Secondly: we must *continually improve*. Finally: we will carry on with the *big moves*. These iconic and, at times, disruptive changes deliberately make a splash.'

Operating such a business-based HR agenda blurs the lines between HR and the business – it promotes new levels of partnership between HR and management.

Success Factors for Outsourcing

Ultimately, HR leaders must ensure that they automate and manage contracts – getting systems designed in the right way. As one HR Director put it, 'If we can't, we're nowhere in the debate.' Similarly, if good outcomes are to be achieved it is important that there is clarity about why the shared services or outsourcing arrangements are being entered into, and what benefits are to be derived. For example are the primary drivers cost, service, freeing up HR resources (and are those resources capable of being upgraded?) or upgrading the quality of information, or all of these? In which case it is important to be clear what tradeoffs may be necessary, since it is unlikely that all are possible without considerable compromise.

HR has to pay attention to opportunities and relationships with third parties, i.e. vendors. Issues can arise over, for instance, ownership of data, accuracy, integration with the system of origin, multiple vendors, legacy systems and other unknown changes resulting from mergers and acquisitions, etc. Unless these are foreseen and managed, the outsourcing service will be less than optimal. There also needs to be capability within the HR function to manage the HR outsourcing arrangements in an efficient and value-added way.

Another Accenture case study organisation – Astra Zeneca – transformed its HR function through introducing centralised HR support. The drivers for the transformation were cost savings and increased customer service (which previously was patchy across the organisation). Throughout the transformation much effort was put into developing the capability development of the HR team for working with third parties. This included improving business acumen, and customer and financial awareness (and other recognised skills including change management, project management and IT skills).

Then HR must relinquish control to line managers and increase their focus on activities that align with organisations' strategic goals. Line manager understanding and capabilities therefore must also be considered when moving to outsourcing arrangements, as their roles can change significantly too. As Martin Tiplady points out, 'The way ahead is about changing the way people and organisations work. This means getting alongside managers, better understanding the business and facilitating its change programmes, improving productivity, and performance coaching, learning and a lot of workforce planning and forecasting. This is what HR is about. And the quicker we realise it, the more secure the function will become.'

The retained HR organisation must be designed correctly to leverage advantages from shared services/outsourcing (Alexander, 2008). As we saw in Chapter 3, the most senior HR executive must have credibility with the company's Chief Executive and the executive team, and in this capacity they act as strategic advisers. HR also has to work differently, for example clearly distinguishing among its various roles: generalist, specialist, business partner and administrator. HR employees then need to develop the deep competencies required for their roles. This should help also clarify and simplify HR career development tracks within and beyond the organisation.

The Senior HR Team

HR leaders who are driving business results also marshal the efforts of their own senior team. When HR is organised into functional silos, for instance compensation, benefits, training, etc. the HR executive can over-rely on balancing resources and priorities within the function. As the SHRM authors point out: this is a trap. It takes real leadership to develop a business-based HR agenda and a high level of discipline to execute this strategy.

At the UK's Ministry of Defence (MOD) Jonathan Evans and his team work as one team. The HR Business Partners (HRBPs) are embedded in the business and report to the line rather than Jonathan. As Jonathan says, 'they're my eyes and ears'. He has tried to take the status out of the way the team operates, making team interactions informal, putting the focus on outcomes rather than inputs. Anne Minto considers putting together good teams of people to be a key strength: In Centrica my team do a great job of working effectively with one another - drawing on each other's strengths and capabilities. There is a great deal of co-operation and coordination between them. We run one People Agenda thus reducing duplication and wasted effort. People will always volunteer to help one another if they have previous experience and knowledge that can make a contribution. Our People Plan is a a shared agenda so that different people champion different workstreams ensuring that everyone takes co-ownership of it'. 'In Smiths my team did not only work hard for me but worked well as a team together so that they were getting the benefits of one another and there was lots of cooperation and coordination between them. There was nobody who was running their own agenda to suit themselves. In Centrica, my Head of British Gas services will always volunteer to help another colleague somewhere else and we tend to divide up our people agenda so that different people run with different parts of it, so that everyone takes a co-ownership of it.'

EXAMPLES OF HR TRANSFORMATION

High-performing organisations use a combination of outsourcing and insourcing so that they have the best processes, technology and practices permeating their organisation (Ephor Group, 2008). Market leaders continually assess new opportunities to outpace their market rivals and this is achieved through interchangeably utilizing insourcing and outsourcing to improve the organisation, combined with employee-centric decision-making (for example on engagement, reward, etc.).

Surrey County Council

In Surrey County Council they've moved very much to a self-service process, where line managers have been equipped with basic HR expertise, or the resource to find that expertise. HR policy and practice is now manager-friendly rather than just HR-friendly and that's using jargon-free language and logic to create understanding. The HR team has worked hard to develop much stronger relationships between managers and unions through the development of consultative groups, and managers are regularly engaging with staff and staff representatives.

To support this work, HR has built a number of critical measures for managers in terms of annual and quarterly surveys and 'health checks' to give managers a regular picture of how their part of the organisation is doing. They've also developed some comprehensive management information reporting which helps managers get a snapshot of what's going on in their service from every aspect including turnover and sickness.

Pfizer

Martin Ferber recognises that in a highly competitive and fast-changing industry such as pharmaceuticals, business needs should be at the centre of HR's efforts. He reports that in Pfizer: 'There is now a very concerted effort to better realign HR to what the business really needs and that coincides with the business itself changing very dramatically in the pharmaceutical industry. Pfizer's one of the big companies at the forefront of making that change and we, as an HR function, are definitely integral to not only making that change ourselves, but supporting that change in the organisation. We are strategically positioned to help in that.'

HR in Pfizer is divided into three groups to reflect the three business units: there's the manufacturing side, the commercial operation and research and development. Each of these business functions has separate HR functions. There are some common systems and policies of course, but they don't necessarily directly correspond or overlap and there are some quite significant differences. Duplications have evolved over the years. As Martin indicates: 'One of the things we're trying to do is look quite hard at that, and there's an intention to drive back to a more coordinated, single "One HR" as we sometimes call it internally. Recognising that the business partner role is very specific, "One-HR" is particularly in the operational or foundational aspects of HR, which could be better harmonised and coordinated, more systematic and ultimately, therefore, probably smaller and cheaper.

I also think that the business leaders want, and have recognised the power and the usefulness of having an HR Business Partner, or the HR leader work alongside them, who really understands their business and can work with them on an equal footing in the context of people issues. I don't mean just being a supporting function, but actually work strategically alongside them in a more consultancy kind of relationship.

But they also recognise they want that foundational, day-to-day, operational stuff that HR does carried out more efficiently and better, whether it be paying people on time, delivering bonuses on time, having good employee relations, environment support, problem-solving and all the other lifetime career management aspects that HR can support. We have had gaps in our organisation in that, and we are working quite hard now with a re-design programme, of which I'm going to be leading the European piece over the next six months to get it kicked off.'

Centrica

Anne Minto describes the process of HR transformation underway in Centrica, and some of the learning emerging from the process: 'In Centrica we started our HR transformation journey 4 years ago – to ensure that we were providing our colleagues with the most efficient and cost-effective service delivery across the company. Four years down the line the business is enjoying the benefits of having created a shared service model and access to on-line tools for people so that at a click of a button managers can process lots of mundane transactions that used to take a great deal of time, paperwork and effort. People have ready access from their PCs and it gives the managers much more responsibility and accountability for their people in a way that perhaps four years ago in Centrica was very much seen as the role of HR.

Managers must manage and be accountable for their people, just as they are accountable for the goods and services that go in and out from their businesses. We are seeing bottom line benefits to the business of that accountability for people. I think that it is simplifying things for people, taking the mystique and complexity out of employment practices and policies is what HR should be doing for all employees. It is making clear and transparent for managers and giving them meaningful management information to make better decisions.'

I think there is much more HR ought to be doing to take away some of the mumbo jumbo and give it much more transparency and clarity for line managers. One of the other things my folks think about now if we are going to bring in something new is – why is it that we need to bring in something new – and if it's needed, that's great. Then – what's going to be taken away? What in the old tool kit is going to be got rid of – not overlaying it with something else again. Right now we've got a project on to try and find the most creative and innovative ideas within HR to simplify processes for our line managers. We have given that challenge to our shared services partners as well and it will also hopefully bring in a lot of cost savings as well.' We are also much more discerning about the changes that we make: why is it that we need to bring in something new? if it is of value or benefit to the managers and employees, that's great. If you introduce new processes, ensure all the old ones are removed - don't keep on overlaying process upon process - keep it simple! Right now we've got a project ongoing to try and find the most creative and innovative idea within HR to simplify processes for our line managers. We have given that challenge to our shared services partners as well and it will also hopefully result in further cost savings as well as time savings.'

And for Anne Minto, handling the process of outsourcing administrative HR is a test which her team has come through with flying colours: 'I am enormously proud in the way that the team has handled the whole outsourcing of our shared service. The implementation of our employee self-serve, and manager self-serve have all happened without disruption to the services we provide our people and that is no mean feat when you have got 33,000 people. Line managers have been hugely supportive of the changes from lending their time on the working groups to benefiting personally from the more efficient services.

For Anne herself, transforming the HR function has been an activity which has taken up a lot time and will continue to do so but more use of technology in the form of online products is not yet exhausted. Meeting our KPI's at stretch is critical to serving our Business Unit customer base. Because 'we are not yet where we want to be. We are pretty far along our journey.

Transforming the Professional Body for HR in UK and Ireland – the CIPD

The development of the HR professional body reflects the transformation of the HR profession itself. Geoff Armstrong was asked to lead the predecessor body to the CIPD (the Institute of Personnel Management – IPM) in 1992. At the time IPM had grown its membership but was not punching its weight, either in terms of member services or income. It had little research base. Its qualifications were respected and widely taken up and it had a good library but it was old fashioned and not geared up to mass membership. It was losing money as a number of investments had failed to pay off and the recession of the early 1990s had led to cut-backs and redundancies.

The IPM board wanted a recognised leader of the profession to lead the IPM. Geoff was appointed to be both the leader of the profession and the leader of the Institute, with accountability across both spheres. Geoff's early decisions were about the orientation of the Institute. He wanted IPM to be more anticipatory and responsive to member needs. He was keen to build customer service and better services, such as later developing Web-based services.

Then Geoff wanted to establish that HR could make a valued contribution to business performance, and for HR to be judged by its contribution to the advancement of competitive business strategies. He wanted HR professionals to be business people first, functional specialists second. He also wanted to raise the evidence base of what does and does not work in different contexts – to build a decision science around people management as a discipline of management, which is no less measurable than other disciplines. He wanted to get the professional standards revised so that they reflected this positioning.

Geoff saw his role as that of ambassador for the Institute, selling the vision across the country, sensing the mood of members, rearticulating their desires in more stretching ways. He deliberately used the various organs available to the Institute, such as People Management Magazine and its predecessor to get messages across. Articles and research featured the growing evidence base; commercial channels such as conferences would include business gurus such as Michael Porter, Gary Hamel; training course materials would include articles from business journals such as Harvard Business Review. The message was about changing the game, creating strategies for sustainable success.

Geoff led the IPM through the merger with the Institute of Training and Development (ITD), dissolving both predecessor bodies to form a new body, which could make the most of the potential synergies and show that people management in all its forms is an integral part of business management. Subsequently, Geoff took the new IPD through the process of becoming a Chartered Institute, a status it obtained in 2000, becoming at that point the CIPD. The CIPD qualification has become a key entry point to professional HR careers. Now with over 130,000 members, the CIPD is globally the largest HR professional body outside of SHRM in North America and is seen as the standard-setter for the HR profession internationally.

Geoff retired in 2008 and the CIPD is now headed up by its first Chief Executive Officer (CEO), Jackie Orme. The CIPD is undergoing its own next phase of transformation in preparation for leading the further development of the HR profession into 'Next Generation' HR.

WHAT DOES THE FUTURE HOLD?

The economic crisis adds extra potency to the argument that HR leaders need to build their organisation's strategic capability. But what that capability looks like will depend on the nature of the organisation and the specific nature of its challenges in an unknown future. Boston Consulting Group (Strack et al., 2009) has developed two main post-crisis business scenarios. In the first, a company will recover and its revenues will regain historical levels sooner rather than later. In the second, a company will recover its traditional growth rate but not see its revenues return to pre-recession levels for a long time, if ever.

Each of these scenarios requires a different approach. Companies which expect their business to recover to historical levels of revenue sooner should explore *flexible solutions that lower costs*. For instance, at a 2009 HRD focus group one participant reports that he is focusing on building the basis of a more agile organisational culture: 'I have three clear priorities in no particular order. One is around simplifying our business, creating a culture where there's less bureaucracy and more simplification, with pragmatic values-based decisions and solutions. The second is around empowerment and how we continue to develop that in the organisation. And the third is around strategic capabilities.'

Companies who fear that recovery will take longer or envisage permanently changed realities should explore *restructuring* and *workforce reduction*. In February 2009, the CIPD carried out a survey of over 3000 UK-based employees to understand how they were experiencing the economic crisis. Almost 25% of these respondents reported that the downturn was having little or no effect on them. Twenty-four percent of people responding in this way worked in the public sector. Then in April 2009, the Chancellor of the Exchequer's Budget revealed the extent to which costs of delivering public services would be pared back in years to come, given the amount of public expenditure which needed to be recovered after the banking crisis. It was at that point that the future prospect loomed of 350,000 public sector job cuts over the next few years.

Organisational Capabilities for the Future

As we have already discussed, a strategic approach to improving the performance of the organisation involves taking into account the external drivers and constraints, identifying the capabilities required for future success and then putting plans into effect to build these.

Public Sector Capabilities

In public sector institutions, the external influences on organisational performance include government and politics; social and economic structures and national and local priorities. And with increasing cost constraints and requirements for better value, a focus on capabilities is a good way of defining where and how HR could contribute to building high performance.

My own research into high performance organizations suggests that all organizations need to build human capital and client relationship capabilities. For high performing government organisations (HPGOs) in particular, Accenture (reported in Linder and Brooks, 2004) have identified the following nine characteristic capability areas:

1. *Strategy and policy-making*
2. *Organisation and process design*
3. *Performance management*
4. *Partnering*
5. *Human capital management*
6. *Information management*
7. *Market and client relationship management*
8. *Procurement and logistics* – HP organisations 'operate flexible, cost-effective sourcing processes and streamlined supply chains' in order to increase 'rigor, accountability and cost-effectiveness to purchasing activities'.
9. *Operations* – all of the organisations' capabilities need to be brought together to deliver the service to the public.

In common with all high performing businesses, high performing government organizations (HPGOs) have clear goals and mission. As well as responding to the requests of stakeholders they try to influence them. They align short-term goals with the long-term agenda. They openly share performance data with stakeholders. HPGOs have flexible structures which stimulate innovation. They assess and review the effectiveness of their organizational processes and use of technology. They have structured processes and cultures in place to encourage information management (both acquisition and dissemination). They operate 'flexible, cost-effective sourcing processes and streamlined supply chains' in order to increase 'rigour, accountability and cost-effectiveness to purchasing activities'.

In terms of client relationship management, all high performance organisations actively use feedback they get from customers to try and deliver what customers want. With respect to their delivery chain partners, they ensure that their partnerships support their strategic objectives and that they capture value from these. Above all, they engage employees, have effective reward systems and operate on shared values.

During the economic crisis in particular, HR leaders need to be thinking strategically, working out the future workforce supply and demand, restructuring the organisation, developing frontline leaders and maintaining employee engagement.

Spotlight Example: Responding to External Demands on the National Health Service

A number of CEOs and senior HR executives based in one of the regions of the UK's National Health Service (NHS) were asked to anticipate the likely external challenges for the NHS over the next few years. Their predictions are as follows:

The main issues include an ageing population and increased demands. These will be set against the need to reduce public spending by 9.6% annually between 2009 and 2018, according to a PricewaterhouseCoopers (PwC) estimate, or else put up taxes by a significant amount. There will be pressure to improve performance, cost-effectiveness and efficiency (and staff reductions can be anticipated). *Therefore NHS executives will need to manage downsizing and learn to do more with less.*

If these are not *tackled upfront*, the traditional means of saving money in the NHS will be used, e.g. vacancy freezes, letting waiting lists grow, etc., which these executives fear will undo all the progresses made as a result of the high levels of investment in the NHS over the last 10 years.

At the same time, there is likely to be *large-scale service redesign* to reduce costs. Foundation Trusts and a more market-based service will change the way NHS managers and staff work. There will be the separation off of Primary Care Trust provider services, whether this is by the creation of new social enterprises or vertical integration with acute services or indeed local authority services. There is likely to be more *streamlining of the commissioning process* and the commissioning/provider interface, getting greater clarity on what is actually being commissioned and expected outcomes.

Therefore the organisational capabilities required will include:

- Building the people and performance management capability in the line management population. HR should do this aggressively. It's not good waiting for managers to ask for help. You need strong pro-active HRBPs to go into business units, challenge managers and get them to tackle poor performance, manage down absence, and face down grievance cultures.
- Change management – managers and staff will need help to cope with the fallout of downsizing. After a downsizing there will be managers who have never had to fire so many people in their lives and staff who have never been through such a change. Both the process and the aftermath of change will need to be handled carefully and sensitively.
- Building commercial skills and attitudes among managers and staff.

Is HR Ready to Exercise Leadership?

This should be an ideal opportunity for HR to exercise leadership and develop a people strategy with line executives which will have supporting metric systems and the ability to demonstrate business impact. But is HR ready for this task? As one HR Director reports, 'From my work in X region there doesn't seem to be much enthusiasm or capability to do this, although from talking to colleagues elsewhere there is good practice going on but just not being shared as well as it might be'.

Continued

Spotlight Example: Responding to External Demands on the National Health Service—cont'd

These directors argue that HR transformation will be vital if HR is to play its part in the challenging context ahead:

- HR needs clarity of objectives and clear targets. The strategy requires diagnostics and empirical evidence (e.g. staff survey feedback) to indicate areas of greatest need/fastest return on investment (time and/or money).
- HR should review internal operations and develop transactional shared services with other trusts, so taking away transactional and even some advisory work from HRBPs.
- Set performance standards and implement, including culture change.
- Culture change requires performance coaching, willingness to have the difficult conversation.
- Develop the skills of (or manage out) the remaining HR staff to become proper HRBPs, i.e. acting as HR Directors for their business units. HRBPs will need more commercial skills, consultancy skills, mental toughness, ability to challenge, breadth of thinking, knowledge of current affairs (read a decent newspaper!) – and of course, the ability to very quickly get inside an organisation and understand what is going on. Some of these skills can be acquired through a mixture of coaching, mentoring and some really well-managed action learning sets. Then just getting out there and doing it.

And there is plenty of room to make a difference. HR should be scoping what the future NHS workforce needs to look like and commissioning education and training appropriately. There is a dearth of training opportunities for nurse specialists and no accreditation process for such posts and yet the whole 'care closer to home' strategy is dependent on having these skilled practitioners in place. There is also very little being done to develop multi-skilled staff who can operate diagnostic equipment, read test results and do hands-on treatment, which will be really important if more care is to be delivered outside of hospital. What all these HR Directors and Executives agree on is that HR needs to be talking this up, really raising awareness of these issues and coming up with ways of tackling them – a real leadership opportunity for HR to grab.

BUILDING EMPLOYEE ENGAGEMENT – HR'S KEY TARGET

The ability to engage employees is a key capability required by any organisation which depends on people for its output. There are many definitions of what employee engagement is and what drives it. Employee engagement is 'the intellectual and emotional attachment that an employee has to his or her work and organization' (Heger, 2007). It is 'passion for work' (Truss et al., 2006). Most definitions suggest that employee engagement is experienced as 'flow' – when people are so pleasurably immersed in what they are doing that they do not notice time passing. It involves both feeling positive about your job as well as being prepared to release discretionary effort to make sure you do your job to the best of your ability.

In recent years, progressive HRM practices have been geared to increasing employee engagement by rebuilding a relational psychological contract, i.e. an employment relationship based on mutual trust and perceptions of a 'fair deal'. Employee engagement initiatives are generally geared to building good employee relations with employees at the individual rather than the collective level.

Links Between Employee Engagement and Performance

High performance theory places employee engagement at the heart of high performance, especially among knowledge workers. A study by Kingston Business School (Truss et al., 2006) found that contextual influences on engagement included opportunities for flexible working; role and occupation; management style and communication and involvement. In the Kingston study, the main drivers of employee engagement were having the opportunity to feed your views upwards; feeling well-informed about what is happening in the organisation and thinking that your manager is committed to the organisation. Line manager positives which impacted on engagement included 'treats me fairly; is supportive; listens to my suggestion; makes clear what is expected of me'.

Perhaps not surprisingly, high levels of engagement have been found to be associated with a whole range of beneficial outcomes, including high levels of performance. The Kingston study suggests that engaged employees deliver organisation performance improvements. It also found that the consequences of employee engagement were individual performance, intention to stay with the organisation and employee well being. Engaged employees were higher performers; loyal; organisational advocates; wanted to stay; took less sick leave and were more satisfied. They demonstrated that commitment to the organisation made them, were more likely to engage in voluntary or citizenship behaviour and to help their colleagues. Previous research for the CIPD conducted by Guest (2004) also suggested that employee engagement is associated with a number of positive factors including an employee's intention to stay with the organisation.

Anne Minto agrees that focusing on employee engagement does pay off: 'In my mind there is a total correlation between people who are fully engaged in the business and superior and performance. You want engaged employees who come to work feeling good about their jobs and the company they work for and wanting to do the best possible job they can every day. Centrica is a very customer-focused business. We want our engineers when they come to people's homes to have a smile on their face and be ready to provide a first class service. We want our call-centre staff to be bright, friendly and alert when they are answering those phones, making sales and sorting out customers' issues. If your boiler breaks down you want to get somebody who is courteous, friendly and helpful at the other end of the phone who is going to empathise with you and is going to fix your problem'.

Employee surveys are a useful means of taking the temperature of how employees are feeling about the organisation and they are used extensively in Centrica, as Anne Minto reports: 'We're big supporters of employee engagement at Centrica and we have fantastic returns on our surveys. We get circa 95% of people completing the surveys which is just phenomenal and we take them very seriously – not the just the good stuff that comes out which we'll celebrate and feel good about, but also the low ranking scores are the ones that are in the plan for next year. If we can turn those scores around then we can tackle those issues that have been highlighted and that will make a difference to people. Our employee engagement scores for commitment are in the upper quartile and we are recognised in the Top 20 'Best Places to Work' surveys'.

However, as we shall consider in Chapter 5, workforces are rarely a homogenous group. Employees have different needs, concerns, life histories and expectations. Increasingly, initiatives aimed at increasing employee engagement are focused on key segments of the workforce, rather than attempting to be universally effective. The Corporate Leadership Council (CLC, 2004) researched the impact of employee engagement initiatives on employees. They categorised levels of employee engagement as follows:

The disaffected – representing 13% of the average workforce, these were the poorer performers who frequently put in minimal effort. These were four times more likely to leave than the average employee.

The agnostics – categorised as 'leaning towards disengagement' (20%), 'neutral' (20%) and 'leaning towards engagement' (27%). The agnostics exhibit only moderate commitment to their work, teams, managers and organisations. They are capable of moving into the disaffected or the 'true believer' categories. Many in fact already lean one way or another.

The true believers – These are higher performers with a lower retention risk (11%). They exhibit very strong rational and emotional commitment to their day-to-day work, teams, managers and organisations.

CLC (2004) argued that the agnostics represent the greatest risk and opportunity. True believers are largely engaged anyway – the challenge is not to create disengagement. To increase engagement among the agnostics the key means is to remove barriers to engagement.

Dr Tim Miller of Standard Chartered Bank (SCB) is one HR leader who is actively seeking to build employee engagement by addressing issues which act as barriers to employee engagement. Tim uses Gallup's Q12 survey to establish a deep understanding of the levels of employee engagement and brand identity throughout the SCB's Retail Bank in its many and varied locations. He has correlated employee engagement scores in different branches with customer feedback and business results. He has been able to refine the focus of initiatives to improve engagement by analysing some of the potentially causal links. Specific and targeted initiatives are then taken to address issues arising from the surveys and subsequent surveys suggest that employee engagement improves as a result.

Establishing the links between improved employee engagement and improved business results makes a powerful, evidence-based statement about the importance of good people management to business success. Managers in SCB's Retail Bank buy in to the idea that engagement scores can be improved. They look forward to receive their teams' survey results because they know this will provide them with meaningful data that they can do something about.

This bears out what Ulrich and Brockbank (2005) argue: 'Value becomes the bellwether for HR. When others receive value from HR work, HR will be credible, respected, and influential.' In the SBC example these approaches to employee engagement are providing strong relevance for the HR role given that HR supplies the tools which help line managers understand where and how to make a difference to business performance.

Putting the People Plan Together Collaboratively

Large organisations depend on cooperation to achieve their goals efficiently. HR can play a key role in modelling this approach by working with line colleagues to design key HR processes such as people reviews and career and development processes, so that corporate, departmental and individuals goals are met. One example of how this can work in practice is the way Liane Hornsey builds Google's People Strategy.

> **Spotlight Example: Putting Together the People Plan in Google**
>
> Liane Hornsey suggests that the process of developing a business-focused people plan is quite straightforward: 'In every company I've worked for I've used the same approach to putting the business plan together. You take the annual attitude survey as a base, because that will tell you quantitatively what your employment base thinks. Then you do some qualitative diagnostics – some focus groups, or some semi-structured or structured interviews, or a mix of all of those. If you've got a free flow in your attitude survey you'll take some comments from that as well, and you do a whole load of analysis.'
>
> **Creating Ownership**
>
> 'And unless you're really stupid as a manager, you'll involve your team in that, and you'll involve your clients in that. So for example what I've done here is to take that data, synthesise it. But don't do the analysis – let your team do the analysis so that they own it. Then let your clients do a bit of the analysis too so that they own it, and then sit down in a room and say, "OK, if X is a problem, let's brainstorm what we need to do to close the gaps, and then let's agree on what we need to do to close the gaps".

Continued

Spotlight Example: Putting Together the People Plan in Google—cont'd

An example would be our latest attitude survey which has just come out in time for us to do our business plans. One of the issues in EMEA is work–life balance, and people are beginning to feel that getting work–life balance is difficult. So what have we done? We've looked at the data, we've looked at the comments, we've run some focus groups and got some rich data, because work–life balance is tricky – you never really know what that means. You know, statements like "I feel I'm working too hard", or "I feel that the company is working me too hard" – well what does that actually mean? What do you want to be different? So you need to do some qualitative research and then you know.

Then you sit down with your team, and you sit down with your clients and you determine what you're going to do. That's when you say, "right, we're going to do ABCDE". Some of that will be HR or people operations initiatives, such as introducing flexible working hours for example. But a lot of it will also be shared measures with managers, because a lot of what you have to achieve in HR is shared with manager behaviour. So if you take the work–life balance example, one initiative I will make happen is a policy on flexible working hours. The much, much harder thing is to get managers to not expect their people to be here at seven, and not to be sending them e-mails at four o'clock on a Sunday afternoon.'

Selling the Proposition

'And then you're back into working with managers – coaching, counselling, making sure that your leadership cadre is everything it should be. I tend to break down the actions into: what have we got to deliver in terms of initiatives? What have we got to do to influence managers? And then thirdly what have we got to do to communicate, because a lot of great HR practice, if it's not sold, there's no point having it. You know I'm an ex-sales person and HR is internal selling. You do great stuff for your people but you tell them you're doing it, you make sure they know you're doing it for them. And you sell, sell, sell'.

DEVELOPING A CLEAR, FOCUSED STRATEGY THAT DELIVERS WHAT IS NEEDED

There are many ways of articulating what HR is strategically focused on.

Increasingly, People Strategies are clearly expressed around a vision to help move the business forward through people. To deliver the vision, a few simple and relevant business drivers are chosen to form the People Mission, for instance having the Best People, The Best Leaders and A High Performance Climate. These provide the parameters for specific people strategies and related processes, such as workforce planning, diversity, talent planning, performance management, change management, work-life balance etc. The strategy is delivered through value-adding activities or 'deliverables'.

In one example, David Fairhurst describes the alignment between the business and people strategies at McDonalds.

Q. How does your job impact on the business aims of the company?

A. McDonald's 'Plan to Win' business strategy identifies five key business drivers: People, Products, Place, Price and Promotion – each with a cross-functional 'P-team' responsible for enhancing the performance of their area year-on-year. It's no coincidence that People always appears first on that list. This puts the People team at the heart of the business with responsibility for one of our key business drivers.

Q. What challenges do you see coming up in the future?

A. Preparing the service sector for the 2012 Olympics. This is the biggest event on the world stage, and the service sector will be the 'face' of Britain in welcoming the world.

Q. What will your approach to those challenges be?

A. We are supporting the sector skills council for the travel and tourism industry, People First (I am Vice-Chairman) and the Employers' association - the Confederation of British Industry (CBI) (our CEO Steve Easterbrook chairs the CBI's Education and Training Affairs Committee) to change attitudes towards the service sector and to play our part in ensuring that we have sufficient high-quality customer-service skills available in the workforce.

Q. What initiatives do you have in place to help the organisation succeed?

We have identified three 'pillars' of activity which provide a focus for our People initiatives: Operational excellence – ensuring we run a really effective business through People; Education – a broad agenda around capability, skills, training and education; and Modernity – ensuring we are progressive. These are not discrete. They naturally overlap and many initiatives sit in two areas or, indeed, all three.

These three pillars are essential for prioritising our efforts. In fact, if an initiative does not contribute to at least one of these areas we will not pursue it. Furthermore, since the pillars apply equally to all of the disciplines within the team, they provide a framework which enables us to share ideas and work together in an integrated way.

Our approach to developing initiatives within the pillars has been threefold. First, to get the basics right. These are the crown jewels and the foundation of all our work. Second, we must continually improve. Finally, we will carry on with the big moves. These iconic and, at times, disruptive changes deliberately make a splash.

Q. Where have these initiatives come from?

A. Constantly searching for insights which will enable us to create value for our People:

- The appliance of Marketing science ... research which delivers employee insights.
- Links with academia, professional bodies, employer groups and skills agencies give us access to both best practice as well as the latest thinking.

- Asking 'what if?' and 'why not?' ... and then keeping our feet on the shop-floor whilst reaching for the stars!

Q. *How do you measure your own success?*

A. Outcomes rather than inputs. Remembering that effectiveness is as much about what we enable to happen, as it is about what we do ourselves.

METRICS

The HR function must be able to measure its contribution to business success. In particular it needs to calculate its contribution to the effectiveness of both its internal operations and the company's overall people strategies. In most companies, the link between HR and strategy and HR and metrics is weak or non-existent.

Anne Minto measures her success 'by the numbers of successful employees that we promote and develop into positions within the company. I measure a lot of my success on my employee engagement scores- that's what I look at and I perhaps expect much more of myself as Head of HR. We also have regular feedback focus groups and surveys with our employees who give us direct feedback on what they feel about the HR function and the services we provide. We also regularly benchmark ourselves externally and compare competencies, service delivery and cost-effectiveness.' then I can hardly go and counsel other people if I am not doing that myself.'

David Smith argues that any business has to be driven by the metrics, and the retail sector in particular tends to have turnover problems: 'so of course we look at our retention and our absence numbers by geography, by age group, by parts of the business. We run an attitude survey called "We're listening" in 30-odd stores at any one time on a rolling basis. So at any one time we're able to say what the morale is like in the business, and we can tell you what our people are feeling about communications or leadership or pay or training or whatever it might be.'

Employee attitude data are then compared with business data to establish an employee–customer-service value chain and it is the frequency with which these data are compared that allows HR to take action based on the feedback from employees and customers: 'We're constantly looking at what's happening in terms of the metrics compared to what we're doing and we then relate all of that to our customer figures. We take these on a monthly basis and they tend to be around actual physical customer numbers, customer complaints, customer perceptions etc. So we're looking all the time at what all of those different care aids and initiatives are doing, what is actually happening to our results based on what we're doing. Only then can you actually tell what's really happening. Our survey is designed not only for quantitative data but we also allow people free comment, so we can get commentary from them in terms of how they're feeling and what they think about what we're doing.'

Liane Hornsey measures her team according to their specific objectives: 'So, for my team actually it's pretty easily, because if you take the staffing team you can measure the number of hires, quality of hires and the time to performance of the hired over time. For learning and development you can obviously do the quantitative measures – the number of learning courses, number of initiatives, number of things designed and number of things facilitated. It's much harder to measure qualitatively in the leadership and development (L&D) area and I think that as HR you have to have a degree of faith. Some of the HR measures that people tend to use can be a little wide of the mark. So I definitely use attitude surveys, and we do look at our attitude survey very carefully. We are going to enter the "Great place to work for" competition in several of our countries. You should be measured by feedback.

In terms of my personal measurement, it's whatever I set out in my business plan at the beginning of the year – did I deliver it? So if I said we were going to achieve X, did we? And a lot of that is quantitative rather than qualitative, which is dangerous, but the most important feedback is much softer than that. It's whether the senior team are coming to my room all the time to talk to me, before they do anything organisationally. That's how I know if I'm being successful of not. Are any of them looking to hire people, or do anything with their senior team, or reorganise something without coming to talk to me? And you know, when you first come to an organisation they're all doing it. When you're a year in, none of them should be. Then you'll know whether you're good or not.'

Hewitt's (2008) research on Next Generation HR has placed bold bets on areas where HR can deliver most value to business. They argue this will be possible when HR can demonstrate a causal relationship between workforce practices and business performance. To create these insights and identify new opportunities HR will need access to advanced data mining and the predictive modelling of human capital processes. In other words, HR will continue its focus on human capital measurement but will shift from 'post facto' measures to more 'predictive' measures allowing management to make better strategic decisions.

CONCLUSION

The HR department needs to be highly efficient, especially in these challenging times. Otherwise HR executives will lose credibility when they try to lead initiatives elsewhere in the organisation. The business downturn provides an opportunity to review what work needs to be done and how, and structure accordingly, weeding out unnecessary processes.

And transforming HR must not become the end in itself but the means to a greater contribution by HR to business success. The success of alternative means of delivering HR administration, such as outsourcing or shared services (HRSS), depends on a good shared understanding amongst stakeholders about what its purpose is. And if having found successful alternatives to delivering transactional work, the remaining HR function fails to establish a high level of strategic business presence, then HR transformation becomes an own goal. Whilst it is early days to judge how HR teams are stepping up to the challenge, a number of reports, such as PwC Saratoga's *Managing People in a Changing World* (2008) suggest that so far HR has generally failed to make the shift to a more strategic contribution. This report suggests that there is little evidence of increased influence of HR in the Boardroom. Its authors have found that CEOs generally have low opinion of HR, and the number of HRDs on main boards of FTSE 100 is down to five. They also report that business partners aren't valued by executives.

So while this raises questions over the future of HR, I for one am optimistic, and so are many of the HR leaders featured in this book, that this will be a significant and positive one. We shall return to the question of 'what is the future of HR?' in Chapter 10. But clearly if HR is going to be part of the solution, rather than the problem, HR leaders and their teams must be able to make the significant and proactive contribution which organisations need from them. We shall move on to look at the key capabilities which form the core of the HR leadership agenda – talent, leadership, culture and change – in the next few chapters.

Chapter 5

Leading the Talent Agenda

'In fact in challenging times, the need for a clear view of corporate talent and tools to encourage employee productivity, morale and motivation becomes imperative.'

Taleo (2009)

Gather together any group of human resource directors (HRDs) to discuss the key challenges facing their organisations and some predictable themes will rise to the surface, not least attracting and retaining talent, employee engagement, change management and the need to build leadership and management capacity. In this and the next chapter we shall look at approaches to leading the agenda for talent management and leadership development.

Increasingly, the terms 'leadership' and 'talent' are becoming interchangeable and two 2009 surveys – DDI/CIPD Global Leadership survey and the BCG/EAPM Global HRM survey (Strack et al. 2009) – found that *talent* is executives' number one business priority worldwide.

And why should these issues be so key and so common in virtually every sector? The need for effective talent management – a company's ability to attract, retain and motivate employees – reflects the labour market realities of today. Partly that is because thanks to technology, globalisation and competition the nature of business, delivery channels, and work are rapidly being transformed, making organisational change and the search for innovation the norm in most organisations. Under these circumstances, the human side of business is *the* key source of competitive advantage but the complexities of today's business environment makes talent management a major challenge. The 24/7 trading environment and the more personalised nature of customer provision are driving the need for greater flexibility, quality and efficiency of delivery, reflected in more complex organisational arrangements and resource requirements, and more varied forms of employment and employment relationship.

The economic crisis brings new urgency to cultivating a workforce that can create sustainable competitive advantage. At a time when people are increasingly recognised as the most important asset for business and organisational success, talent and leadership are becoming scarcer resources than ever before, as demographic shifts change the nature and flow of the talent pipeline.

The growing importance of knowledge-based services and products within the global economy as a whole is driving the need for higher level specialist skills in industries as diverse as construction, pharmaceuticals, defence and high technology that are already experiencing serious shortfalls of available global talent, with even greater shortages predicted thanks to the growing impact of demographic trends. In such a context, 'the war for talent' is once again with us.

In recent years, organisations have competed for the best talent, and HR strategies have been geared to finding ever more innovative ways to attract, motivate and retain key talent for the future. For Ulrich and Brockbank (2008), HR professionals must evolve into being the best thinkers in the company about the human and organisational sides of the business. HR professionals must master theory, research, and practice in both talent management and organization design. Talent management focuses on how individuals enter, move up, across, or out of the organization. Organization design focuses on the capabilities an organization has that are embedded in the structure, processes, and policies that shape how the organization works. As Ulrich and Brockbank suggest, HR is not just about talent or organization, but about the two of them together.

In many organisations, the link between talent and business success is now so visible and direct that the need to source scarce talent is high up amongst board priorities. Google for instance is growing so fast that its senior managers spend 30% of their time interviewing prospective employees.

The internet giant receives on average 250 applications for every vacancy.

Each successful applicant will have a minimum of four interviews, with Liane Hornsey herself endured 14 before landing her job. Company founder Larry Page signs off every single hire, at a rate of more than 100 a week. So great is the need to plug the talent gap that some companies are experimenting with potentially costly solutions such as locating work where skilled employees prefer to live, rather than where other logistics dictate.

Employer branding is another device to attract potential recruits with a strong 'promise' reflecting what the employer stands for and the employee value proposition on offer. And there is growing evidence that the criteria used by younger workers, in particular, to select their future employer include the values, even more than the pay on offer. Organisations that are demonstrating links between brand and HR and who have transformed their employer brand include Orange, easyJet, Accenture and McDonalds. Branding is being used in all communications used to attract and recruit employees and is evident in the redesign of Websites, interview processes (Whirlpool), candidate management processes (e.g. Whirlpool, Starbucks), induction processes (easyJet), reward (easyJet) and career development (McDonalds, easyJet).

Given the premium placed on skilled workers in many industries, retaining them is another headache. Employees increasingly want the same kind of individualised attention that customers receive and skilled workers can and do exercise their options if they are not happy with their lot. In common with other forms of branding, if the lived reality of the brand is different from the promise, the customer–employee goes elsewhere. Furthermore, the old truism about people leaving their managers appears to hold true. A focus group of HRDs confirmed that improving the quality of leadership and management is central to employee engagement and performance. For these HRDs talent management, employee engagement, leadership and business success are inextricably interlinked.

A DISCIPLINED APPROACH TO TALENT MANAGEMENT

Talent management requires a disciplined and rigorous approach in the same way that organisations manage their supply chain for products and services. One of the reasons that companies find managing talent so difficult is that it is a complex, multi-layered issue. BCG/WFPMA (Strack et al., 2008) identifies five distinct but inter-related activities in the talent management process: identifying, attracting, developing, retaining and handling the departure of talent. While the first four steps are widely recognised, the fifth is often neglected.

Any talent management strategy needs to be a business strategy, not an HR strategy. Boards and leaders of companies need to be significantly engaged in and take ownership of talent and leadership issues, with senior executives ensuring that HR and people strategy is the cornerstone of their corporate strategy.

Identifying future talent needs means that HR leaders need to carry out strategic workforce planning in the light of longer term growth projections and other strategic business requirements, such as the desired pace of growth or targeted future locations. To drive a continuous supply of talent, HR leaders not only have to look at new talent acquisition, but also at articulating future critical competencies required by the business, creating mechanisms for the assessment of internal talent on these competencies, developing internal talent, creating workforce planning frameworks and determining market pay levels. Performance and competency assessment should be used as a means to segment future potential and top talent.

Attracting and developing current and future leadership is a key aspect of talent management. A Group HRD for instance will typically focus on succession planning for the top team across the Group, on the management of high potentials, on executive compensation and on any employee relations issues which might affect corporate reputation, i.e. if any potential industrial action is brewing.

Lower down the HR organisation, HR professionals will be involved in dealing with similar issues. The focus of the talent strategy will include the recruitment and retention of high-potential managers and specialists for key positions. Graduate recruitment, resourcing major projects, career development, reward strategies and bonus arrangements for specific groups. Increasingly, too, organisations are defining what they mean by 'talent' more broadly, beyond high potentials to include people with specialist skills that are in short supply.

Retaining talent means making sure that the employer brand promise is delivered, especially as far as high-potential employees are concerned, i.e. making sure that the employee value proposition acts as a 'hygiene factor', if not a motivator, resulting in employees who are satisfied, committed and engaged with the organisation. As workforces become more diverse, the nature of what amounts to an enticing employer brand may vary from group to group and individual to individual. Therefore, delivering on the employer brand promise involves having the right reward and recognition schemes, as well as creating and implementing development strategies that provide stretch and career opportunities for different groups of employees, not just those deemed to be of high potential.

Talent – A Global Issue

Whatever is taking place in HR is now a global issue. In a globalised economy, HR leaders will need to be prepared to manage a global workforce. Staffing becomes more complex. Today's talent can be sourced from across the world and organisations also want to spread their knowledge across the different regions in which they operate. Talent management and organisational development are intimately interconnected in achieving these goals be proficient at developing and promoting talent from anywhere, moving talent across borders and creating the infrastructure to build a high-performing global workforce. This will mean managing new types of relationships and adapting to a diverse population in terms of needs, business requirements and cultural expectations. Moreover, in global organisations, HR leaders need strategies that build a culture that pulls employees together, creating a brand that is consistent throughout the world.

ANTICIPATING NEEDS

Companies can start to lay strong foundations for creating people advantage in the future – and that means building and maintaining an active focus on talent management, even in troubled times.

Managing Demographics

As workforces become ever more diverse, one aspect of diversity, which is giving rise to particular concern because of its implications for the supply of labour, is age. The size of Europe's workforce is set to decline as a result of falling birth rates and the rising number of 'baby boomers' entering retirement. Since the workforce is ageing, and since skills shortages can be envisaged over the long term, competition for talent is as fierce as that for customers. Generation Y is said to be increasingly choosy about their employer, and although the current turbulent employment market situation is unlikely to ease for a considerable period, for people with talent, there are still career opportunities to be had.

At the same time, many older workers want to carry on working beyond traditional retirement ages. There are two key aspects of managing risk with respect to the ageing workforce: managing the loss of productivity as employees age and managing the loss of capacity as employees retire. Currently, many companies are starting to deal with both issues by offering extended or flexible employment options to attract or retain semi-retired or retired employees.

An Age-Diverse Workforce

Although generational stereotypes can be sweeping, they are also a helpful starting point to understand what people may want from work and the broad influences that may have shaped them. Previous research has demonstrated that each generation has different attitudes towards their work and the workplace, differing, for instance, in view of whom they are loyal to and how they view their career progression. Their views are defined by their formative years and the nature of the economy when they joined the workforce. Each generation creates its own traditions and culture through shared attitudes, preferences and dispositions. Such differences can be lifelong and are influenced by a combination of:

- Societal trends around raising and educating children;
- Traumatic social events;
- A significant change in the economic cycle;
- The influence of significant leaders and entrepreneurs; or
- A dramatic demographic shift that influences the distribution of resources in a society.

Generational Stereotypes

'Baby boomers' (born between 1945 and 1965) are often described as the generation of the workaholic. Rather than retire early, many are likely to want to carry on working, given current pension annuity rates. Stereotypically ambitious and optimistic, service oriented and idealistic, they value teamwork and cooperation, can be judgmental of differences and are uncomfortable with conflict. Money and security are important to them, according to Tamara Erickson's research (2008). Their drivers for satisfaction include having the power to make decisions, being in charge of a team and determining targets or goals.

Generation X (born between 1965 and 1979) is high on self-reliance, with a strong mistrust of institutions. For them, having options is a metric for success. They value flexibility and gain a sense of security from having diverse skills and networks. **Generation Y**, or 'Millennials' (born between 1980 and 1995), have grown up in a period in which terrorism and school violence have been a regular aspect of the news. Seemingly 'random' events – inexplicable things – can happen anytime. Millennials, therefore, tend to live in the moment. They are optimistic and have been brought up in a pro-child culture, with working mothers. They are great users of technology. They want important and challenging work and success represents opportunities to learn.

There is also a new generation soon to enter the workforce. **Generation Z** (born between 1996 and 2010) are under 16 years and are typically finding their first jobs on leaving school in retail and hospitality organisations. Tamara Erickson (2008) refers to these as the 'Re'-generation because during their lifetime they have experienced the growing resource shortages – energy, recession, refinancing and housing crisis, the quest to reduce carbon emissions. Their expectations may be tempered by hard truths – reality, restraint, renewal and regeneration. They may well look for security and sustainability. As the economy moves through the recession, this will be a key formative difference between this generation and the one before them (Generation Y), who have been used to a long period of economic growth throughout their working lives to date.

The different generations in the workplace also bring divergent skills, learning styles and expectations around reward. However, as with all stereotypes, the Gen Up (CIPD/Penna, 2009) research found diversity within each generation to be as significant as across generations.

STRATEGIC WORKFORCE/TALENT PLANNING

Managing demographics is an ideal opportunity for the HR function to actively collaborate with the corporate strategy staff to understand the future demand for employees derived from the corporate strategy. Ideally, organisations will carry out scenario planning to create advanced models through which they can estimate demand and supply for certain types of future jobs and skills.

Demographics may be best managed at a job-group level, because in some job families there will be a surplus while in others there will be a major shortfall. The workforce should be assessed by projecting the average age and the age breakdown of the workforce in 5, 10 and 15 years, taking into account factors such as retirement, attrition and recruitment rates. Modelling labour demand by job families over the same period involves categorizing functions into job groups which are jobs that require similar skills, and examining strategic growth projections at function, family and group level. By so doing, HR can estimate expected the future needs, labour shortfalls and surpluses for each job group and job function.

In general companies use internal training to prepare for the future more efficiently, including retraining and redeploying employees who have obsolescent skills but who have the potential to make a useful contribution over time in other roles. But training and transfers may not be enough to resolve future needs specific to job families. Some shortfalls may need to be made up by hiring from the outside or by pursuing alternative strategies such as outsourcing to reduce the demand for staff. One company using proactive and innovative thinking about its recruitment challenges is Infosys, which has a heavy need for technologically skilled graduates and is in a worldwide competition for such skills. Infosys has partnered with 60 universities in India, sponsoring its own business partner outsourcing module and is therefore able to attract and recruit prime candidates.

Managing capacity loss will be an ongoing challenge. Simultaneously, companies will have to think about how they handle the loss of productivity of older employees. Some companies are offering older employees the opportunity to rotate between jobs that involve varying degrees of physical labour.

Capacity Shortfall Solutions – Recruiting Older Workers

ASDA became well known for being in the forefront of employing older workers some years ago. David Smith read the trends in the labour market well and acted before the competitors in ways that directly benefited ASDA. As David explains, 'The world is constantly presenting new challenges. In particular the nature of the labour market in the UK is changing. One of the things that I did 10 years ago was to start recruiting people aged 50 and over. In my view the labour market was already shrinking back then, and the birth rate has certainly been shrinking since then. We've seen a lot of immigration to fill that particular void.

At ASDA we've had a tremendous amount of success recruiting in the 50 plus market - we're the largest employer of the over 50s. We employ 24,000 people with tremendous life skills and we've had great customer service on the back of that particular strategy. I think that the labour market challenge will become ever more acute. One of the emerging challenges for the future which you can see now in the population is that people are:

a)   Needing to work longer; or
b)   Wanting to work longer; and
c)   Able to work longer than people ever used to do before. I think employers that don't value the diversity of the population are going to be in trouble.'

Need for Fresh Thinking on Employer Brand

If you want to demonstrate how your HR initiatives are aligned with overall business strategy then strategic workforce planning is a great way to do it. Wise employers also understand the importance of having a strong employer brand to attract desired recruits. An employer brand is at its most powerful when it aligns people processes, business goals and employee needs and expectations. This is when the employees want what the organisation has to offer and vice versa, and when the implicit or explicit 'promise' at recruitment forms the basis of a 'deal' – legal and/or psychological – that is successfully delivered to employees through its HR programmes, including career development, learning, reward and recognition, structure and processes and systems. The very nature of this alignment tends to lead to engaged employees and a high level of business goal achievement.

Developing an employer brand that appeals to different generations is no mean feat and the nature of employee expectations is constantly changing. For instance, Anne Minto points out one of the specific challenges of recruiting young talent into the oil and gas industry. Centrica operates in a very competitive environment. Gas and oil prices fluctuate daily, which affects Centrica's business: 'ultimately you have drive more efficiency through the people you employ, so you have got to be constantly ensuring you are employing and recruiting the best possible people and also that their training is absolutely 'fit for purpose'.

One of the biggest people challenges we have is recruiting in specialised skilled areas where we have gaps. I think that the oil and gas industry is seeing less people coming into it. It's not seen as the frontier business that it was 25 years ago when people flocked into it. We are competing with other large companies to get the best geologists or power engineers and that is a real challenge for us.

In parts of our upstream business, for example, there are just fewer and fewer qualified engineers in the hydrocarbons area.

Those graduates and young people are making very different decisions to what Generation X or the Baby Boomers did. When they come for interview, it is definitely a dual interviewing process: we might be interviewing them but they are certainly interviewing us. The environment and business ethics are all topics that are high on Generation Y's list of things to ask about.' In recent times many engineering graduates have gone to work in the city or in consultancy, but with the economic downturn we hope to see more of those coming directly into our industry.

Building an Employer Brand to Make the Most of Generational Diversity

The varying needs of different generations of employees mean that employee value propositions and management approaches must be constantly under review. Increasingly, segmentation approaches borrowed from marketing are applied to understand the needs of different talent groups. Stereotypically the generations vary in terms of what they want from their job - the degree of freedom they expect to exercise, the amount of team interaction, risk-taking etc. they are also likely to vary in terms of what they expect in terms of the 'value proposition' or 'deal' they expect. Components of the deal are likely to include salary, pension, learning opportunities, flexible working etc. Some will be happier with deferred compensation than others for example. They will also vary in terms of their preferred style of management-formal or informal- and type of hierarchy as well as in the nature and frequency of communications, and the degree of alignment to shared values they expect.

Understanding the needs of the different generations is a growing research theme internationally with researchers such as Frank Bournois, Tamara Erickson and others examining the implications for employers of managing a multi-generational workforce. The following 'value propositions' draw on their work to varying degrees. For instance, the Gen UP research (CIPD/Penna, 2009) explored the needs of the different generations currently in the workplace and considered how organisations can develop tailored value propositions to meet the different needs. By doing so, the authors argue, employers can harmonise the workforce generations to bring about sustainable high performance.

The Baby Boomer Value Proposition

Baby Boomers seek authority to make decisions. If they have challenging work, then Boomers are more likely to feel engaged with their organisation. Baby Boomers want work–life balance. Half would consider working beyond their expected retirement age. They want to feel personally valued by those around them, but currently under half of them do. Just under half feel people take note of their opinion and ideas. Boomers are more engaged if their organisation demonstrates social/environmental responsibility. Access to personal development engages them, for example, if they feel able to be successful and if there are excellent job opportunities available, though only one in five are positive about job opportunities.

The Generation X Value Proposition

Generation X seeks authority to make decisions and thrives on feeling challenged. They also want work–life balance. Generation X have reacted against the 'face time' culture and often look for more of a work–life balance which gives them flexibility and freedom. They are more concerned with outcome than process. Half feel their job allows them to have an appropriate balance between work and personal life. They want to be personally valued by those around them and tend to be more engaged if there is a sense of team. Currently, half feel people take note of their opinion and ideas at work and this too is similar across sectors. They value feeling able to be successful in their organisation. Access to personal development opportunities includes 'on the job' growth combined with excellent job opportunities within their organisation.

The Generation Y Value Proposition

Generation Y seek to be part of a team, have fun and make new friends. They feel more engaged to perform better where they can access this team work. Three in four feel part of a team at work while half feel their organisation is a fun place to work. This environment is consistent across sectors. They also feel more engaged if they have challenging work, feel able to get things done and feel a sense of challenge. They also want work–life balance. They are more engaged with their employer if their overall benefits package meets their needs and if they have access to personal development, for example, being able to be successful and having ample opportunity to grow. These opportunities include specialist skills development.

"Our number one objective is to hire the right Googlers," she said. "We never just put a bum on a seat. This ensures we only recruit high-potential, culturally compatible staff - 100% talent."

Once a new employee's contract is signed, the company sends them presents every week before they join and invites them to lunch with their managers.

"On their first day, the 'Noogler' [a new employee] finds their desk festooned with balloons, gifts and T-shirts," said Hornsey. "So they already love us - and why would they ever want to leave?" As a result, staff turnover is just 3%.

Training and development is largely an on-the-job experience. Google operates a 70:20:10 policy to encourage innovation. Some 70% of an employee's time is spent on their day job 20% is spent on project work and 10% (or one day a fortnight) is spent working on whatever the employee wants to do.

"If someone thinks we should open an office in the Congo, they can gather a team and research the opportunity," said Hornsey. "And if they conclude we should, then they can go and do it."

All this emphasis on people development requires a hefty HR resource. In the EMEA region, Google has 300 HR staff as part of a total workforce of 2,500.

Is There a Generic Value Proposition That Works for All?

Core to the generic value proposition is the need to offer a 'competitive deal' and job security. These expectations are consistent across different industry sectors. However, the way these needs are expressed in terms of value proposition varies. For instance, some Baby Boomers are interested in long-term reward packages, while there has been a shift for Generations X and Y to focus on shorter term pay/benefits deals. This may be in response to the loss of final salary pension schemes. Employers are offering pensions, childcare vouchers and buying/selling holidays to meet the needs of the different life-stages of their employees.

Having a good reputation as an employer attracts and engages employees from all generations. A good employer will offer jobs with a sense of purpose and challenge. They are also considered to treat people with respect and offer employees recognition and credit for their achievements. Many employees expect an organisation to offer personal development opportunities as part of the value proposition, though the nature of development preferences varies between generations. For example, Baby Boomers and Generation X consider these opportunities to include internal job moves within their organisation. Generation Y is more interested in being given specialist skills training and ample opportunities to grow 'on the job'. This is likely to reflect the growing emphasis on 'employability' – enabling employees to maximise their value in the employment market.

Are Organisations Getting This Generic Value Proposition Right?

There are clear opportunities to harness the engagement and performance of each generation. Yet it seems few organisations are responding to the diversity of attitudes and needs and consequently may be disappointing many employees. The Gen Up survey looked at how well organisations are perceived to meet these core expectations that vary by generation and found some key factors on which generational differences appeared most marked in different sectors:

Pay

For Boomers, pay is seen to be most competitive in the public sector. For Generations X and Y, those in the professional sector are the most positive about receiving competitive pay from their employer. Workers in the service sector are generally less positive than others about their 'deal' meeting their needs.

Job Security

Although many seek job security from an employer, Generation Y is more optimistic than the other generations. Six in ten of both public and financial sector workers feel their job is secure. This is to be expected for the financial sector, given the current economic situation. However, this is perhaps a surprising finding, given the general perception that the public sector offers significant job security.

Reputation – A Great Place to Work

Professional sector workers are generally the most positive about their organisation's reputation as a place to work. Generation X in the service sector are also likely to feel that their organisation has a good reputation. Conversely, Baby Boomers are less likely to feel that their organisation has a good reputation, particularly if they are based in the public sector.

Treated with Respect

Baby Boomers are less inclined to feel that people in their organisation are treated with respect. Around 7 in 10 workers across each generation feel a sense of purpose in their work. Employers in the public sector seem to be doing best when it comes to personal development for all generations. Baby Boomers are amongst the least happy in the UK workforce in terms of personal development opportunities.

Squaring the Circle?

Effective diversity management is about creating choice for people, but building tailored employee value propositions and at the same time ensuring equity and affordability is a difficult balancing act. Inclusiveness rather than exclusion should be the watchword in policies and practices. This approach can be extended to managing across different cultures, genders and other demographic differences. Total rewards are an excellent means of providing both tangible and intangible rewards, many of which have few cost implications but provide maximum benefit to employees. HR needs to work closely with line managers to ensure that key talent, in particular, can achieve some satisfaction of their needs and expectations in return for their part of the employment deal.

Rewarding Knowledge Workers

When Jon Sparkes worked as HRD for Scientific Generics, a Cambridge (UK)-based firm specialising in devising ingenious solutions to difficult technical or scientific problems, he had the challenge of devising a reward system that could retain the talented individuals who worked for the firm and who were being constantly poached by competitors in the area.

Jon's solution was to work in partnership with employees, and having deeply understood their motivators, he designed a reward process that could meet the needs of both the business and employees. The company created an intellectual property (IP) consultancy to maximise the inventions being produced and developed spin-out companies which involved licensing, with inventors given 10% of royalties. Spin-out creators were given 10% of shares of the company without having to be involved in day-to-day operations.

Commercial back-office staff sold services to spin-outs. These were free to a new spin-out, then sold to older and better spin-outs who could afford to employ their own organisational development (OD) specialists because they had the budget.

Generics was a hotbed of innovation, with the City of Cambridge forcing the pace. Jon was recruited to get growth in headcount (15–20% p.a) to generate the IP. He had to go global to find the people he needed – he wanted polymaths, since innovation happens on the boundaries between disciplines.

As Jon says, 'HR creates the thing to support the strategy. Now the process is one of perpetual renewal. In Generics, the link between people and organisation and the business strategy is so strong.'

RECRUITING FOR ATTITUDE

A traditional approach to recruitment is looking for cultural fit. This is the approach taken by most HR leaders. Indeed David Smith considers that part of ASDA's turnaround in the early 90s was due to the strategy he developed of hiring for attitude and training for skill. For David, it is extraordinarily important to get the right kind of cultural fit of people at all levels. He said that 'if you're working in a mundane job at ASDA you need to enjoy mixing with the public, as there's little else that will help stimulate you. To this end, ASDA runs a half-day assessment centre for hourly paid people.

'Something that we kicked off in those days and still stands today, is the recognition of individuals; this whole idea of listening to people, seeking their help on business issues and taking their ideas on board is massively important, much more so than your formal remuneration strategy. This is about how people feel about the business they're engaging with, whether they feel that their ideas and their contributions are recognised – those are the things that stand us in good stead. I think the whole piece has been run on communication.'

Anne Minto and her team have taken a 'drains-up' to the way they recruit people in the first place. Recruiting for attitude is the primary driver in the recruitment of front-line staff. To become an engineer, clearly one has to have the technical capabilities either to be able to operate quite complex IS systems or to train technically. As Anne says, this approach is paying off: 'Actually recruiting for attitude has made an enormous change in our ability to deliver service to our customers and that is something HR training has had a huge influence on.'

Anne is very proud of Centrica's on-line recruitment, especially for graduates and apprentices. Five years ago, when she went to Centrica, they had no capacity for on-line recruitment but since going on-line, even though they still experience problems in filling all of the specialist positions, they attract a very healthy number of graduates and they have diminished a lot of their problems in recruiting engineers. This is because people who are just surfing the net see the site and the jobs and apply. They have recruited all kinds of people who have changed career and come to work for British Gas as engineers because they happened on the recruitment site.

Spotlight on Google: Culture Fit at the Heart of Recruitment and Retention

As Liane Hornsey says, 'I only hire people who are compatible with this culture, I think that's always something you've always got to look for, I think people really whither on the vine when they're wrong in the culture.'

Background

Google has grown rapidly exponentially since it was founded 10 years ago. Its technology is absolutely cutting-edge and it needs very bright talent to keep generating great ideas and great technology. By accident, rather than design, the types of people they have employed have been young, technically savvy and often straight from university. This is because they have the skills and ideas needed – but their objective is to recruit clever, innovative people who will fit the Google culture, regardless of their background and level of experience.

The Google culture is slightly anarchic, informal, relaxed and friendly. People are not spoon-fed – they are expected to stand on their own feet and use their initiative. With their phenomenal growth and increasing competition, they have an ongoing need for new talent. They aim to present the Google 'brand' to people they want to employ now and also those who may join them in 5 years' time. The impression they make at any touch point in the hiring process is very important, as are word-of-mouth and reputation as a good employer.

Approach

- Created a 'house-style' look and feel for offices – the Google primary colours, lava lamps, massive Google current search and Google Earth screens in receptions, chill out areas - which encourages a relaxed (although highly focused) working environment.
- Every employee can have three free, high quality meals a day in a lively canteen, plus open access to lots of areas with free drinks and snacks. This leads to informal social and business interaction and, hopefully, healthy employees.
- Culture Club – lots of special interest groups to engage broad range of interests, both professional and social.
- There is absolute consistency across all global locations in terms of technology and an office pass which can be used anywhere – so wherever people go they can plug in their laptop and work.
- The recruitment process is very personal and consistent globally. After a telephone interview there are a number of one-to-ones with different people. The process suits all ages – but possibly is more favourable to experienced people. However, new graduates need to be able to deal with it. The objective is to ensure not just skills match, but also culture fit.

Outcomes

- Still attracting incredibly talented people
- Excellent retention rates
- No. 1 employer graduates want to work for

Sources: Liane Hornsey and Gen Up, CIPD/Penna, 2009

DELIVERING ON THE EMPLOYER BRAND

While creating an exciting employer brand to attract bright new talent is one challenge, in practice, building the commitment of a diverse workforce requires some fresh thinking. David Smith argues that this is needed – and lacking – because employee needs and expectations are constantly changing, and HR initiatives are not keeping pace: 'Because when we first started calling people by their first names and taking an interest in them, that was a wow. Now they say, 'well you can read my name on my badge, impress me in some other way', so their requirements are continually rising.'

Changing Careers

And careers may be changing in ways that we don't expect. Graduates of Generation Y (often referred to as 'Millennials') in particular appear to want a flexible model of careers, where they can work in a project environment and move in and out of responsible career roles. Balancing the needs of the business for more flexibility, and the aspirations of employees for more flexible working can be a big challenge for HR and the demand for flexible career paths is likely to grow.

As David Smith comments: 'If you think about Generation Y, and certainly Generation Z when it comes along, people's expectations will be enormous in terms of what a working career and job and occupation will provide for them, whereas the Baby Boomer generation was much more content to do what they were told, and be much more loyal naturally. Now I think people are more disloyal naturally and they want to know what your ethical policy is and what you are doing about saving the planet. I think the future of business is much more around people understanding and being comfortable with your ethics behind the scenes than ever it used to be. And that's a good thing but it's also something you have to think about for the future.'

Improving Work–Life Balance

Given that most sections of the diverse workforce want to achieve better work–life balance, building options to help people achieve this will reinforce the employer brand. Offering flexible working is the commonest means of managing work–life balance. HR leaders use employee surveys and assessments to determine the options that employees and recruits are looking for with respect to work–life balance. They then develop key performance indicators to measure work–life balance and its influence on business, such as the voluntary attrition rates of high-talent employees. The portfolio of work–life balance offerings should be frequently and widely communicated to employees. Line managers should be trained in work–life balance initiatives to ensure that they incorporate the initiatives in their businesses.

Delivering on the employer brand requires a laser-sharp focus on the effective implementation of the employer brand promise. Typically, this requires HR processes and practices that allow experiential learning opportunities for talent and high potentials, together with the use of variable compensation to motivate employees. The majority of people in each generation are likely to seek development in their specialist area of expertise.

Currently Google is one company intent on delivering on its employer brand promise – and is doing so in part through learning and development (L&D).

Building a Learning and Development Department at Google

At Google, there have been many HR initiatives over the last 2 years, but the one that stands out for Liane Hornsey was building an L&D department. When she arrived at Google, there were a number of training initiatives in place, such as product training, new starter orientation and a bit of skills training, which involved, for example, people putting their hand up for presentation skills. But beyond that, in Liane's words:

'The L&D function, the HR function didn't exist. There were a couple of HR people but they were very employee relations sorts of HR people. I've supplemented and complemented these people them with some internal business partners who understand how to consult, who have OD and other backgrounds, but who really have an OD expertise.' Liane hired a leading edge development director, and together they spent a lot of time strategising on what the learning and development needs were, and then they've put together a whole strategy around project working, coaching, development, talent managing succession planning, blended learning, and so on.

'And I've built a really stunning, I mean a fantastic learning and development department, I've hired a lot of people, I've built the organisation up from scratch really, and I have this big department because we're growing very, very quickly. By the end of this year it'll be about 130 people. Because we have some very, very capable people at Google and the key to keeping them highly motivated is to keep the totality of our client base learning, so the learning and development department is really important to us.'

DEVELOPING THE MULTI-GENERATIONAL WORKFORCE

Providing development opportunities is a key means of delivering on an enticing employer brand promise. Devising development strategies to get the best out of a multi-generational workforce calls for real creative thinking underpinned by good data. Marketing techniques, such as segmentation of the workforce can be valuable in helping create a better understanding of the needs and aspirations of specific employee groups. The Gen Up study found that for all the generations there is significant demand in terms of L&D for:

- People management skills including customer service skills
- Different uses of technology

- Leadership development
- Knowledge about their organisation's wider business

But what are the best ways to provide development that is tailored to different needs and motivations, flexible and affordable?

Forms of Development Practice

Perhaps the most effective way of providing wider development to the workforce is through managers and HR can develop managers of multi-generational teams to get the best out of the people they manage. While training is still the most common development practice, leaders in a CIPD/DDI study find special projects, mentors and personal coaches more effective. Often, the main benefit of training is exposure to new networks and to ways of thinking that stretch perspectives, yet can also be applied in practice.

Formal development methods in recent years have tended to favour behavioural (situational leadership) approaches and self-awareness raising using psychometrics and emotional intelligence-based instruments. Contemporary development methods include coaching, action learning, 360-degree feedback, opportunities for learning and self-development, integrated with career planning and challenging job assignments. Other common methods include job shadowing, secondments, off-the-job development, networks and visits. Volunteering is increasingly being used as a means of both developing individuals and teams and fulfilling an organisation's social responsibility to the community.

Development opportunities appear to be most enriching if they provide people with access to new, varied challenges, where there is a degree of difficulty in the task and where outcomes are important and highly visible, especially if success is by no means guaranteed. Even hardship can be developmental, according to previous research by the Centre for Creative Leadership.

TALENT MANAGEMENT IN THE DOWNTURN

In 2009, as the economy cools, organisations have to cut costs and realign their goals. Usually the first casualty of a downturn is people, but there are dangers for organisations that cut their workforces too swiftly. While people may be in greater supply than jobs at the moment, the tide will soon turn thanks to the demographic forces that threaten to strangle global talent supply lines. At times like these, companies need to start paying even more attention to retaining and developing their top talent, and considering how they can motivate and keep the commitment of key employees.

In practice, in the 2009 recession, it seems that employers have taken on board lessons from previous recessions – when talent processes stalled and large-scale redundancy programmes undermined the talent base and commitment of 'surviving' employees – and this time, it seems that many employers are trying hard to retain as many staff as possible.

Employers generally seem to recognise that the right talent and the right HR strategies will be required to bring organisations successfully through the downturn. Talent is very much still on the agenda, and currently the focus is mainly on retention of key talent. Employers appear to be very conscious both of the value of skilled and experienced employees and of the cost of replacing them when the longed-for economic recovery happens.

BT Group chairman Sir Michael Rake (and Chairman of the UK Commission for Employment and Skills (UKCES)), in a letter to the Financial Times (27th February 2009), urged employers to be more forward looking, to continue their investment in skills to survive the recession and to be well-positioned when the economy picks up. And at a CIPD February 2009 round-table discussion of senior HR and executives from the public and private sectors, trade union representatives and policy experts from employer bodies, there was strong consensus that an unrelenting investment in people is what is will help organisations to sustain their competitiveness. Similarly, continuing to recruit new talent to bring in needed skills and expertise will remain important even though organisations may be downsizing.

This is borne out by findings from the CIPD's Employee Outlook survey of employees in UK-based organisations, carried out in February 2009, to find out how they were experiencing the recession. On the one hand, many of the organisations that took part in our data gathering were focusing almost entirely on managing for survival of the business in the immediate short term. One notable element is that many of the managers and trades union officials who are having to deal with the challenges of the recession have never before been through such a downturn and therefore lack previous experience of how to handle situations that occur as a result of the slump. However, this may actually be an advantage if it opens up the way to more collaborative solutions than in previous recessions. In particular, although many organisations taking part in the survey were preparing for redundancies or had already restructured, there appeared a genuine attempt to find alternatives to redundancy where possible.

Organisations have acted swiftly to get their costs under control. Many of the cost-saving measures have been developed jointly by managers and unions or staff groups. Mostly these have revolved around variations on flexible working, such as short-time working. Other cost-cutting measures include pay and recruitment freezes and deferred graduate recruitment. Employers are placing less emphasis on investment in L&D, employee well-being and diversity initiatives. In fact, the most popular planned action by employers, according to a BCG/EAPM survey (Strack et al., 2009) is cutting back on recruiting. But organisations should cut back with caution. In the aftermath of previous recessions, many companies found themselves without the skills they needed. This time the skills shortages are likely to be even more acute, with fewer younger people entering the workforce and greater numbers of older people entering retirement, resulting in likely skills shortages in key areas.

Clearly, a major motivation for finding alternatives to redundancies is the desire to retain a skilled and talented workforce for when the economy picks up. Some of the dilemmas employers are struggling with include:

a) How to lose cost and surplus capacity, but still keep employees engaged, committed and performing. Understanding potential growth opportunities and restructuring for these is a key concern.

b) When an organisation's strategy is in 'holding pattern' because of the context – how to keep people motivated when there may not be major projects to keep people energised and delivering at full stretch. Employee engagement is therefore a key concern.

c) When an organisation is in full growth mode – how to recognise and develop skills needed for future success while people are extremely busy now. Building and maintaining high performance is a key concern.

Many employers are also looking to strategically restructure, find greater value from what they are doing currently, including stronger performance management and retain a focus on talent and development. These challenges will be at the centre of many HR leaders' preoccupations, especially as they all have longer-term capability and performance implications.

Retaining a Focus on Talent

CIPD Employee Outlook survey (McCartney and Willmott, 2009) respondents recognise that bringing organisations out of the downturn will require having the right talent and the right HR strategies. Respondents from all sectors predict that the biggest issues for their organisations over the next 5 years will be improving the quality of leadership, keeping the most talented employees and improving customer service. Additionally sectors are grappling with:

- For nationalised/public corporations the biggest issues are the introducing new technology, and becoming more innovative.
- For public sector organisations introducing new technology.
- For charities and the voluntary sector generally becoming more innovative.

Impact on Learning and Development

Conventionally, when organisations are cutting costs, investments in training and development are usually the first to be cut. And while there are cuts in training budgets, they were not as draconian as might be expected. The CIPD 2009 *Learning and Development Survey* (April 2009) found that around half (51%) of respondents reported that funds for L&D stayed the same for the past year, with 45% believing that funds will remain the same in the next 12 months, although 44% of respondents expected a decrease of 40% or more to their budgets during the same period. Similarly, the CIPD's Employee Outlook 2009 survey reports cuts in training (17% in total, 25% in nationalised industries), while 38% of respondents report that investment in L&D is carrying on at much the same level as before the downturn. However, the median training spend per employee has dropped from £300 per employee last year to £220 this year.

- Gearing development more closely to tomorrow's business needs

With respect to training and development, the CIPD study, *Fighting Back Through Innovation* (July 2009) reports that many employers are attempting to balance the immediate business critical needs with long-term sustainable business needs. For example, National Express is continuing to train managers in 'recruitment behaviour' so that they are ready to recruit the best when recruitment picks up.

Seventy percent of Employee Outlook respondents agree that (L&D) continues to be a high priority in their organisation and 76% say that it is seen as part of business improvement. Looking to the future, 65% anticipate that L&D will become more closely integrated with business strategy, and 60% feel there will be greater emphasis on evaluation. The majority of respondents believe that leadership skills (81%) and strong commercial awareness (67%) will be most important in meeting business objectives in the next 2 years.

Many employers are concerned about the risk cuts to L&D budgets pose to healthy leadership and talent pipelines. Trainer development is expected to suffer, with 25% of companies planning to reduce efforts in this area, along with coaching and development at the top of the business with 22% making cuts here. 'Soft' skills and teambuilding are the most likely to suffer, with technical skills and leadership development more likely to be preserved, in that order.

Deriving more value from training

Where training is still on offer, HR teams are reported to be focusing leadership and management training on priority areas such as change management, stress and conflict management, talent management and development, people and performance management, decision-making and difficult conversations (Employee Outlook survey). Some are also providing bespoke support to line managers in a number of areas, including downsizing, advice on talent and performance improvement, employee relations and increased communication and information.

L&D professionals report that they want to derive more value from spending on training and to secure greater return on investment, with training focused most on managers and individual team members where there is greatest potential to drive business growth (*Source: Cegos Survey, November 2008*). The same survey predicts that the biggest growth area of training will be e-learning, set to increase 18 points in 2009 from 55% of organisations using e-learning in June 2008.

Organisations that are aiming for high performance need to be agile and to harness different capabilities. For organisations in every sector skills in digital technology, information management and entrepreneurialism need to be mixed with change management and customer service ethos.

Building a customer service ethos has been the driver behind many of Centrica's training programmes. These have been revolutionised as Anne Minto describes: 'We have far shorter programmes in our call centres now before people actually get out on to the telephones. So instead of doing 9 weeks of theory and then getting to the phones you are having trials on the telephones by week 4 and that's made an enormous difference to people because they can consolidate what they have learnt in the first 4 weeks rather than thinking by week 9 "what did I learn in week 1?" That means that our attrition rates have gone down as people stay longer and we are not having to deal with this constant change-over of staff. It has been a major goal to reduce attrition because we want consistency and we need our customers to feel that the people they are dealing with on the telephones are helpful, courteous and knowledgeable abt the products we are selling to them.'

Organisations are also generally more focused on sharing learning and pooling development resources across different departments. For instance, when Gala Group merged with Coral Eurobet in October 2005, different processes continued to exist in different parts of the business. Currently, Heads of L&D across the business meet regularly to share learning and reduce spending by removing duplication, thus leading to greater efficiency and effectiveness.

For all the challenges of the recession, there are opportunities too. And while many employers may have to make some redundancies at least in the short term, it is not only *what* organisations have to do but *how* they do it which will affect employee engagement and the possibility of sustainable performance for a return to growth.

Example: LEGO – Development with the longer-term in view

One company that is planning to maintain its investment in training and development, despite the downturn, is Lego, the Danish toy manufacturer. In the last few years, Lego has been competing with computer games and mp3 players. Traditional toy sales have decreased but Lego sales increased in most of their markets in 2008. Lego reports its greatest current threat to be the worldwide recession which is expected to increasingly affect the toy market. However, they still expect to see a moderate increase in sales.

Lego is looking to the long term and plans to continue its investment in sales, marketing and production in line with this expected growth. Lego has a strong interest in stimulating learning, and they also plan to maintain their investment in human capital, with competence development activities and individual development plans, ensuring it has a supply of intellectual capital and technical competence for the future. Lego has also undergone some restructuring and has in-sourced its production to increase flexibility and efficiency. All of which suggests that Lego is looking to the future, at what the organisation will require in the long run rather than cutting back spending in a knee-jerk reaction to the current climate. Based on source: Leroux, M. (2009).

IMPACT ON THE EMPLOYER BRAND

In the past decade, many employers have sought to differentiate themselves in the recruitment market by building strong employer brands – typically implying a fair 'deal', strong values people can relate to, opportunities for growth, etc. How are employers remaining true to their employer branding promise? Are they maintaining their focus and determination to live their values, to build their talent base and to improve the quality of management and leadership, or will short-term expediency push these out of the frame?

In general the answers are encouraging. Practices suggesting that a focus on employer brands is being maintained are reported in the Employee Outlook (2009). They include 'Giving employees training to make them more employable' and 'Recognising the need to keep managing talent and provide development opportunities, up-skilling on the job floor, rather than sending people on external training courses'.

BUILDING TALENT MANAGEMENT CAPABILITIES

Looking ahead, in preparation for the recovery, organisations must continue to build their talent management capabilities. Especially for those organisations that find themselves in a 'strategic holding pattern', it will be essential to find ways of stretching and motivating key talent, preferably by involving them in finding and exploiting opportunities for the business in ways that create first-mover competitive advantage. BCG (Strack et al., 2009) make the following recommendations:

- Assess future talent needs in the light of strategic and business require-ments, such as the desired pace of growth or targeted future locations.
- Monitor and manage the pipeline of future leaders.
- Ensure that the plans for talent succession are in place and that candidates for key positions are tracked as part of a regular process.
- Match talented individuals with key positions within the organisation and implement mentoring programs.
- Carefully monitor programs for managing expatriate employees, including those working abroad in any talent management planning and ensure that their return home is managed professionally.
- Continually adapt career tracks to address internal shifts in the workforce or business strategy and external client needs.
- Separate long-term planning decisions from short-term activities so that, for example, valuable job-rotation activities are unhampered by any short-term implications for profit and loss.
- Identify the specific types of employees sought and the best avenues for reaching them.
- Offer potential and current employees a value proposition that aligns closely with their desires as well as the employer's brand.

CONCLUSION

In the downturn, many of the talent practices that had been operating before the recession – such as developing employer brands – are at risk and the widespread process of change may undermine the emotional attachment of key employees to the organisation. While the recession is a global phenomenon, employers who remain true to their employer brand and continue to deliver their people promise will be likely to keep their employees engaged and performing. Talent management must remain in focus – HR must continue to build career paths, integrate business-relevant learning and identify development opportunities that will prepare both individuals and the business for the recovery. The good practice which is evident in the way many organisations and their employees are responding to the challenges thrown up by the economic crisis suggest that a strong foundation of good employee relations which can be built on to mutual employee-employer benefit in the post-crisis era. And in particular, HR must focus on building the leadership needed to take organisations forward into the next phase of business growth. It is to the topic of leadership that we turn next.

Chapter 6

Building Leadership Capability

'The ultimate test of practical leadership is the realization of intended, real change that meets people's enduring needs.'

James MacGregor Burns

That we are experiencing uncertain economic times few can doubt. At best it would seem that developed economies are in for a period of weak growth over the next few years. The impact of globalisation and technology has also to a large extent reframed the environment in which organisations create value and change is the order of the day. Arguably it is precisely when times get tough that leadership is most required, especially leaders who can lead people through uncertainty, keep people engaged and focused on performance. Indeed, in such situations, wise counsel would suggest that this is the time to invest in developing leadership.

But what kinds of leadership will be required if we are to prepare organisations to seize the opportunities of the recovery? On the one hand, effective leadership at the top can also be a powerful organisational performance enhancer. Warren Bennis (speaking at a CIPD Conference in 2004) argued that the impact of effective top leadership can increase shareholder value by 11%. On the other hand, various theorists argue that new forms of leadership will be needed to cope with a fast-changing context. As Hamel and Breen (2007) put it, 'management is out of date'. Markides (2009) and others argue that we need to move away from the old model of a single charismatic leader towards a collective leadership, where it is the everyday efforts of employees that produce high-performance organisations. The response of markets, analysts, shareholders, customers, employees and the public at large to the leadership of major financial services organisations such as Northern Rock, Citi, HBOS, Lehman Brothers, Merrill Lynch, RBS and UBS will testify to this.

And if business leaders own the talent agenda, HR leaders must own the leadership agenda – ensuring that their organisation has the forms and quality of leadership required for sustainable success. That means that HR leaders need to know what forms of leadership will help their organisation to succeed and then be able to source and develop these. This can prove difficult because as Augier and Teece (2005) put it, 'As a scientific concept, leadership is a mess'!

LEADERS AND CULTURE

It is particularly in changing times that leaders need to pay attention to building healthy and adaptable cultures. There is a growing consensus that organisations now cannot afford to have work cultures burdened with politics and power conflicts where creativity is obstructed and where managers have no cultural awareness. To create what Sujansky (2006) describes as a 'vibrant entrepreneurial organization' leaders must be able to share the vision, encourage employees to take risks, set the right example, stretch employees, provide work–life balance, establish productivity standards and feedback, recruit and retain winners and celebrate victories.

Similarly, today's workforce is becoming increasingly diverse and work patterns are changing. What employees who are working flexibly or remotely may need from their managers may be different from what conventional teams co-located with their manager may need. Above all, in a global business context, leaders must become 'intercultural ambassadors' (Loubier, 2002). They must understand that the very concept of leadership, and therefore its practice, varies between cultures. This understanding is an essential factor in possessing intercultural leadership competence.

WHAT KINDS OF LEADERS ARE NEEDED FOR TODAY'S ORGANISATIONS?

Quite what is required to successfully lead in today's organisations is less clear. One of the themes emerging from an extensive review of management and leadership literature (2003–2006) is the need for new or evolved forms of management and leadership, more suited to the demands of a complex, fast-changing knowledge-based economy, whose focus is on engaging with employees in ways which produce discretionary effort.

Hamel and Breen (2007) argue that 'old' management and leadership styles (i.e. which they refer to as 'Management 1.0'), which are based on a convention of low trust/high control, sit uneasily against a paradigm of 'volunteer' knowledge workers, who are expected to be accountable and empowered, willing and able to create shared learning and intellectual capital. Hamel and Breen argue convincingly that 'what ultimately constrains the performance of your organisation is not its operating model, not its business model, but its management model' and that 'management as currently practised, is a drag on success'.

'MANAGEMENT 2.0'

They propose that new forms of leadership ('Management 2.0') are needed for today's and tomorrow's organisations. They want to reconstruct the philosophical foundations of management. To build companies fit for the future, they argue, we need not only new management practices, but also a new statement of principles. Without such a foundation, innovation will remain limited to incremental tinkering. They argue for instance that management education privileges decisiveness over reflection whereas what should be encouraged is deeper, more multidimensional thinking, embracing systems, values and the right, as well as left, side of the brain.

Hamel debated the components of a management innovation agenda with a range of eminent leaders and academics at a conference at Half Moon Bay (US) in 2009. The goal was to pinpoint the twenty-first century's most important management innovation challenges. In particular, the challenge was to identify the make-or-break steps that would dramatically improve the capacity of organisations to fulfil their obligations to society, adapt in the absence of crisis, unleash the power of innovation and become truly inspiring places to work. The following related challenges (and others too) emerged from the discussion (Sources: LabNotes 5 (2009) and Hamel, (2009)):

- Fully operationalise the ideas of community and citizenship. Manage as if everyone matters (because they do). Recast stakeholder relationships as fundamentally interdependent and work to maximise system success.
- Seek orientation in a higher and broader purpose. Purpose generates energy, passion and commitment. Managers must become entrepreneurs of meaning, interpreting and translating purpose for different stakeholders. As other researchers, including Nigel Springett and myself are finding, alignment around a meaningful purpose can be the 'glue' which binds employees to the organisation throughout periods of change. The task of leaders is to make sure that people can retain line of sight to the purpose in their day jobs.
- Distribute (share) the work of creating direction and strategy finding ways of working with weak signals and experimenting with many people to generate vibrant alternatives. The use of organisational development methods for engaging employees in strategic change will be discussed in Chapter 7.
- Increase trust, reduce fear. Create cultures of trust and transparency that reduce the penalties for speaking up.

Such a powerful leadership agenda will require leaders who are willing and able to change, see their role as organisational leaders not simply as business leaders. It is HR's job to build the forms and practice of leadership that will equip their organisations for tomorrow. As Hamel argues, the executive time-frame and perspective should be stretched. Incentives should be changed to reward those who nurture the small projects that have the potential to become the big ones over time. And the financial crisis has amply demonstrated the damage that can be caused to entire systems by rewarding executives for short-term activity without any thought of longer-term benefit or consequences.

Similarly more holistic performance measures should be used to capture for instance the Return on Investment (ROI) of investments in human capital and the value of unique customer experience.

These themes are reflected more widely in the leadership literature. One strong theme emerging from recent leadership literature is the need for individual business leaders to have strong values and to exercise moral leadership, perhaps not surprisingly in this post-Enron age. For Tubbs and Schultz (2006) the leader's values strongly shape behaviours of people around them. Forms and styles of leadership are variously described as *'moral'*, *'grown-up'*, *'versatile'*, *'differentiated'* and *'prosocial'* leadership. A leader's authenticity is a very strong theme in the literature. Goffee and Jones (2005), amongst others, argue that leadership demands the expression of an authentic self. People want to be led by someone real. People associate authenticity with sincerity, honesty and integrity.

And, given the context of almost constant change, various authors argue that authentic leaders must learn to embrace paradox and be versatile: strategic and operational, forceful and enabling. The emphasis is as much on emotional intelligence as on intellect. The literature suggests that leaders handle uncertainty by reflective conversations, that they must find sources of advice they can trust and that the first step of any leadership development journey requires leaders to look at themselves intensely and critically, i.e. leaders have self-insight and grapple with their shadow sides; that leaders need moral codes that are as complex, varied and subtle as the situations in which they find themselves.

Collins (2001) is not alone in pointing out the almost altruistic nature of 'great' business leaders. Collins suggests that the 'level five' leaders he describes in *'From Good to Great'* work for others and themselves; they recognise the intrinsic worth of employees and other stakeholders, support the development of associates, and bring both hope and pain by the changes they bring about.

Moreover such leaders fully embrace their role as organisational leader, whose focus is on building a culture which is sustainable. They develop the culture consciously, using symbols and dialogue to create moral solidarity and enriching the culture by telling stories. Effective behaviours include understanding the bigger picture, demonstrating a compelling and achievable vision, inspiring others, active listening, reframing, encouraging others to be creative, creating transformational change and developing a team-oriented culture.

However, leaders need to strike a balance between the needs of the business and the organisation – that one should be a means to the other. As Covey (2004) suggests, in business you need to focus on mission (purpose) and margin (profitability) – one without the other doesn't work. Ulrich and Smallwood (2007) suggest that leadership is about getting the results organisations need, in the right way. Ulrich also promotes the idea of creating a leadership brand as an identity throughout the organisation. For Ulrich what is required is an appropriate blend of leadership roles – organisational strategist, organisational executor, talent manager, human capital developer – underpinned by high levels of personal proficiency.

Collective Leadership

The importance of leadership (rather than leaders) in culture building is a growing theme in recent literature. Increasingly, leadership and leadership development are seen as inherently collaborative, social and relational processes. Leadership will be understood as the collective capacity of all members of an organisation to accomplish such critical tasks as setting direction, creating alignment and gaining commitment. Leadership is variously described as 'shared', 'we', or 'distributed'. According to Spears (2004), 'We are seeing traditional and hierarchical modes of leadership yielding to a different way of working – one based on teamwork and community, one that seeks to involve others in decision-making, one strongly based in ethical and caring behaviours.'

There is a strong emphasis on employee development and on managers creating the environment to allow staff to release potential. Indeed, a strong sub-theme is about building communities of leaders at every level who can proactively shape some of the context around them, and deliver successful implementation through high performing, highly motivated and committed teams. Raelin (2005) for instance argues that 'leaderful' organisations see leadership as concurrent, collective, collaborative and compassionate, in contrast to more traditional leadership which tends to be thought of as serial, individual, controlling and dispassionate.

Defining What Is Required of Leaders

Defining what is required of leaders, individually and collectively, and the processes for developing leaders, is very much a matter of debate and fashion. For instance theorists and practitioners increasingly argue that the leadership competency approach is limited. Instead of focusing on only the competencies of the leaders, leadership is increasingly defined not as what the leader is or does but rather as a *process* that engenders and is the result of *relationships* – relationships that focus on the *interactions* of both leaders and collaborators.

One clear articulation of this trend is in the guidance provided by Norwich Union to its future leaders: 'When we look for leadership we look for …

- *Evidence* in the *outcomes* your leadership produces (not your rank, role, experience, psychometric profile).
- *Performance over time* across outcomes we value: sustained performance (not a one hit wonder).

- *Learning agility* achieving outcomes in the face of change (not being stuck in one way of doing things).
- *Authenticity* that increases your impact on outcomes – being yourself more, playing to your strengths, with skill (not acting a role).
- *Followers* who are engaged in the outcomes we value and excited to exceptional performance (not subordinates who comply).
- *Behaviours* in line with our *values* (not outcomes at any costs).'

Given that in practice much leadership development happens on the job, it is vital that people with leadership potential have the opportunity to deliver real results in positions which are central to the company's business challenges.

Despite this, leadership competencies remain a key tool in the leadership toolkit in many organisations, but with a growing focus on the competencies required to lead in a fast-changing context. The shift is to focus on the organisational capabilities which appear to underpin corporate agility, i.e. leaders who can lead beyond the short term, transform cultures, stimulate innovation and also drive a successful business agenda.

Need for New Skills

Although the field is moving away from viewing leadership in terms of leader attributes, skills and traits, leadership competencies remain a core dimension of leadership development activities in most organisations. HR leaders aiming to improve leadership development should create a leadership profile that describes the specific leadership capabilities an organisation requires to be successful. These are likely to include the ability to think strategically, enable organisational agility, foster engagement and drive accountability for superior performance.

Professor Jean-Marie Hiltrop and Sheila Udall (2008) identified the following mix of skills and competencies as vital to sustaining organisational competitiveness:

- *Visioning and planning*. Providing a clear view of a future for the organisation, together with plans to translate the overall vision into operational reality, is crucial as a point of focus and commitment for staff.
- *Information handling*. Clearly companies need to be able to use new technology to generate, select and digest the information they need.
- *Leadership and motivation*. Companies will find themselves increasingly relying on these skills as the new generation enters the workforce and relationships with employees are becoming more transactional.
- *Creativity and learning*. Most organisations say they value, even require creativity and innovation. But in reality they discourage risk-taking and have a culture that does not tolerate mistakes.
- *Change and adaptation*. Organisations need to improve their ability to cope with rapid and complex change in an increasingly turbulent environment.

The general 'ideal' is for leaders who have strategic anticipation and insight, enabling them to shape as well as respond to the changing environment; who have core skills of communication, collaboration and empathy; and who are versatile, resilient and emotionally intelligent, thus enabling them to tailor their styles to specific people and situations and cope with the multiple demands of leading others through change. These are likely to be leaders who are curious, responsive to markets, ambitious beyond their current role, able to change, are ethical, have high integrity and are able to mobilise employees to higher level efforts. In other words, both trait and situational leadership theories are alive and well.

A Leadership Development Strategy

Crafting a leadership development strategy involves making choices. HR teams may find the following questions helpful in clarifying both the options and potential implications of the choices they make:

- In making our talent management decisions, how much should we put the business needs first above the individual context/requirement?
- How do we spot talent (given that people do not come wearing badges); should we grow our own?
- Should we favour internal versus external talent?
- Should we be aiming for the cadre development of the many versus the special high-potential few?
- What do we need to emphasise more – long-term/strategic thinking or short-term operational excellence? How do we strike the right balance?
- And how do we ensure that we are operating to high standards with respect to equality and diversity when identifying and developing our leaders?

Identifying Potential Leaders

HR should lead the process of identifying and developing leaders. A joint DDI/CIPD leadership survey report (2008) suggests that the best way to assure a qualified cadre of leaders in the pipeline is to begin by developing potential leaders at the bottom of the leadership pool, whereas the general practice reported is about development being focused on those at Head of Department level or above. As the report points out, failing to assure that those with the highest potential rise into each rung of management could leave UK organisations with a less than optimal pool of candidates for higher-level positions.

But how to identify and develop such managers and leaders?
Improving leadership development should start with an assessment of the types of leadership capabilities that are needed, then comparing those needs

with the capabilities of the leadership team. In creating a management and leadership development strategy, development should be focused at the right level. Leadership development efforts should be focused on executives who are receptive to training or coaching and are able to close the gap between current and requisite skills. The strategy should also focus on what can realistically be developed. Tubbs and Schultz are not alone in arguing that some aspects of leaders are more or less fixed (core personality), while others can be developed (behaviours). Conventional skills alone are unlikely to equip managers for their roles in years ahead and leadership and management skills need to be advanced in order to create the vision, culture and change necessary.

Succession Planning

While many studies of long-lived organisations suggest that the more successful tend to grow their own leaders, the nature of succession planning required for twenty-first century organisations is the subject of much debate. Succession planning – and the need to keep a supply of good people coming through the talent pipeline, not least in HR itself – is a particular challenge for many HR leaders.

While 'ownership' of succession planning is widely recognised as residing with business leaders, responsibility for the process and quality of outcomes rests with HR. Focus group members point out the importance of engaging key stakeholders in the process of clarifying what being a 'good leader' means and creating answers to the what, why, who, how and how well questions.

The challenge is that tomorrow's leaders are likely to be very different from today's – yet today's leaders get to choose what 'potential' looks like. And while many of today's leaders may be busy focusing on execution, tomorrow's leadership challenges may call for new sets of skills and approaches. Getting the right mix of skills and approaches across leadership groups will be important.

Gone are the days when organisations could protect their futures by nurturing a chosen elite for future senior roles based on early assessment of potential and followed by deliberate development via a succession of broadening moves and opportunities across the business. While such development models still exist, today's high potentials are likely to have many alternative options and are unlikely to pursue their career in any single organisation. Succession planning has to work for both the organisation and the individual leader.

Instead, or as well, the focus is increasingly on growing a broad talent pool, as well as 'buying in' new leadership talent. The talent pool should consist not only of those designated to have high potential from the outset but also people who are perceived to have the latent ability to lead in new ways but who may not previously have been designated as 'high potential'. 'Latent ability' suggests that individuals are able to develop and use the skills regarded as 'key'; therefore the definition of potential should not be based only on current skill levels but also embrace what can realistically be developed. Again while theorists may agree that intellect alone is not enough to suggest potential for future leadership roles, debates rage about for instance how much leaders can develop self-awareness, without which other aspects of emotional intelligence are unlikely to be effectively applied.

Another debate is about whether succession should be planned around roles or around building broad senior leadership capability. Competencies are often used as a means against which leadership potential can be assessed. Dave Ulrich argues that leadership competencies should be deduced not from some ideal competency template, but from the results leaders will have to achieve in their context. These need to correspond to the organisation's particular strategy and business model – specific to their distinct business challenges and goals. This 'leadership brand' perspective connects leadership development to business, organisational and individual performances. The prevalence of formalized succession planning practices in organizations appears to be increasing, largely due to changing demographic and related trends. However, many organization leaders report low levels of confidence in their succession planning systems and processes. Best succession and talent management practices can help organizations achieve significant benefits, including improved financial performance.

A typical 'leadership brand' succession planning process involves first anticipating changes in markets over the coming 5 to 10 year period, then to envision where the organisation wants to be in those markets. From that, it should be possible to envisage what potential leaders will need to deliver in 5 years and start to identify and develop leaders with the qualities and abilities to operate in the ways which will deliver success.

Looking ahead to how managers will produce the results expected of them in the future, managers will typically be required to manage more diverse workforces, including age diverse, to manage at a distance, across different time zones and cultures. These will be leaders who can develop flexible structures and roles with a line of sight to the customer, coach and develop their teams, create a shared sense of direction in the face of ambiguity, be credible and demonstrate their values through their actions and behaviours.

Hiltrop and Udall (2008) argue that succession planning should focus on positions rather than generalised cadres but specifically those positions defined as 'core'. These they define as scoring highly on three sets of criteria – strategic impact, discretionary impact and replacement risk – and ensuring these jobs are filled by the most talented individuals. Then, having identified core positions, the existing talent pool should be reviewed and talent aligned with positions as much as possible. This alignment is a never-ending process, as is the assessment of potential.

Ulrich also advocates assessing key positions and assessing people along dimensions of performance (past) versus behaviour (potential) using a customer/results-based competence model. Assessing the current leadership pipeline involves clarifying expectations and gaps in skills, knowledge and perspective by key transitions and building career paths in a systematic manner.

'High-Potential' Development

Similarly, how to define 'high potential' is a challenge for many organisations that struggle to differentiate performance potential versus readiness for a specific role or general progression. High-potential development programmes are common in large UK organisations and usually involve a formal assessment of strengths and development needs, more than typical general leadership programmes. The DDI/CIPD study found that this discrepancy between high potential and general leadership development programmes is evident in other ways too. UK organisations generally do a better job of aligning and monitoring their high-potential programmes than their regular programmes. Not surprisingly leaders were more satisfied with high-potential programmes because they perceive them to be much better executed than programmes designed for typical leaders. On the other hand, accountability, especially among senior managers, is reported as weak (23%), trailing the global average for high-potential programmes (44%).

DEVELOPING LEADERS

And there is no shortage of opportunity to make a difference to the quality of leadership practice through development. A large DDI survey (Pomeroy, 2006) found that only 61% of global business leaders feel that they have the skills to 'bring out the best in people'. Moreover managers and leaders may need ongoing development if they are to acquire the entrepreneurial mindsets required for success. Although collective and collaborative leadership is increasingly considered desirable, still the greater focus in most organisations is on developing individual leaders. And while leader development is a well-trodden field, many of the approaches used for developing leaders remain either contested or unproven in terms of their effectiveness. Even if more HR professionals from the UK rate their programmes as high quality than do their counterparts globally, this number is still small (41%). Moreover, only two in five UK leaders are satisfied with what their organisations offer in the way of leadership development.

There is clearly little room for complacency. While the DDI/CIPD survey suggests that UK leaders are better performers, on average, than their global counterparts, the proportion considered very good or excellent (44%) is still below the standards needed to grow and compete successfully on an international stage. Indeed when asked to rate the overall quality of leaders in their organisations, only a disappointing 8% of UK leaders rate them excellent.

Even when organisations are clear about what leadership potential looks like in their context, the question is how can evident and latent potential be realised?

For some pundits leadership is not a set of techniques or a position; it's a way of 'being' that results when leaders embark on a developmental cycle of 'awakenings' (Locander and Luechauer, 2006). For others leadership is a skill like many others, something you have to practise before you become proficient.

An effective management and leadership development strategy will include HR developing the skills to coach managers and will create genuine development opportunities – and encourage risk taking. And ultimately leaders need to be able and willing to develop themselves on an ongoing basis. Yet continuous professional development seems not to be in the DNA of many managers and leaders, and the skills of leadership still seem to be taken largely for granted.

DEVELOPMENT METHODS

Methods of management and leadership development appear caught in a time warp and alternative forms of development through technology remain in their infancy. Using the best methods to achieve the right outcomes means that a blend of opportunities may be needed. While training is still the most common development practice, leaders in the CIPD/DDI study find special projects, mentors and personal coaches more effective. They recommend job rotation and on-the-job training, and tailoring these to employees with different levels of seniority.

On-the-Job Development

How can future leaders learn to both execute effectively in the short term and also develop their strategic capability? Simply moving high-potential individuals around the organisation at speed may not be the best way of developing them or assessing whether they do indeed have the potential to build sustained performance; in fact it may actually prevent them from developing and applying their skills in ways which put them to the test and improve business results. Members of the CIPD focus group recommend keeping high-potential employees longer in development posts so that they can deliver meaningful performance before progressing on to the next experience. This not only increases future leaders' credibility with staff, but also helps to close the common gap in understanding between those at the top of organisations and those lower down the hierarchy about how to make things happen.

But if future leaders are to learn most from experience they need to consciously learn from mistakes about what not to do next time and this is where a 'sink or swim' approach may be unhelpful. The DDI/CIPD study also found that UK high potentials are much less likely to get sufficient feedback about their performance than those in other cultures. Similarly, fewer UK high potentials get clear communications about the importance of their development, and fewer describe their programmes as aligned with the performance management system.

Providing deepening and broadening experiences, such as participation in special projects and opportunities and linking up with international counterparts, should be part of the development mix. Other methods may include job shadowing, secondments, coaching as well as off-the-job development, networks and visits.

Development opportunities appear to be most enriching if they provide access to new, varied challenges, where there is a degree of difficulty in the task and where outcomes are important and highly visible, especially if success is by no means guaranteed. Even hardship can be developmental, according to previous research by the Centre for Creative Leadership. However, some support can make the difference between success and failure and the development of multinational leaders appears to be a universal problem. Nearly 71% of the UK multinational leaders in the DDI/CIPD survey describe their preparation for their assignments as fair or poor, which makes these less useful as development experiences and which might make it extremely difficult for them to succeed.

Formal Leadership Development

Formal leadership development takes many forms in large organisations yet conventional methods of management and leadership development often appear caught in a time warp. Only 42% of the UK leaders surveyed are satisfied with what their organisations offer to develop their leadership.

As various studies have found, training is still the most frequent development practice, yet sometimes the main benefit of training is exposure to new networks. In recent years behavioural (situational leadership) approaches and self-awareness raising using psychometrics and emotional intelligence based instruments have found favour. The focus on self-awareness, while important, can sometimes be at the expense of helping leaders understand the art of motivating and mobilising others, especially in a context of change or where innovation is needed. This is particularly important for people who find themselves in leadership roles by dint of their technical expertise, rather than through evidence of their ability to bring out the best in others.

Increasingly high potentials and would-be senior leaders attend MBA and other strategic programmes at leading international business schools where many large organisations also sponsor bespoke programmes for cadres of leaders. In the DDI/CIPD study, UK executives give more priority than other global executives to building new company capabilities, defining a clear or new company strategy and managing new acquisitions and mergers, and curricula tend to reflect these priorities. In comparison, they are less concerned with operational excellence, such as improving quality and related people processes. Unfortunately, as with competencies, the jury is still out as to how effective these forms of development are in developing empowering and transformational leaders.

Indeed, critics of business school education argue that the curriculum of many business school programmes, with their focus on business models and challenges, may contribute to what Jeffrey Pfeffer (2000) describes as the 'knowing-doing gap', i.e. the lack of translation of knowledge and insight into leadership behaviour and action. In Bennis and O'Toole (2005), 'How business schools lost their way', the authors argue that the critical issues of leadership are indistinguishable from the critical issues of life, and that these are addressed best in great literature. They argue that business schools should offer a more humanistic study of leadership and recommend that MBA students increase their self-knowledge and gain a deeper understanding of human nature by looking at literature. They also argue that business schools should provide more chances to learn hands-on management skills – perhaps by running actual businesses, which students would help oversee as part of their coursework (just as law schools sponsor legal clinics).

Informal Development

Informal development is a key theme in leadership literature, as is the idea that leaders become leaders through their own efforts and choices; as Gandhi said, 'you must be the change you want to see in the world'. However, the first step of any leadership development journey requires leaders to look at themselves intensely and critically, and many people don't want to do this. Denial is a main form of self-protection for managers, according to Locander and Luechauer (2006). Similarly, the focus on emotional intelligence and good relationship management is evident in much leadership development. Badaracco (2002) argues that while empathy is good, it cannot replace confrontation with the darker sides of one's own self – taking responsibility means coming to grips with your 'secret' side, your shadow side and your reflective side. Leaders need to build fierce self-awareness of the way they behave around people and methods such as coaching, multi-rater feedback and action learning groups can provide useful insights.

Handling Uncertainty

Self-awareness is one thing: being able to lead in a constantly changing context is another. The twenty-first century will mean rapid changes that cause confusion and leaders may feel under pressure to always have the answers. Jentz and Murphy (2005) argue that managers will increasingly be measured not only by what they know but also by how they behave when they lose their sense of direction and become confused. Many managers respond to confusion by denying they are confused. Reflective Inquiry and Action (RIA) is a five-step process to handle the confusion credibly:

- Embrace your confusion;
- Assert your need to make sense;
- Structure the interaction;

- Listen reflectively and learn; and
- Openly process your effort to make sense.

Such a process is completely in line with the aim of helping leaders develop self-awareness, authenticity and participative styles of management. In turn leaders who exercise these more open forms of leadership, are likely to be better able to build trust with employees.

Handling Uncertainty by Reflective Conversations

Much recent literature emphasises the social construction nature of much leadership development. Productive deliberation is a chaotic process of zig-zagging between feelings, thoughts, facts and analysis. It resists the temptation to grasp hold of a single grand principle and allow it to tyrannise all other considerations. The best reflection involves dialogue with others.

Sources of Advice

Joni (2004) argues that leaders cannot succeed without developing relation-ships with people they can trust.

According to Joni (2004), there are three fundamental types of trust as follows: *Personal trust* – based on faith in a person's integrity. It develops in the workplace through shared experiences and knowledge of colleagues' charac-ters. *Expertise trust* – is reliance on an adviser's ability in a specific subject area. S*tructural trust* – informed, disinterested advice from sources who are committed to a leader's success, but who have no personal stake in it. It provides leaders with a source of insight and information.

Sources can be academics, consulting and professional-service firms, family and friends, alliance/partner contacts, corporate peers and coaches and Board members – each have something to offer and potential pitfalls. It is through such relationships, that leaders can obtain feedback and input from third parties. This can enhance leader behaviour, development and decision-making. For a short period in the 1990s, a few large organisations created the role of 'corporate jester', to act as trusted adviser to a powerful chief executive. This was usually an external consultant who worked within the organisation, acting as the CEO's eyes and ears, mentor and challenger. In the UK, executive coaching is more commonly used than in many other countries (DDI/CIPD survey). Leaders must be careful that structural trust does not erode as advisers are exposed to the abrasive forces of politics and personalities. For those at the corporate pinnacle, high structural trust with most insiders is difficult to sustain. They are surrounded by people who want to protect them from distractions, unpleasantness or any undue influence other than their own. The result is an isolated leader exposed to limited perspectives and subsisting on a diet of artfully prepared 'truths' that may be anything but.

A Blend of Approaches

Achieving the right outcomes may require using a blend of opportunities and methods. As a global Head of HR interviewed in a study of international human resources management (HRM) conducted for the CIPD by Paul Sparrow and Chris Brewster (2008) comments:

> 'So you identify out of your regional structure the people who are really strong and show the capability and develop them... you coach them, give them stretch assignments. Our basic model of adult learning is 70% of what you learn, you learn on the job, 20% you learn through networks, coaching and feedback, and 10% through formal learning processes.'

Contemporary development methods include coaching, mentoring, action learning, multi-rater feedback, online communities, opportunities for learning and self-development, integrated with career planning, and challenging job assignments. Other common methods include job shadowing, secondments, visits and networks and engagement with the community. Volunteering is increasingly being used as a means of both developing individuals and teams and fulfilling an organisation's social responsibility to its local community.

DEVELOPING COLLECTIVE LEADERSHIP

Developing communities of leaders requires great communications, strategic conversations and the creation of cross-organisational networks united by shared purpose. This requires a deep understanding of the role of organisational systems and culture in leadership development (Van Velsor and McCauley, 2004). Increasingly, organisations use consultants and facilitators to help senior teams work through major strategic processes and decisions, and into the bargain develop top teams and individuals.

Organisations are also increasingly involving large numbers of employees in 'town hall' style meetings where they have the opportunity to better understand the organisation's strategic challenges and work through them, feeding in their own ideas. Organisations in sectors experiencing rapid change find such large-scale interventions highly effective in developing a willingness to change, proactivity and broader employee engagement. Covey and Crawley (1999) suggest the following process:

- Do some 'city planning': define borders and boundaries. Determine who you are and who you are not. Have a master plan for 5 years.
- Focus on what you share in common: unite people by focusing them on common causes and concerns.
- Celebrate success: be positive, focus on the strengths of individuals to make their weaknesses irrelevant.
- Take pride in new products and services: build traditions by having ceremonies and annual events.
- Have fun at work: play and socialise together.

- Take care of your own: when members of the community feel cared for, they will be more willing to care for others. Inspire people to give back to the community.

Above all, these authors suggest building meaning into work; being passionate about some shared vision or mission, tying every new venture to the mission and seeking alignment of personal interests behind the vision. Again, the notion of shared purpose as the key unifying factor in an organizational community comes through clearly. A community of leaders can be developed in other ways too. Mirvis and Gunning (2006) describe how 200 executives across Asia formed a community of leaders. They went to ashrams, hospitals, schools, micro-enterprises and charities in India and used their experiences to re-examine their own community and reconsider their corporate purpose.

Communication is integral to building community. The community of leaders use 'dialogue' methodology in groups of varying sizes (see Chapter 7). The creation of a collective 'us' is what Scott Peck calls 'group mind'. Howard Gardner was the first to propose that great leaders combine intellect, creativity and ethics. Gardner and Laskin's 'Leading Minds' (1996) showed that great leaders relied on storytelling to inspire followers.

Assessing impact is important; in particular, ensuring that leaders are performing more effectively as a result of development. The strongest pressure facing leadership developers will be demonstrating ROI according to Hernez-Broome and Hughes (2004). Human resource directors (HRDs) advocate the setting of outcome targets which reflect what should be expected of managers as a result of development, such as developing their own staff to their full potential, and then rewarding leadership excellence.

This is where many UK organisations score badly compared with their counterparts elsewhere. The real test of leadership is the way leaders affect performance. Proficiency can be assessed in terms of a leader's impact on performance outcomes, measured through leadership surveys and employee satisfaction, customer advocacy and business results.

The DDI/CIPD survey suggests that UK organisations are particularly remiss in areas such as not holding senior managers accountable for leadership development, being inconsistent in the way they deploy programmes across locations and failing to measure the results of leadership development. Thus, despite the efforts that UK organisations put into clarifying and aligning their message about leadership development, their failure to assure that development takes place through proper follow-through and measurement is likely to be a barrier to gaining the results they want.

Reinforcing leadership through training and other HR systems is essential. For Pearce and Manz (2005), the organisation reward system needs to emphasise team-based rewards as well as recognition of individual initiative that contributes to overall team performance.

Spotlight on: Angela O'Connor, Head of HR Profession for the UK Police Service

Angela is currently Chief People Officer at the National Police Improvement Agency (NPIA) since November 2006. The NPIA was set up in 2007 to create a national set of management, training and Human Resource standards within the service, as well as coordinating a National information technology (IT) infrastructure. It works with a number of partners, including the Association of Chief Police Officers, police authorities and the Home Office. Angela is head of HR profession for police HR staff in England and Wales and leads on Police Learning, Development and Leadership and People Strategy. She is responsible for the development of people processes to underpin ethical policing in the UK, including leadership development at senior levels.

Career summary

Angela's own experience is wide-ranging and her career journey to her current sectoral leadership role for HR has been across sectors. Following a number of years in the private sector Angela has spent the majority of her career in the public sector. She has been in senior HR roles at three London local authorities, Haringey, Hackney and Enfield.

Her HR teams have been recipients of numerous awards for equality and diversity, recruitment and innovative HR practices. She was headhunted from Enfield to the Crown Prosecution Service (CPS) in 2002 where she led a national team determined to ensure that CPS became a world-class prosecuting authority.

She was named Personnel Director of the Year in 2005 at the Telegraph Business Awards and HRD of the Year at the Personnel Today awards. A fellow of the Chartered Institute of Personnel Development and she appears frequently in the lists of top HR 'power players'. She is a board director of Skills for Justice and has recently been elected as vice president for the CIPD Police Forum. Angela is past President of the Public Sector People Managers' Associations (PPMA) and she was the first Civil Servant President in the organisation's 30-year history in 2006/2007.

Early career

Angela's early career was not planned. The daughter of immigrant parents, Angela inherited from them a strong work ethic. She knew she wanted to work rather than carry on with school studies and left school without taking 'A' Levels or going on to a degree at that time. At that early stage she was keen to have a local job which would not interfere with her social life and her first real work experience came at the Department of Health and Social Security, working in reception. It was there she developed strong views about the way people should be treated and honed her philosophy about the public sector. She learned that when people are in difficulties, they can often be isolated from the state and she knew that she wanted to make a difference.

Continued

**Spotlight on: Angela O'Connor, Head of HR Profession
for the UK Police Service**—cont'd

From there Angela moved to Reed Employment where she learned about customer service and the bottom line, about the importance of answering the phone within three rings (she still does). She became interested in marketing and sales and the link between customer service and good customer service training. She recognised that in the recruitment business, people were a commodity, albeit a lively commodity. She discovered that she was good at sales and found that it was easy to make good money and bonuses. She loved working with employers and stayed for 5 years working as a troubleshooter at branches which were struggling. This meant that sometimes she would have to close down branches and make staff redundant, a process she found upsetting.

Moving back into the public sector with a job in Personnel for Haringey Council, Angela's job involved providing personnel advice to grant-aided voluntary sector organisations such as the network for elderly Asian and Caribbean women. This was a time of some turbulence in Haringey, with riots in Tottenham and the first Lesbian and Gay Unit being established by a UK local authority. Angela was keen to get involved in some of the 'meaty' issues but recognised that most of the more interesting work went to men, most of whom had an industrial relations (IR) background and personnel qualifications.

Angela decided to do something to improve her own prospects and went to night school to complete her school education. She then took a Post-Graduate Diploma in Labour Studies as a mature student in London, covering law, industrial relations and gaining exemptions from the CIPD qualification. Angela found that she loved studying and was horrified about the lack of rigour amongst many young students. For her, studying had been inspirational, opening the door to how organisations work and how things come together. She wanted to explore what HR/Personnel could really mean – how HR could make a difference.

A formative period

Angela moved to Hackney to progress her career. Such is her work ethic that she took only one week off from night school when she had her baby daughter. She returned to work as a job sharer for a year (as did her husband). At Hackney she had the most meaningful career experience.

It was a roller coaster of political in-fighting. People worked all day and often until the early hours of the morning. There were major policy changes weekly, resulting in chaos. At the time the Inner London Education Authority (ILEA) was being disbanded and its responsibilities were being transferred to local authorities in central London. Angela managed the transfer of staff from ILEA to Hackney, from a strategic and tactical standpoint – at one point going to Woolworths to purchase cleaning materials for the education department offices. At that point staff had no faith in Hackney and 400 education workers were protesting as the payroll failed. For Angela this was a very formative period, and everything was being developed on the hoof.

The teachers' pay issue was a major learning experience. Angela employed a county hall official as she needed this person to come and work in Hackney

**Spotlight on: Angela O'Connor, Head of HR Profession
for the UK Police Service**—cont'd

Education with her. Angela wrote her a contract on a serviette in a local cafe due to the need to close the deal quickly due to the need to close the deal quickly. She led the negotiations with the Teachers' Unions, sitting with the teachers in the classrooms, getting to understand their point of view.

Lessons in leadership

Angela realised that the role of head teacher was extremely influential and wide-ranging – from chief educator to CEO. The head teacher could make the difference between success or failure. Some were incredible heroes and heroines, who could turn schools around, engage parents and do the best for the children; others could cause the school to be destroyed in a very short period of time. This led Angela to realise not only the difference individuals could make but also the impact of selection and promotion on a school's fortunes. A 'tick box' mentality would not work. Leaders needed to make strong connections and to have the ability to impact on communications.

Angela moved back to the Centre as Head of HR for Hackney. She found some staff complacent, an issue which had not been tackled by management previously, so set about 'kicking butt'. This allowed the 'brilliant staff' to be given what they needed to do their jobs well.

Following her career in local government and a successful role in the CPS, Angela moved to the Policing NPIA.

The NPIA

Angela's role as Chief People Officer for the NPIA is a new role in a new organisation with a new brief. Angela's job is to be the head of the HR profession for the police force in the UK. The CEO of NPIA needed a seasoned HR professional who could create people processes to underpin an ethical approach to policing which would be policing-led and owned. Angela's task is to develop a national people and organisational development strategy for policing – a tough challenge given that the 43 police forces are independent of one another. She is also responsible for health and safety above the levels of individual chief constables. She therefore has to create a strategy which produces coherence between and above these levels.

Angela is responsible for ensuring effective learning and development (both tactical, such as firearms training, and operational, such as management development) as well as leadership development across the 250,000 strong police service for England, Wales and internationally. The training and development takes place at sites throughout the UK.

Hers is a lonely, hard job at times. As Angela is the first to point out, everyone who moves into a job at a very senior level goes through this, and she was glad of support from other senior professionals such as Martin Tiplady, HRD for the Metropolitan Police. At the start there was no infrastructure or clarity about budgets and nothing worked. It was tough trying to create a new body from a range of legacy bodies. And while Angela generally thrives on big challenge, it was particularly tough for the

Continued

Spotlight on: Angela O'Connor, Head of HR Profession for the UK Police Service—cont'd

people who had worked in NPIA's predecessor bodies who found the chaos involved in creating a new world hard to deal with.

Working with stakeholders

This is a highly sensitive role, and where the issues on her agenda produce a large number of parliamentary questions. Angela has to pull together the views of all the key partners/stakeholders – the Home Office, ACPO, the senior police officer group and the Association of Police Authorities (APA). Working with partner bodies can be complicated and Angela has had to learn the history and motivations of each partner group. Angela particularly enjoys gaining insight into the day-to-day issues facing the police force and will often spend time 'on the beat' to see for herself what needs to be done.

Her role as head of profession for HR in the police is proving a pleasure. The HR community has been welcoming and Angela is determined to give them something in return; in particular to deliver on the common HR challenges across policing. Her early data gathering suggested that there were some significant issues to be dealt with, and that a purely logical approach to resolving these would not work. Some were simple things, such as the fact that the providers of the service had not fully engaged with the customers. In terms of police officers and staff, some ranks were overloaded with development while others received none. On the whole there was little effective development of key skills such as business, political, community engagement and ambassadorial skills. Others were issues which made little sense, such as the pressure to always train staff and police officers together, which Angela describes as 'tree huggy'. ICT challenges were a 'mess'.

On the other hand there were some real 'jewels' such as the Strategic Command Course and tactical training (firearms). There was plenty of potential in a new High Potential Development Scheme and plans for a new graduate scheme. All of these factors contributed to Angela's vision for the kind of development which could deliver the ethical policing at the heart of her and the NPIA's mission.

Building ethical policing

Bramshill in Hampshire is the new National Police College and will be familiar to many police officers above a certain rank. The NPIA runs much of its development from there. Angela introduced annual conferences and the NPIA has an annual chief constable's commendations ceremony to celebrate achievements in line with the capabilities and values underpinning effective and ethical policing. In deciding what the focus of development and awards should be, Angela's view is that you need to be clear about how people will feel when the vision has been delivered and work back from that. And that image is reinforced in many ways, practically and symbolically. For instance symbols of policing which had previously been discarded have been reinstated at Bramshill. A DVD has been produced to remind people of the history and 'soul' of policing.

Spotlight on: Angela O'Connor, Head of HR Profession for the UK Police Service—cont'd

A year on, NPIA has produced on behalf of the tripartite a national strategy for leadership and a national people strategy, both have been agreed by the Home Secretary and the national police board. Both featured large in the recent policing green paper and it has been announced that a national college of police leadership is to be created with its HQ at Bramshill.

Angela is starting to feel that she and her team are making progress and also making a difference, connecting well with HRD colleagues across the police forces. She consciously and deliberately builds trust by admitting when she has made mistakes. She tries to walk the talk on development and arranges dinners for colleagues and brings in external speakers to expose them to leading-edge practice. In all of this Angela believes that what goes round comes around:

'You owe something to the community who supported you. You should give a leg up to others too – always in a mentoring relationship. I gain from this as much as they do every time'.

Other challenges this year include getting people thinking about the opportunities an economic downturn brings to create better value ways of working. Raising productivity and cutting costs to increase value will be critical this year: 'To say we are busy is an understatement but I see all of this as a mark of confidence in the work we have already done. I have just been elected as the vice president of the CIPD police forum and will succeed to president in due course. I am delighted with this confidence shown in us by the police HR community.'

CONCLUSION

An effective management and leadership development strategy will therefore include HR developing the skills to coach managers to manage performance and handle change effectively. HR leaders must look to create genuine development opportunities – and encourage risk taking. To be seen as credible suppliers of excellent leaders, HR departments need to model the performance and good practices required of all leaders.

The real return on investment for leadership development will be when leaders are held to account for closing the knowing–doing gap and putting their development to good use. And the good news is, developing good leaders pays dividends. Not only does field study evidence (Barling et al., 1996) suggest that leadership behaviours and effectiveness increase following training, the DDI study (Pomeroy, 2006) found also that the companies that develop leaders well have high RoEs and profit margins.

And – who knows? – it may be too much to expect that by developing leaders at all levels, HR will be potentially winning the war on talent, but at least it should help organisations become more agile, reinforce the employer brand and help create better employee engagement. A prize worth going for!

Chapter 7

Leading Change

'Leadership is the ability to step outside the culture...to start evolutionary change processes that are more adaptive.'

Edgar Schein (1992)

In today's challenging economic climate, organisations in every sector are experiencing severe competitive pressure. With markets in downturn globally, cost-cutting and restructuring are the order of the day. Employment is a major casualty, with pay and recruitment freezes, restructurings and redundancies are now commonplace. And as we have seen in previous downturns, disruptive change such as this can significantly damage productivity and innovation. Employee engagement in particular, which is thought to be the driver of sustainable performance is potentially at risk in times of change. But must organisations be doomed to repeat the mistakes of the past, and lose organisational knowledge (corporate amnesia), waste opportunities for synergies and shared learnin, become siloed, stale and slow to change?

Even in 'good' times the typical management focus and time-span are very short term, for a variety of reasons. Indeed, periods of strong growth can often mask the need to do anything different and can breed complacency. In the recession, the focus is likely to be exclusively on the present. More generally, a fast-changing context highlights both the risk of organisational implosion and the need for different and longer-term thinking and practice.

HR leaders will be in the thick of change and transformation. They will be at the forefront of integrating organisations after mergers and acquisitions (M&A) implementing restructurings and relocations. HR leaders need to be good at four fundamental practices (strategy, execution, culture and fast and flat structure) and four further secondary practices (talent, leadership, innovation and growth through M&A and partnerships) that need to occur at the same time if organisations are to outperform their competitors and get extraordinary returns (Joyce, 2005).

And as HR leaders know well, managing change is not only a strategic process but also a profoundly human one. Even when the right decisions have been taken, the way the human aspects of change are implemented can cause change to come unstuck. So is it possible to make sure that organisations are ready for growth when the markets pick up again?

In the current economic climate there is a real opportunity for businesses to break out of vicious cycles of wastefulness and short-termism. This highlights

137

the need for a different approach to managing change, one which takes the human equation firmly into account from the outset. But this means taking stock and making any tough restructuring and downsizing decisions with a view to what will be needed to help the organisation recover and improve when growth returns.

If HR leaders are to prepare their organisations to survive and thrive in the future, they need to not only manage change effectively, but also build agile workforces and change-able cultures which can respond to change and equip the organisation to compete successfully over time. HR leaders therefore must lead the process of culture change, building adaptable and resilient structures, systems and behaviours.

In this chapter we shall consider how to both bring about change and build the ability to keep on changing into the DNA of organisations by taking an organisational development (OD) approach to change. OD's focus is on facilitating human development for organisational, community and social gain. OD recognises that organisations are complex, adaptive and essentially human systems, and are influenced by their past as much as by the present. Without sufficient energy for change there is little hope of change being sustained organically. OD therefore puts human dynamics firmly in the foreground of any change process and group as the primary unit of change.

BUILDING CHANGE-ABLE ORGANISATIONS

The sheer speed and volume of change are evident in Anne Minto's reflections on the business transformations at Centrica: 'I think one great success has been our agility to accommodate a rapidly changing business model. We have come from being a business 5 years ago that had a very diverse portfolio including British Gas Services, the AA, The Goldfish Bank, Onetel – to forming ourselves into an integrated energy company. During that time we have disposed of those businesses whilst still maintaining customer service. This has been a massive challenge for our front-line staff. Additionally we have kept our HR team together and pushed through our own transformation in the midst of all this business change.'

The CIPD's Employee Outlook survey (McCartney and Willmott, 2009) asked its 3000+ respondents from all sectors the following question:

Looking ahead 5 years, what do you predict will be the main business issues facing your organisation?

These were:

- Forty-five percent of survey respondents predict that adapting the business to the new economic conditions is going to be the biggest issue over the next 5 years, especially in the private sector (51%), voluntary sector (48%) and nationalised industries (47%).

- *The need to find new ways of doing business*
  For some organisations this means more emphasis than in the past on restructuring (38%) and looking for new markets (37%), particularly within

the private sector (44%). Other responses include improving customer service (33% overall; 40% in the private sector); introducing new technology (30% overall; 43% in the private sector) and becoming more innovative (27% overall; 36% in the private sector). M&As remain a firm feature of the business landscape and cross-organisational collaborations are on the increase, especially with respect to public sector delivery.

Success in the future will require organisations to operate as collaborative communities, to have agile cultures, more adaptable business models, flatter hierarchies and distributed leadership.

LEARNING FROM PREVIOUS DOWNTURNS

Change management has been the subject of management fad and fancy for years. The last major downturn in the 1990s coincided with an explosion of 'guru-led' change management theory. Many of these change approaches could be described as 'left brain'. They focus primarily on metrics and measurements, technical systems and process design, linear pathways and evidence-based decision criteria. The unit of change is generally business process improvement or organisational structure and correspondingly headcount, roles, skills and capacity. Reengineering for instance became popular with executives who liked the idea of being able to improve processes, while saving headcount and other costs.

The real challenge of course is that countless studies suggest that many of these 'top-down' change initiatives did not work. The promised improvements and savings however often failed to materialise. Implementation usually proved far harder to achieve than was thought once the consultants had left, and change did not 'stick'. No wonder many executives found themselves wondering why there was no energy for change beyond the change proposers. Why was the level of conflict/resistance so hard to contain? Why didn't people 'get it', that this change was ultimately for the good of everyone, and for the long-term viability of the organisation?

Worse still, when growth returned, employees who had survived the cull often demonstrated symptoms of 'survivor syndrome' as reflected in a lack of commitment to their employer and unwillingness to 'go the extra mile'. Job losses and the added pressure on employees who remained, allied to job insecurity, gave birth to the long-hours' culture. This was also the era when employers told people that they should manage their own career. As a result, employees got the message. Disgruntled and over-stretched, many often took the first opportunity to look for better jobs elsewhere when growth returned, taking their skills and knowledge with them, leading to what Arnold Kransdorff (1998) called 'corporate amnesia' and causing 'wheels' to have to be expensively 'reinvented'. 'Lean and mean' approaches also led to 'corporate anorexia'. Consequently, organisations found themselves without the talent needed to fuel growth. This also led to what McKinsey dubbed the 'War for Talent' at the end of the 1990s, as businesses competed with each other to attract and retain the best talent.

And things are not much better these days. A 2008 study found that companies surveyed in the UK lost £1.7 bn a year from failed change initiatives. Among companies surveyed across Western Europe, approximately 10 bn Euros per year are being wasted on ineffective business process change projects (Logica Management Consulting and the Economist Intelligence Unit).

RISKS TO EMPLOYEE ENGAGEMENT

Before beginning a culture change process, HR leaders need to address questions such as:

- How much change is necessary? How much is imposed? How can the pace of change be modulated?
- What needs to be in place to enable flexibility? How flexible are roles?
- How clear are people about the rationale for change? How much do they 'buy-in'? What 'bottom-up' changes which benefit the customer are we encouraging?
- Is there a way to harness conflict/resistance and move forward in a productive fashion?
- Is there an easier way to create ownership of the change agenda and how do we get people to be willing to implement the solutions?

Rather than change being imposed from the top, the workforce as a whole needs to see the rationale for change. This will require leaders and the workforce as a whole to be capable of strategic anticipation and innovation, with employees who are willing and able to gather and share market intelligence, mechanisms to involve employees in rapid execution and a greater focus on customers – at all levels. This willingness by employees to 'go the extra mile' is a symptom or by-product of employee engagement. Employee engagement is a key indicator of a company's culture: how employees are treated in bad times will be remembered by them in good times. Therefore employee engagement is an essential element of a change-able organization since by building and maintaining good relations with employees, during times of change leaders enhance employee commitment, capability and performance.

Various studies hint at the positive link between employee engagement and performance. From a study of the drivers of employee engagement by the Institute of Employment Studies (Robinson et al,) a clear view of the behaviours demonstrated by the engaged employee emerged:

belief in the organisation
desire to work to make things better
understanding of business context and the 'bigger picture'

respectful of, and helpful to, colleagues

willingness to 'go the extra mile'

keeping up to date with developments in the field.

Engagement has clear overlaps with the more exhaustively researched concepts of commitment and organisational citizenship behaviour, but there are also differences. In particular, engagement is two-way: organisations must work to engage the employee, who in turn has a choice about the level of engagement to offer the employer. In times of change, many of the drivers of employee engagement can be undermined.

The effects of employee disengagement are detrimental to the organizations. Flade (2002) concluded from the Gallup Organization's Employee Engagement Index survey that more than 80% of workers in Great Britain are not committed to their jobs and are not actively engaged. According to this piece poor management is to blame for the lack of employee engagement. Crabtree (2004) also used the results of a survey conducted by the Gallup Management Journal which surveyed 1,003 employees nationwide and examined the differences in responses between engaged, un- engaged and actively un-engaged employees. There was a strong correlation between employee engagement and positive workplace relationships which suggested that fully engaged employees have positive relations in their workplace and are more productive in their jobs.

One of the main risks to successful change is when the 'psychological contract' between employers and employees gets undermined during the process of change. Guest argued that employers are increasingly seeking high levels of discretionary behaviour (i.e. engaged performance) from their employees, consistent with psychological contracts which are 'relational', i.e. based on *mutual trust*. The concept of the psychological contract consists of the *perceptions* of both parties to the employment relationship, organisational and individual, and implies a set of reciprocal obligations, reflected in an unspoken, implicit, assumed agreement between employers and employees about what employees perceive they owe to their employers and what their employers owe to them.

Exchange theory suggests the psychological contract works on the principle of reciprocity. When people enjoy a trusting relationship with their employer, they tend to work hard and well for their employer. Conversely, when the contract is 'violated' – such as when perceived mutual obligations are not delivered by one party or another – reciprocity is broken, trust is lost, and the psychological contract tends to become more transactional. Employees may resist or decommit if they do not trust management. As David Fairhurst suggests, if employee relations (ER) are to work: 'There has to be mutual trust between employees and the management of the organisation. In that light, if you are relying on conflict resolution skills and arbitration then it's already too late!'

Rising Insecurity?

Cappelli (1997: 8–10) argues that new forms of high-performance work organisation require committed, flexible and highly trained employees and that their diffusion is hampered by worker insecurity. It has also been argued that an essential precondition for business strategies which emphasise quality enhancement and productivity growth is a stable, secure and trained workforce (Brown, 1995; Edwards et al., 1998; Kochan and Osterman, 1994). Of course fast-changing circumstances threaten the basis of stability and job security, potentially putting employee engagement at risk. Therefore, engaging employees in turbulent times will be challenging, especially in a context of uncertainty where people may be losing their jobs.

In a CIPD poll (April 2009), 61% of respondents agreed that rising levels of job insecurity are making it difficult to maintain levels of employee engagement. If redundancies continue to increase throughout 2009 as is predicted, the effect on engagement could be potentially corrosive.

If organisations are forced to restructure and continue to lay off employees, this is likely to undermine employee trust and the stability of team membership, which are important to the success of High Performance Working Practices (HPWP) – unless employees have a continuing basis for trust. According to Clark and Payne (1997) and Osterman (2000), employers must offer a quid pro quo of job security if they want to get employee commitment, something that would be very hard to do in the current climate. Godard (2004) found that although workers and unions may initially decide to co-operate in the adoption of HPWP, they may respond with apathy or resistance if management violates the psychological contract through lay-offs.

Engaged employees, who are willing to go the extra mile, will be vital to business survival and success in times of turbulence. They could help organisations make the performance improvements they need to survive, or better still, help to create innovations required to achieve competitive edge in a tough business climate. Professor Jeffrey Pfeffer forecasts that only major companies which remain focused on customer and employee engagement, and true to their values, such as Southwest Airlines and Toyota, will successfully remain in business in the future.

Obviously, while it may not be true that in all instances treating employees well will result in better business results, Lawler (2003) argues that there are numerous instances in which the two factors are mutually reinforcing so that a kind of virtuous spiral is created. Consequently, if current circumstances undermine the basis for employee engagement, it might be argued, there are risks to performance. And while there is still as yet little empirical research which suggests how a good psychological contract and employee engagement affect performance positively, there is an increasing body of research which suggests the harmful effects on performance of a poor psychological contract.

NEED FOR A RETHINK!

So while there may be many merits to traditional 'left brain' approaches to change, what they are not well known for is a focus on cultural alignment and behavioural shift – which often hold the keys to sustainable change outcomes. Failure to focus on the 'people bit' of the change equation is what can turn a change process into a major liability.

This is where OD approaches can complement traditional change management, turning the process of change into a powerful driver of performance, especially in tough times. In contrast to traditional change management OD practitioners believe you can't plan, predict or determine a change of culture – you get the culture you deserve. The task of OD is to create the conditions for change to emerge rather than dictating its content.

WHY IS OD NEEDED NOW?

In today's fast-changing context, especially when the focus is on survival in the short term, organisations can lose sight of the bigger picture and undermine their potential for renewal and future growth. It is still quite rare for leaders to deliberately embark on organisational development/culture change initiatives in order to build some new capability. More generally, opportunities come disguised as other problems – something is not working, a process is broken, employees are demotivated, the organisation is losing customers, etc. HR leaders must recognise these as the systems issues they are, diagnose the core problems and work collaboratively with business partners to identify solutions to questions such as:

- What are the right skills to drive my organisation forward?
- How will tomorrow's leaders need to be different from today's leaders?
- How do we engage the people we needed to deliver success?
- How do we speed up processes?
- How can we break down siloes and break up large, unwieldy units that are slow to change?
- How do we ensure that front-line employees understand the business well enough to be able to make trade-offs in real time?
- How do we create collective leadership?
- How can we embed customer focus in the organisation's DNA?
- How can we create and transmit values which bind the organisation together?
- How do we create a climate for performance and innovation? How do we unleash human imagination, create slack that gives people time to reflect, dream and innovate; reward much more small-scale innovation?
- How can we manage change effectively and not 'throw the baby out with the bathwater'?
- How do we maintain trust and keep people motivated through change?

HR leaders focus on both/and – understanding that what why they do in the short term helps build capability for the longer term. That's why any change must be treated as an exercise in building a sustainable business culture.

WHAT IS AN OD APPROACH TO CHANGE?

In OD the emphasis is mainly 'right brain' – on imagination, engagement, participation, moving and mobilising, empowering – at least as much as 'left brain'. It involves a dedicated effort to keep a balance of content, process and people in its change approach. While strategists and senior leaders generally prefer to take a planned approach to change, OD recognises that in human systems, logical planning alone rarely determines what actually happens *and* that change often 'emerges' when people are actively engaged in the change processes. In OD the key principle of participation is given, not a choice; as Weisbord (1978) stated 'people will support what they help to create'. The task of OD is to create the conditions for change to emerge through people engagement rather than dictating its content in a rigid fashion.

OD works from the 'end-up'. People need to understand the business case, then they can work out the implementation. That is why it is so important that diagnostics and implementation are rolled together, and that people have the chance to understand why change is needed and help shape their destiny. You can start anywhere – at the strategy, leadership development or operational effectiveness levels. It's about working with the positive energy within the organisation, dealing with real issues, knowing where to connect, working across the whole system and looking for the change levers. It's about trying to create the conditions but not attempting to drive the outcomes.

For the OD practitioner it's about being resilient, holding the paradox – people crave clarity and certainty, but for change to emerge which is truly 'owned' by those who implement it, you have to live with the messiness. You don't necessarily need a grand master plan – simply working with the leaders who in turn work with their teams creates 'bottom-up' change. At the same time it's about staying pragmatic, recognising that OD is about managing the both/and world of expert change management and OD approaches to change.

This approach takes time, some may argue, but if you want change to 'stick' you may have to go slowly at first in order to go fast in a meaningful way. And by the way, effective change need not take a long time to stick if employees feel they 'own' the change. That's why, particularly during a downturn, when speed and effective changes are needed, successful change requires a combination of change management and OD.

CHANGE PRINCIPLES OF OD

Since Linda Ackerman Anderson (an OD practitioner) coined the term 'change management' in 1968, the field has matured in its thinking about the nature of change, change processes and change implementation. The following key OD change principles are likely to produce different/better outcomes than simply sticking to traditional expert-led approaches:

1. **Be clear about the nature of change required: focus on the 'end game'**
   In a downturn, there is only so much change that organisations can absorb or even need to engage in. It can be helpful to establish criteria for deciding the nature and amount of change required. Using a big system OD framework such as those of Burke–Litwin, Nadler and Tushman can help distinguish between at least four categories of change:
   - Externally driven change which is non-negotiable both in criticality as well as in timescale;
   - Externally driven change which is negotiable, again both in timescale and criticality;
   - Internally driven change that is non-negotiable (double check whether the non-negotiability is due to personality power or due to organisation survival issues); and
   - Internally driven change that is negotiable because they are just someone's personal agenda.

   Each type of change agenda may need different treatment. A typical OD methodology involves steps of progression: needs assessment, diagnosis, design, implementation and evaluation. Using such frameworks will provide the diagnostic data needed to manage the suite of change coming at us and also give us confidence that we're focusing on the right issues. As Anne Minto says: 'It's making sure we are doing the business critical work. We cannot do everything at one time – we just don't have the resources.'

   OD focuses on the 'end game' but change can start anywhere – for instance by working on issues relating to strategy, leadership development or improving operational effectiveness. It's about working with the positive energy within the organisation, dealing with real issues, knowing where to connect, working across the whole system and looking for the change levers. It's about deliberately involving people in identifying the collective desired outcomes and then trying to create the conditions to work towards those outcomes. By focusing on the 'end game' and maximising involvement, OD is as much about institutionalising change as initiating it.

2. **Secure the engagement of people**
   By securing the engagement of people likely to be affected by the change and tapping into the energy available for the change agenda, change will have a higher chance of success. Since OD always starts from the 'end game', at the beginning of any change initiative we need to ask:
   - Who are the KEY individuals/groups on whom the successful implementation of the change project depends?

- Who else holds data that we, the top or the change team do not have?
- Whose perspectives do we need to solicit to ensure that we have a more robust way of thinking about this change?

Having identified those groups of people, we then need to enrol them in actively taking part in the change process.

In one major FMCG company, the Executive team went out to employees to hear what people had to say about some proposed changes. They then invited the top 180 managers to help them extend the process. Each of the 180 managers held meetings in small rooms with people who had volunteered. In a real sense people were given permission to be engaged. As people became more confident about challenging, managers said, 'We hear you. This is crap. Will you help us sort it?' A 'bottom-up' network of about 500 people was formed to help drive the changes, taking people's views and ideas into account as much as possible.

3. *Use high leverage change methodologies*

The term 'high leverage' change methodology was coined by Holman and Devane (1999) to mean methodologies that 'create high energy and yield extraordinary, sustainable results' or 'create the highest possible value for the effort invested'. They, together with the work of Bunker and Alban (1998) and of Wheatley(1999), have crystallised for us the characteristics of this type of methodology which have been proved to reduce implementation time by half over more directive methods. They are highly people focused and emergent in nature and their features include the following:

- *Dialogue based* – Involves collectively exploring, surfacing and testing each others' assumptions since change challenges people's personal world view or paradigm. Changing people's paradigms requires more than 'tell and sell'; it requires a structured dialogue and inquiry, therefore it is important to use dialogue to invite participation, particularly to unleash seven types of freedom: freedom to have voice, to be heard, to dream, to be passionate, to co-construct, to participate and to contribute (from Appreciative Inquiry). The role of change leaders is to suggest their own view as a means of inviting people to co-construct the new.
- Most HR leaders get to understand what's going on in the organisation by actively connecting with people at all levels. For David Smith of ASDA this is about getting out on the shop floor and listening to people: 'One of the things that I deliberately do all the time is walk about a lot, I get out into the grass roots of the business and talk to people and I listen to people a lot. Never a week goes by without me getting feedback on all of the things that the business is doing. And people generally come up and tell you how wonderfully things are going because – well they would, wouldn't they? They want to tell you how hard they're working, and that their initiatives are working really well, but you need to find out

from people five or six layers below, "well what do you think of this particular thing that's happened?" And then you get the real feedback which enables you to make a much more educated decision on whether you think it's working or not.'

- Similarly Anne Minto takes a lot of interest in getting out and around the businesses: 'Three or four days per month I spend in one of our business locations -one of the call centres, an engineer focus group, meeting with the graduates or the apprentices or I am overseas. I'm getting out and about, understanding exactly what is going on in one business better than another. At the end of the day you have to be talking openly and regularly with your employees'. You can't delegate that to some other third party. It's your responsibility to communicate with your employees.'

- And Martin Ferber talks of 'humanity in work', and the need for an HR leader to be genuinely interested not only in the business but in people.

- *Whole system based* – People will support the change more if they have the opportunity to share data/understanding of the need to change, analyse current reality, identity what needs to change, generate ideas on how to change and map out a possible implementation plan. Therefore it is important to bring together from the outset all those who will need to own and support the successful implementation of the change to achieve joint ownership of the solutions and an agreed approach to implementation will be important.

- David Smith describes the process used at ASDA to engage employees in cultural change: 'Lots of businesses have undergone a cultural change. Most retail businesses won't tell their shop floor people what the sales figures are, they'll not talk about profitability, they'll not talk about the issues, for fear that people will ask for more money or debunk some of the stuff to the competition or whatever. That's not the way it's been here, it's been communications-led. In the early days of the turnaround in the business at shift change we would "huddle" as we'd call it. This was a 10 minute debrief of what was going on, what the numbers where, what the issues were, giving people an insight into what was going on. That carries on today as a central bit of the business. We're still, as a business, very, very open on the basis that if you can get people involved and get them to understand then they will care more and make their contribution. That's one of the basic principles that run true to what we've been trying to do really.'

- *Engages multiple perspectives* – In change, one should expect that people hold different meanings and interpretations of what's going on, so in order to produce the greatest benefits, it is important to use processes that actively seek out the greatest diversity that exists, and give different stakeholders the opportunity to influence each other. This can strengthen the debate, unleash creativity, and help find common ground in the midst of diversity.

- For David Smith hearing directly from customers is vital to get a rounded perspective on how things are going: 'I spend a lot of time in customer groups, listening to what customers are saying about the business. Getting radar from people who have no axe to grind is vitally important, because the more senior you get in business, I find, the higher up in the clouds you can get therefore you can't see the ground'.

- *Encourages the various bits of the system to connect with itself* – Using group dynamics such as large scale gatherings to increase the number, variety and strength of connections within the system will help to increase the fuel to drive change and optimise the synergies. So instead of change leaders attempting to influence the system, processes should be created to enable the different parts of the system to influence each other. By maximising the group interface, no group is given the opportunity to stay rigid. As a result, a collective view will emerge as to how best to create the desired future. For Martin Ferber this is about 'coordinating, being sensitive to things that come up, raising awareness making connections between the organisation and between people; sometimes stopping people making some dreadful errors because they don't understand how different it can be somewhere else, because they're not experts, they haven't had the time....'

- *Manages emotion*
  Managing emotion is another focus of OD. This is especially crucial during a downturn, since negative emotions and change fatigue tend to flow through the organisation. When these emotions are not managed properly, no matter how strategic the change, its outcome will be at risk. People have a huge life urge to shape their own destinies; if they understand why and where change is needed, they can work out the implementation and are more likely to support the change than if they are simply told what will happen. It is therefore important to involve key individuals in the diagnostic process and invite them to put forward their voices about how to plan for implementation. In that way diagnosis and intervention are rolled together to speed up the change, and ideas and emotions are harnessed positively to help change succeed.

  Anne Minto argues that there is also only so much that line managers and employees can take in terms of the change agenda: 'So I think that as a line manager one has got to be conscious of how much change you can actually shower on to people before they say "hey hang on a minute here, I can only cope with so much". And that is something that I encourage my line managers and HRDs to be constantly looking out for – that overdose of change – because in this modern world we live in, some people are less able to cope with constant change than others. You have to keep eyes open and hope that you can spot things before they become a real problem. It's not just the pressures people are under at work, it's the pressures generally in their lives; they have all kinds of other things going on – children, families, divorce, bereavements – and now increasingly people have financial problems. Many people struggle with this whole concept of work/life balance: what is that and how can I achieve it? It's nice to say it, but how can people achieve it on a personal level when the business environment of necessity has to be agile and able to change rapidly.'

- *Manages the covert aspects of change*: Bob Marshak in his book 'Covert Processes' (2006) states clearly that any attempt to manage change as a rational process alone will not work: out of six dimensions of change he identifies, five are covert. Therefore any change practitioner needs to work beyond the level of reason (the rational and analytic logics) but also at the levels of organisational politics (individual and group interests), inspirations (values-based and visionary aspirations), emotions (affective and reactive feelings), mindsets (guiding beliefs and assumptions) and psychodynamics (anxiety-based and unconscious defences). These five dimensions of change, Marshak argues, often dictate the outcome of any change exercise.

- *Focuses on multiple levels of system intervention*: To bring about successful change, OD interventions usually focus on a minimum of three levels of intervention, e.g. intrapersonal, inter-group and total system. These multiple levels of intervention are a trademark of effective OD change support.

When Graham White came to Westminster council in January 2008, one of his big tasks was to launch a cross-council pay review. He knew it was going to be a sensitive issue because pay is very emotive. As he says: 'I knew that if the review was to work we had to get the engagement right.' But the question was how to do so when the Council's 5000 staff were spread across many sites and offices.

While Graham used traditional tools such as cascaded briefings to managers, union meetings and 'open-house' briefing sessions, he did not want to use exclusively measures which appear to come down from 'on high'. So alongside these measures, he decided to turn to the power of Web 2.0, i.e. applications featuring user-generated content – anything from Wikipedia to community threads. Using technology in this way allowed relative accessibility since most of the office staff have computers, many have computers at home and there is access for all to computers in the city libraries.

Graham worked on the project with the in-house communications team and the council began an online discussion forum that was accessible from the council's intranet. When the forum opened, Graham was careful to stress that anyone could initiate a thread, not just members of the HR team. This was a good way of seeing employees' concerns and allowed him to set the record straight if there was any confusion about the proposed pay structure. What was even better was that if an employee did not understand a particular issue, their colleagues would respond with an explanation on the forum without requiring input from HR. As Graham says, 'It has much more impact and credibility when it is a colleague explaining this than when it is coming from the boss in HR.'

Additional benefits were that Graham and his team were better able to understand the mood of the organisation and its values from the comments posted by staff members in their own language. In surveys carried out to measure engagement between 70 % and 80 % said they were well informed about the pay review. And since the review has finished, the Forum has continued to serve as a platform for eliciting views on other issues, though Graham is clear that this is only one of a number of barometers of opinion that it is important to pay attention to. (Based on Allen, A. [2008]

- *Focuses on the transition process rather just the change outcome*: According to Bridges (2003), it is not the change outcome that trips people up – it is the transition journey that does the damage. OD change processes therefore focus on people's transition experiences and are concerned to deliver change in such a way as to ensure there is a 'safe arrival' experience.

In short, any methodology which focuses on *distributive leadership, engagement, participation, multiplying imagination,* modelling and empowering will secure implementation outcomes faster than change methodologies that are mainly expert-led, formula-led, or assume a system/machine paradigm (Holman and Devane, 1999).

EASYJET: EMPLOYEE ENGAGEMENT IN FAST CHANGE

In common with other airlines, easyJet has been facing a highly competitive environment made all the more challenging by the recession. Mike Campbell, easyJet's People Director, describes how the company has remained focused on employee engagement throughout this difficult period: 'Employee engagement is crucial to us. We've been wrestling with the issue of whether or not to implement a pay agreement we reached with the pilots 2 years ago. The agreement is based on RPI which last October was 5% and now is negative. The question at the time was, do we say that we'll go ahead, even though the cost will be damaging for the business, or not? We decided to go ahead with the agreement. Integrity is one of our values and we were not prepared to go back on the deal and sacrifice our values. In any case, we would lose any basis for people to trust us.

When we launched a cost improvement programme in October last year we ran a communication at every base over 3 consecutive days explaining what was happening and why, and the impact on staff. One of the executive team delivered this communication at every one of our 19 bases across Europe. There were extremes of reaction, from pilots (many of whom are shareholders) ranging being concerned about the impact on share price, fuel hedging policy etc., to cabin crew who were interested in roster patterns and the potential affect on their day-to-day activities.

Over the last 3 years we have worked hard to increase the percentage of employee shareholders with schemes based on BAYE and SAYE as well as a free share programme for all staff when we gave everybody 2 weeks' worth of pay in free shares as a thank you for the record performance in each of 2006 and 2007.'

BUILDING LINE MANAGEMENT CAPABILITY TO MANAGE CHANGE

Managing people through a recession is not an easy task, and poor management will undermine employee engagement. Different circumstances call for different mindsets, and many managers will struggle with the demands made of them; after all, few of today's generations of managers, employees, HR professionals and union officials will have previous experience of ensuring business survival in such a volatile context.

HR has a special role to play in developing line managers who are able to cope with the demands made of them today. The new realities require managers to drive down costs, focus on the short term, take quick and potentially tough decisions. Business as usual must be maintained, even if organisations are merging or downsizing, so a rigorous focus on customers and improving customer service will be vital. Good communication will be vital for keeping people informed and aware of priorities.

According to Claire McCartney (2009) while 51% of HR respondents to the CIPD's Employee Outlook survey feel that line managers are equipped to manage talent in the recession to some extent, only 6% suggest managers are equipped to a great extent and 13% feel they are not equipped at all. And while good managers know instinctively what to do, as one senior HR professional put it, even some very good managers when faced with major ambiguity, can be caught like rabbits in headlights, uncertain which way to jump. And as with rabbits, failure to act quickly enough can in many cases prove fatal. So how can HR support line managers to manage people in these changing times?

Supporting Line Managers

Managers will be in the front-line of handling redundancies and their conse-quences, both in terms of workload and staff morale. Managers may need more support in managing talent and keeping staff engaged when many people (including managers themselves) may be nervous and insecure. When redun-dancies are under way, the way people are treated will determine whether or not 'survivor syndrome' kicks in.

HR can coach line managers in how to handle these challenges (i.e. how to manage change) and provide practical support such as 'business as unusual' workshops where managers can openly discuss not only how they are feeling but also what they need to know to manage their own teams through the transitions they face. They can help managers develop effective communications processes, clarify short-term priorities, etc.

HR leaders must also act as advisers to senior management with respect to redundancy choices and processes. As Martin Ferber points out: 'We as HR leaders have to constantly get the message through to our leadership about just how complex these people things are, and that if you don't tackle them correctly, you will not solve your business problems.' HR leaders can advise on the nature of communications required to keep the organisation functioning as well as possible during tough times. They can also use their skills in organisational design to help senior managers to devise structures which will equip the organisation for the recovery and ensure that staffing decisions are taken accordingly. They can keep top management alert to how people are feeling and guide them as to where senior managers in particular need to be seen to lead.

- *Equipping line managers to manage stress*
  Line managers have an important role to play in helping manage stress levels within their own teams, but it is important to recognise that many line managers are themselves under considerable pressure. Many will need support and development in order to be able to deal with the people management demands placed on them. There is a strong business case for helping line managers to manage stress. Under 'normal' circumstances, a symptom of lack of engagement is when employees choose to leave an organisation. Previous CIPD research findings show very clearly that poor and unsupportive management and stress will damage retention. Positive employee mental health/well-being and the prevention of stress are also now recognised as significant determinants of performance and success in the workplace (Dame Carol Black's report on the health of Britain's working age population, 2008).

  CIPD and the Health and Safety Executive (HSE) have examined the capabilities required to help managers manage workplace stress – their own and that of others. Some of the personal barriers include personal/home life issues, own levels of stress and pressure, and perceptions of lack of competence and confidence as a manager. The CIPD/HSE research has led to the development of a line manager (pilot) training programme which is already proving helpful in equipping line managers to manage stress. Results suggest that managers who have been trained in appropriate techniques can reduce stress levels in their teams. Getting senior managers to role model positive manager behaviours was identified as important to encourage these behaviours at all levels of management. However, few of the stakeholders felt that senior managers in their organisation were providing this kind of role model. (CIPD/HSE, 2009: *Preventing stress: promoting positive manager behaviour*).

- *Training line managers in conflict management*

  Given that many employees have concerns over their job security and may be experiencing greater pressure in the workplace, it is possible that many organisations will see an increase in conflict during this challenging period. As with stress, managers have a clear role to play in identifying and managing conflict. Improved consultation with managers in day-to-day management activities is highly regarded as a means of helping line managers prevent and manage disputes. Providing managers with training in conflict management is likely to reduce an organisation's number of disciplinary and grievance cases, as well as improve employee morale.

INITIATING AND CHAMPIONING CHANGE

Responding to the need for change can be difficult enough; initiating and championing change is even more challenging. But if HR leaders are going to drive performance and build sustainable business cultures, that is precisely what they need to do.

In the following spotlight case, the focus of the changes Geoff Armstrong initiated went beyond the organisations in which he worked, and had an impact on changing the overall system of industrial relations (IR) in the UK from the 1970s on.

Spotlight on Geoff Armstrong: Tackling Whole System Change

Geoff describes himself as a classic Baby Boomer – born in 1946 in Bootle, Merseyside, grammar school educated and stepson of a skilled metal dresser in Merseyside shipyards. Geoff has always been driven to succeed, though he did not take the conventional route to career success at the time he left school. Instead of taking up the offer of a degree course to study French at University, Geoff took himself off to Portsmouth Polytechnic to do a sociology degree instead. Geoff specialised in industrial sociology. At the time this seemed rather a rebellious move but Geoff was interested in, and wanted to study the processes of organisations, rather than the welfare aspects of labour, and wanted to understand how organisations in various walks of society could work more effectively.

In the early late 60s graduates had plenty of job offers from employers during the 'milk round.' On graduation Geoff was keen to move into an Employee Relations (ER) role and he chose to enter the motor industry where the hottest IR issues were at the time. He joined Morris Engines at Coventry, a subsidiary of the British Motor Corporation (BMC) as 'graduate trainee.' There were 6000 employees, 5000 of whom were in blue collar jobs. As trainee Geoff initially moved around the various departments, carrying out assignments, including a stint as assistant to the Welfare officer, which meant that he accompanied his colleague to employee funerals and always had a black tie at the ready. Then he became Assistant (or 'Bag carrier' as Geoff describes it) to the Personnel Manager for the whole site. This was a forward-looking man who exposed Geoff to new experiences, in particular meetings with the Unions.

Continued

Spotlight on Geoff Armstrong: Tackling Whole System Change—cont'd

Piecework

This was a turbulent period to be in ER in the UK. During the 1950s and 1960s British manufacturing was struggling to emerge from the legacy of the war years when much major manufacturing had been turned over to the war production where volume had been the key criterion. In the Midlands motor industry in the late 1960s the piece-work principle which had been applied since the 1920s still predominated, so employees were paid extra for doing more work, therefore people would only do more work if they were paid.

In the post-war period the former Axis countries, especially Germany and Japan had received massive re-investment via the Marshall plan in their largely destroyed industrial infrastructure. In Germany in particular, a structural approach was taken to rebuilding the industrial base, especially motor manufacturing, with employment relations treated as a 'greenfield site'. The Germans learned what they did not want to do from examining what was happening in the UK and doing the opposite. Early in his 20s Geoff recognised that piece work was 'no way to run a ship'. Procedure agreements were not effective when change was needed. Piece work meant that nothing was ever settled and effectively became the way in which the workplace was regulated. Any new piece of work needed a piecework price, based on the 3Ms – means, materials and methods. Whenever there was any change, the price needed to be constantly renegotiated, and established for different levels of worker. Given that the world is constantly changing, piecework represented a stranglehold on change which was controlled by shop stewards. These could ensure that the price would be pushed up by manipulating for instance the number of parts which would be produced for the same price, or by demanding higher manning levels for the same job and other 'spanish customs' were common. The recognised way of proceeding was to only enter negotiations with management once the price had been paid.

In Geoff's view, the whole management ethos was heading in the wrong direction since customers were entirely invisible in the process and the entire focus was on the interests and expectations of the workforce. The organisation as an end in itself was no way to be competitive but this approach was common in British manufacturing and traditional industries such as the docks at that time. Geoff spent 3 years with Morris and learned a lot, not least from the experience of driving in to work through his first picket line. As a member of the management side, Geoff saw it as his job not to concede. But what Geoff realised was the power and responsibility of working in Personnel and IR – that these did effectively determine how the factory ran. He was also conscious that his responsibility extended beyond the factory walls and that a strike at the factory could also lead to thousands of people working for suppliers also being laid off.

British Leyland came into being in 1968 as an agglomeration of the British-owned motor industry. The hope was that this would enable volume and economies of scale. In 1970 Pat Lowry was appointed to the British Leyland main board as its first Industrial Relations Director. For the first time BL had a strong central figure whose job was to make sense of this complex organisation. At the time BL had 200,000 employees based at 100+ factories working for a confusing array of brands.

Spotlight on Geoff Armstrong: Tackling Whole System Change—cont'd

Pat Lowry built a small team to help him with this task, and Geoff joined this Head Office team, reporting directly to Pat as his 'bag carrier'. At this was the time of the first Equal Pay Act, Geoff wrote BL's first equal pay policy, as well as BL's first company-wide redundancy policy. With his boss, he was involved in discussions with powerful Union leaders such as Hugh Scanlon and Jack Jones.

Joint regulation of the workplace by collective bargaining was widely seen as the way of getting people working harder and had remained largely unchanged since the National Agreement of 1922. In the post-war period, unlike many other European countries which operated on forms of partnership working between trades unions, employers and the government, and where the working assumptions were that the interests of employees and employers were the same, in the UK industrial relations were more adversarial and interests of employees and employers were assumed to be fundamentally different.

By the 1970s in the UK, the old practice of negotiating 'mutuality' and 'status quo' agreements meant that negotiations would be entered into but change was not effected until the piece-work price had been agreed. Essentially employees always had the veto. Pat Lowry's team worked hard to reverse these long-established practices and achieve a procedure agreement to effect change first and discuss after, rather than stopping work before any change could be implemented. So embedded were these practices that status quo agreements were supported by various politicians and questions about proposed changes were regularly asked in Parliament. The team worked to negotiate.

This was a brutal time in UK IR industrial relations. Geoff felt strongly that the old practices were not only unhelpful to management and stood in the way of competitiveness, but they also worked against the interests of employees. For instance, the rigid hierarchies of skilled labour meant that trades-people were usually labelled by age 21 if they had not reached skilled level and would be condemned to semi- or unskilled work for the rest of their working lives. Many managers viewed people as the 'irrational, bolshy awkward squad' who got in the way of the machinery. They did not see employees as contributing but as a necessary evil. Training was seen as a cost to be minimised and there was little management interest in helping people develop their careers or gain individual fulfilment. Even managers who understood the problem and wanted to do something to improve things were impotent to challenge such a powerful system.

Geoff was coming to an articulation of the problem over time, trying to make sense of it and challenge the unions. IR issues were high profile. The collective mindset at all levels – government, academics, managers and unions -was outdated. Jack Jones the powerful T&G leader was a huge influence on the UK economy and a powerful proponent of the piecework /mutuality principle. The prevailing belief was that organisations should be run in a collectivist way.

Pat Lowry asked Geoff to move to Leyland Truck and Bus as IR Manager. There were 12,000 blue-collar workers and 4000 white-collar workers. This was Geoff's first leadership role and his task was to make sense of the antiquated procedures, try and work out what he could do to persuade union officials and employees, as well

Continued

Spotlight on Geoff Armstrong: Tackling Whole System Change—cont'd

equip managers, to take up new ways of working. In his 3 years at Leyland, Geoff became Personnel Manager. His was a daunting task and he spent many days over that time locked in smoke-filled rooms arguing with different parties. He wanted to change the strike propensity and resistance to change built into the system.

Though Geoff describes himself as still 'green' in understanding what it took to manage an organisation well, one significant achievement was the 'little blue book'. This was Geoff's articulation of the required new working practices, together with a new pay and grading system. He sent a copy to every employee at their home, over the heads of the union leaders, a move which did not endear him to the unions. However, the new system was a success, and relations became more orderly, though Geoff feels that even more success would have been possible had the company invested more in manager training and employee communications.

Then Geoff became Group IR Director for the Truck and Bus Company as a whole. He now had overview of all 12 factories throughout the UK and Ireland. His task was to effect change at the Truck and Bus Group as a whole. The competitive and IR climates at the time were very challenging. Geoff worked hard to convince people that there were better ways of working; in particular he worked to get managers to adopt a more strategic approach and personally negotiated with the trades union, acting as the troubleshooter of last resort. The atmosphere was war-like and his own office was like a command centre. His role was one of fire prevention and though Geoff feels some progress was made, again the size of the issue was such that Geoff feels he was scraping the surface.

Geoff then moved to British Leyland Cars (then led by Sir Michael Edwardes) to carry out the Group ER Director role. British Leyland Cars had even bigger battles with the unions than the Truck and Bus Company. He was based at Longbridge and his role was most of what would now be thought of as Personnel. Geoff wanted to inject some order into the way in which IR operated and to take away the strike propensity. He increased the amount of training and the IR climate improved, or at least, as Geoff puts it,' people stopped killing one another. Group companies such as Jaguar, Land Rover and Unipart were established and Geoff again sees his efforts as a partial success. As Geoff says, 'It's hard to imagine now how dramatic and radical what we were doing seemed at the time. People everywhere wanted to know how we did it'.

However, in Geoff's view success was not as a whole sustainable. The company's problems were so great, and relations between unions and management were very enmeshed and adversarial. There was such a lack of investment and lack of management capacity. Moreover the problems were being acted out in a political maelstrom under the magnifying glass of media attention and under the public gaze.

This attention made Geoff something of a public figure. British Leyland's management was under pressure for their supposed macho management and Geoff gained the soubriquet of 'The Iron man of British Leyland'. Geoff's wife often found out whether or not to expect Geoff back for dinner by watching the early evening news. 'On the balance of probabilities', in place of the existing clause - 'beyond all reasonable doubt', it became front page news. Indeed so intense was public interest

Spotlight on Geoff Armstrong: Tackling Whole System Change—cont'd

in what was happening in the motor industry at the time that when annual negotiations were underway, there would typically be over a dozen newspaper journalists and several television and radio journalists door-stepping the negotiations. Geoff was routinely interviewed by industrial correspondents and often found himself debating issues with politicians and ministers – who were intervening often from a naive or politically interested perspective- both behind the scenes and in public discussions. The level of scrutiny was such that when Geoff drafted a new disciplinary procedure which suggested that an employee could be dismissed for wrong doing.

As Geoff says, 'There was a sense that what we did made a difference. We were tackling some long-standing company issues. It was very pressurised and there was lots of animosity, but it felt worth the candle. It was good to bring relief to managers who were under pressure. I think if we had been even bolder and more ambitious at expressing the nature of the problem we might have achieved even more. At the same time you had to be reflective. I was conscious that the things I said could cause people to lose wages or their jobs if they did not agree with what we were saying.' For instance Geoff had to announce 25,000 redundancies and factory closures, including the Morris Engines factory where he had begun his career. He had to be tough and persuasive in making the cases for these closures and tried to communicate fully, explaining the competitive context and the business imperatives for the closures, using the local media as a key means of getting the message heard by workers.

Essentially there was increasing recognition that this was not a sustainable way to work and achieve competitive advantage and this, together with the growth of political will by Conservative governments to break the old practices signalled the beginning of the end of the old IR era and the dawning of the new which would be marked by human relations management as opposed to collectivist relations practices. This meant that Geoff was not only trying to influence and improve IR practices at British Leyland but was essentially challenging the whole IR system in UK manufacturing at the time.

Personal leadership

In a very real sense Geoff exercised personal leadership. As Geoff says, he never felt like a functional specialist – he was part of the business team who happened to be in one of the most important jobs – his challenge was how to create a sustainable business for the future. In a very real sense HR was the business since what happened in IR terms could make or break the business day by day and could be the biggest impediment to running a successful business.

What helped Geoff lead this change to the system was getting to understand the nature of the problem to be tackled, seeing the big picture, not just a series of fragmented episodes. This required clarity of vision and commitment to the purpose even when people resisted or vilified the approach. He worked hard to communicate why he was doing what he was doing, and showing that he was not just being 'bloody-minded'. Geoff exercised personal courage on many occasions, addressing mass meetings, crossing picket lines and burning the midnight oil in negotiations because 'it was important to do it'.

Continued

> **Spotlight on Geoff Armstrong: Tackling Whole System Change**—cont'd
>
> Geoff's courage was put to the test in one particularly challenging incident. In 1981 while he was still at British Leyland Cars, Geoff agreed to speak at a Junior Chamber of Commerce meeting in Dublin on the subject of IR in times of change. BL had two factories in Dublin and advice was that there was no need to worry since the 'Troubles' were in Northern Ireland. This was however a very fraught time – Bobby Sands was on hunger strike and the infamous H-Blocks were constantly the focus of protest. Geoff was partway into his speech when he became aware that something was amiss from his audience's reaction. Three men in balaclavas and paramilitary uniform appeared on stage to the side of him. One approached Geoff and opened fire at close range with a 2.2 pistol, hitting Geoff in the legs three times. The shooter (who was subsequently sentenced to twelve years in jail) declared that the shooting was a demonstration in support of the hunger strike in the North. The trio had apparently chosen Geoff simply because he was a high profile senior British business man. Ironically, the 'Iron man of Longbridge' received a sympathy vote for him and his family as a result.

CONCLUSION

A proactive and determined approach to initiating and implementing change is what distinguishes leadership from followership. And while it is to be hoped that few HR leaders will be put to quite such tests as Geoff Armstrong faced, nevertheless courage and determination are vital ingredients of bringing about successful and sustainable change. Given the dynamic environment, the ability to change needs to become embedded in organisational cultures. Given that HR leaders should be experts in the human and organisational dynamics of change, they should bring their insights into what will work from a whole systems perspective to the challenges of restructuring, downsizing and integration. In other words, they should bring an OD perspective to strategic change.

The benefits of an OD approach in fast-changing times are significant. Participatory processes led by key stakeholders will mobilise the system and unleash energy. When any change process put people's engagement at the heart of it, using high leverage change methodologies, connecting different bits of organisation together, working through multiple perspectives and keeping the WHOLE SYSTEM together, the change effort is likely to stick.

So in times like these, people should not fear experimenting. After all, the golden rule to follow is as follows: if after trying something three times it does not work, stop and try something else! Perhaps if all of us improve in our 'human dynamics' savvyness, and ensure that we have some OD practitioners in our HR community who can help leaders to focus not just on the technical solutions (content of the change) but on the degree of cultural acceptance of the solutions, then change will not need to be cajoled or coerced, but can simply be unleashed!

Chapter 8

Building Healthy and Ethical Organisations

'Academics call this the "soft" side of leadership. It is anything but soft. It is a lot more difficult to gain alignment of employees around mission and values than it is to meet quarterly numbers or to cut expenses.'

Bill George (2007)

As we know, the banking crisis and subsequent recession have pushed ethics to the top of the agenda for business and society as a whole. Poor corporate practice is now recognised as a key factor in causing the economic crash and the ability of (financial) markets to self-regulate has been exposed as a sham. Organisations are under media scrutiny and pressure to respond to social and public policy expectations.

In the wake of these events, previous reforms of board governance and financial checks are likely to be revisited and strengthened, since the current system clearly did not protect the consumer and other stakeholders against risks they were unaware of. So great has been the damage to some corporate reputations that a few brands have been indelibly tarnished. And while whistle blowing has its place, more generally people are looking for greater transparency for 'truth' rather than spin and accountability as a reasonable basis to trust again.

And many of the factors which must be more closely attended to within the remit of HR. Executive compensation and the big bonus culture are manifestations of market-driven (reward and cultural) practices which have contributed to the banking crisis and broader economic problems. And whilst it may be hard to regulate for bonus payments, something will have to change. If not, and if the impact of downturn on national economies worsens further, the inequities inherent within the system could come more sharply into focus and provoke stronger reactions – e.g. reported risk of civil unrest in Ireland; increasing union militancy which is likely to grow further as public sector cuts start to take place. The basis of UK employee relations – which until recently has rested on HR management (HRM) approaches to employee engagement rather than collective bargaining – may become unsustainable unless lessons are drawn from what has happened and better practice implemented.

So HR is intimately connected with the issues which need to be addressed to improve the overall system. HR will need to lead the search for more sustainable practice. Sustainability involves more than building environmental or social responsibility policies. It is more than ensuring that employees are treated fairly. It is fundamentally about ensuring that the organisation has an ethical basis for its existence and that the organisation delivers on its promises to all its stakeholders, including society at large. It is about equipping the organisation to meet the needs of customers who will continue to buy the organisation's products. It is about developing healthy and innovative cultures in which people are well led and give of their best.

HR's role is to act as builder of healthy and sustainable organisational practice. For Ulrich, an HR leader must act as a *culture and change steward.* Webster's defines steward as 'a person morally responsible for the careful use of money, time, talents or other resources, especially with respect to the principles or needs of a community or group'. What Webster's does not define is how to exercise stewardship. And this is where HR leaders have choices. Will HR be part of the problem or part of the solution?

A 'COMPANY POLICE OFFICER' ROLE?

At one level, a steward can be reactive, controlling, sanctimonious even. If this is the approach taken, HR's role simply becomes that of 'company police officer' who demands compliance with a set of regulations, and adds little real value because – as has already been seen – poor practice can exist even though the regulatory boxes have been ticked. Geoff Armstrong points out the dangers of this approach to HR's reputation: 'If we just stand on the sidelines, sanctimoniously or procedurally, seeing ourselves as custodians of health and safety, etc. we'll be accepted but resented. We'll be seen as the Function that keeps us out of jail, that likes to say no.' Similarly, if HR simply becomes the risk management function, their procedures are likely to kill off the innovation and entrepreneurialism needed for business success. As Pfeffer (2000) points out, much of what HR does kills off innovation.

In today's organisations, ensuring compliance with ethical standards cannot be achieved by command and control. After all, there is an increasing bifurcation with respect to means of exacting compliance – from electronic means of surveillance of employee activities to highly dispersed work forces working from home and never seeing a manager. And there is potentially a vicious circle at work: the less employees are trusted, the more alienated and untrustworthy they may become. With social media making it possible for employees to send damaging images and messages around the world instantly, building a trusting, positive relationship with employees is as much about risk management/ damage limitation as good practice. Once damaged, brands take a long time to recover.

ACTIVE STEWARDSHIP – BUILDING ETHICAL, SUSTAINABLE PRACTICE

To build a sustainable organisation requires HR to take a much more proactive approach to stewardship than mere compliance. I prefer Ulrich's definition of what good stewardship involves – it is about facilitating change, valuing, crafting and personalising culture. Although HR is within the organisational system, HR leaders need to actively intervene in the system to improve organisational health and effectiveness.

This involves identifying and wrestling with dilemmas arising from today's complex organisational environment, such as how to balance risk management and innovation and how to both compete and collaborate. Such dilemmas do not lend themselves to easy solutions and reconciling them can involve cutting across vested interests. This requires HR leaders to operate from a strong value base and be willing to persist in challenging or promoting ideas and practice in the face of opposition, even at some personal cost.

And what qualifies HR for this cultural stewardship role? On the one hand, HR leaders can have no superior claim over other members of management teams to be the moral arbiter and Geoff Armstrong argues strongly that HR must not position itself as such. On the other hand, HR leaders are the organisation's custodians of values. HR leaders must step forward, monitor and govern work (Losey et al., 2005). HR has many tools with which to intervene in the system. And HR is in a better position than most to know what is really going on, but that knowledge can present HR leaders with sensitive choices into address tricky issues. They need personal courage, pragmatism and political expediency and good judgement.

Better Governance

In the past, HR's role in governance processes might have seemed peripheral, but increasingly HR must play a key role in governance. Governance issues are important (for example, moving the organisation in the direction of what is in the long-term interest of customers and shareholders even if these conflict with, or are at odds with Senior Management interests). HR leaders must act as active stewards, creating culture and practices that encourage candour/openness and build trust between managers and employees, the organisation and its customers, investors and other stakeholders. HR should pay attention to the processes for decision-making and communication. Are people getting the information they need to do their jobs, are they involved in implementation decisions, how can technology assist, is there a good balance of reflection and action, could meetings be more productive? All of these are within the HR leader's organisational design and development remit.

HR also needs to understand how to act if different stakeholder interests get out of synch at any point (Becker and Huselid, 2006). Beatty et al. (2003)

mention financial measurement and reward systems as an example of where things can get out of synch. These are intended to reward deserving leadership but if poorly designed they can allow certain individuals (usually management) to 'cook the books'. And Jackie Orme raises the question, given the part played by executive bonuses in the recent economic crisis: 'Have we developed, promoted, incentivised and rewarded the leaders we deserve?'

Beatty et al. (2003) also identify three different areas of focus for HR with respect to the wider organisational behavioural standards and practices they must design and introduce. These cover lawful behaviour, ethical behaviours and vocal constituencies (to ensure that strategic unity isn't lost). The second and third of these are harder to address (not the least because they have different significance in different cultures and for different individuals) but have important consequences for reputation, branding and engagement.

So how can HR leaders demonstrate active stewardship in day-to-day events? Take a disciplinary situation, for instance, in which the HR leader suspects that a line manager has contributed as much to creating the problem as the person who is being disciplined. Jackie Orme argues that there is, in practice, a distinction between approaching a disciplinary scenario wearing a compliance 'hat' – acting as an HR officer merely carrying out a disciplinary procedure – and a strong, independent HR leader who is acting as steward, making sure the right thing is done. The latter involves understanding what values mean in a disciplinary context – saying to a line manager, 'This is wrong' – having the courage to challenge and hold your position.

What about when leaders step out of line and violate cultural norms? Do we address the situation directly or do we accept? Do we try and challenge/change/force out individuals? Active stewardship requires that we do. This is a real test of integrity and moral courage, especially when, as HR professionals, we are essentially enmeshed within the system.

Of course, playing this role is not popular – after all, failing organisations, CEOs and even governments have not wanted to tackle such issues. But if an HR leader has strong values, especially if these are stated, they are something to hang on to. Jackie Orme for instance has been prepared to do this from her earliest career days. She has found that speaking out openly in an informed and balanced way about issues of culture/leadership/values, in the context of healthy peer relationships defined by respect for one another's ideas and initiatives, has produced dynamic tension but led to positive change.

Jackie Orme argues that it is only very occasionally that organisations think about HR's role through these lenses and that when this happens, shareholders and CEOs have very high expectations and provide significant share of voice for HR, seeing it as one of the most important functions in the enterprise. In such circumstances, HR becomes less politicised and is strategically positioned to both deliver the HR agenda and run a commentary on the current and future health of the organisation. Jackie suggests that HR must act as balanced advocate of competing needs of stakeholder groups within the organisation and steer a course through competing commitments that enable the medium or longer-term view to be taken.

More broadly, an HR leader contributes value by instilling within a culture the values, accountability norms and standards of behaviour which create healthy and sustainable organisations. Such organisations actively serve the needs of all their stakeholders – internal and external. The guiding principle should be to support the building of longer-term value.

Many HR leaders themselves can and do take an active role in the governance of other organisations by acting as non-executive directors. By developing a holistic view of another organisation and using their insights to add value, HR leaders not only bring benefit to the organisation but also develop their own strategic ability by exposure to the entire governance process.

Employee Engagement

HR leaders need to build and sustain a workforce environment that fosters engagement and is attractive to potential employees. The volume and pace of change can make the task of aligning employees to the organisation very challenging, especially in large organisations. Martin Ferber comments: 'I think that staff can feel increasingly anonymous and isolated, a cog in the wheel, in these large fast moving companies where people come and go from jobs much more quickly than they used to. You don't necessarily know your colleagues for very long, then you've got another colleague, another report, another boss. It's far more turbulent, and I think the word is turbulent rather than changing, than it used to be.'

Given the growing body of evidence that employee engagement is the major factor in performance, such disconnection could be significant. SHRM (2002) argues that this has many implications ranging from employee well-being, performance and customer loyalty. Towers Perrin (2008) considers employee engagement as comprising three components: rational/cognitive (understanding the organisation's strategy and how they can contribute to it); emotional/affective (to the strategy and their potential contribution to achieving it); and motivation/willingness (to go the extra mile). Others define employee engagement as composed of three elements - intellectual, social and emotional.

Organisational Design

Towers Perrin (2003) identify the main aspects of the work environment to affect employee engagement as strong leadership, accountability, and a sense of control over the work environment. This suggests that employee engagement is closely linked to both leadership and organisational design. Providing a sense of belonging is important if employees are to engage with the organisation at all the three levels. Jamrog et al. (2008) carried out an empirical global survey to discover components of high-performance culture. They found that the following practices were key to engagement.

- 'Walking the talk' and behaving consistently;
- Understanding customers' needs and focusing on meeting those needs;
- Sharing information with employees and developing great supervisors;
- Creating an environment of focus and teamwork;
- Designing processes that unite people;
- Clear measurement of performance;
- Treating employees well; and
- Behaving with the highest possible standards.

HR leaders must design organisational structures and practices which meet the needs of stakeholders, especially customers.

Leaders – Align, Empower and Serve

Leaders are the biggest factor affecting engagement in most studies of the subject. Bill George (2007) argues that successful organisations of the twenty-first century – those that sustain superior results year after year – will be led by authentic leaders who know how to motivate this new group of employees and gain their full commitment. For George, these leaders will align, empower and serve. They will align by uniting the entire organisation around a common purpose and values; empower by motivating employees to step up and fulfil the organisation's purpose; serve by dedicating themselves to all the organisation's constituencies – customers, employees, investors and communities. Building such leadership capability is a key responsibility of HR leaders.

Alignment With a Higher Purpose

And while many design elements can provide the basis for good employee engagement, for a real affective attachment to the organisation a higher purpose provides the glue which binds employees to a common effort however disparate their talents and roles. Employee engagement is not a mechanical system. It is a psychological construct which exists within a company culture. Simply measuring employee engagement does not produce engagement – potentially the opposite. HR leaders must focus on a process of co-creating an Employee Value Proposition which can truly connect and engage employees. They must also ensure that employees have the basis of what Coats (2005) describes as 'Good Work' – where employees feel they are treated fairly and have the chance to participate – i.e. they have 'voice' and 'equity'.

HR leaders have a key role to play in helping identify and create alignment around a higher purpose. Real engagement occurs when people feel uplifted by their organisation's purpose and their part in delivering it. Purpose acts as emotional and connective component of organisation, creating an 'identity' that employees value and that also supports the strategy and defines what you 'stand for'. Companies with a higher purpose tend to have not only a better reputation but also more loyal workers and customers. Such organisations strive for better performance at all times.

CUSTOMER PURPOSE AND SUSTAINABILITY

Of the various forms of organisational purpose – serving the needs of staff, community, shareholders and customers or balancing the needs of different stakeholders – customer-intensive purpose appears to be the most motivating and most likely to result in innovation, speed and sustainable business results.

Moreover, customer-focused organisations are more sustainable than others. There are many studies which suggest a strong correlation between employee engagement and customer satisfaction. Two well-known companies with a strong investment in both employees and customers (and who achieve high performance) are Southwest Airlines and Tesco. HR leaders, therefore, focus on the question how do we position ourselves to be sustainable, and get customers coming back to us?

Companies whose products, processes and people deliver excellence at every touch point of customer contact are simply less vulnerable in the marketplace. These companies exhibit resilience, and this 'stress resistance' translates into an ability to not only withstand transient economic downturns, but also to maintain consistent levels of market capitalization in the longer term. (McEwen and Fleming, 2001).

Of course, for HR the employee is also the customer. Geoff Armstrong argues that organisations have to reposition themselves to deal with (internal) customer demands since they're more reliant on the discretionary contribution of people: 'It is the ability to engage the willingness of individuals to anticipate and feed back what customers are saying, to reconfigure and apply this research fast to maximise the customer repeat order.'

This customer-centric view involves HR 'working with management to develop policies, practices and philosophies geared towards creating a truly motivated and dedicated workforce' (Wharton on HR, 2007). Geoff Armstrong argues that 'This requires a lot of evidence-based knowledge around the practice of management of people, not just the 'programme of the month' or the latest idea out of HBR, etc. It has to be an explicit, ongoing process – how we position ourselves to be sustainable, and get customers coming back to us.'

Building a customer-focused organisation means that HR must use data and tools to understand what is needed to create alignment and a sense of fair deal. And most of these tools are directly within HR's remit – reward systems, communications, policies of many sorts, opportunities for development, team working and well-being. Managers and leaders have a significant impact on employee engagement. HR has the ability to influence both – it has both the sanctions and the levers. The real challenge is to use them to build healthy practice.

Delivering Public Value

In the public sector for 'customer', substitue 'citizen', 'end user', 'public', 'politician'. Public leaders are charged with delivering 'public value' (Moore, 1995), i.e. they should use their resources to maximise their contribution to the public realm and to the achievement of outcomes valued by the public. To achieve this objective they need to engage with their citizens and direct customers to agree what constitutes public value in that specific context. It is this which determines how public sector leaders gain legitimacy and suggests a shift towards meeting the specific needs of the communities being served rather than just government funding departments. The public service leader or manager has to consider the following dimensions in developing a course of action.

- *Authorising or political environment* – do decisions have legitimacy and support? Are they politically sustainable?
- *Operational capacity* – are plans feasible? Does the organisational capacity exist?
- *Public value, strategic goals* – mission and purpose. Is the offer possible?

The proposition is that purpose, capacity and legitimacy have to be aligned in order to provide the public service leader with the necessary authority to create public value through a particular course of action. In much the same way, HR has its own internal 'public value' to deliver, and the same dimensions apply to people strategies. Moreover, public sector HR leaders can deliver not only organisational capacity to deliver public value but also the OD expertise to dign processes which help managers engage effectively with stakeholders. By so doing they contribute directly to the shaping and delivery of public value.

Putting Something Back – Corporate Social Responsibility (CSR)

Giving something back is known to be a factor which matters to employees and companies with active CSR practices tend to produce strong employee engagement and better brands as well as benefiting the community. HR leaders must ensure that the external brand promise is matched by internal brand realities. They must also ensure that the organisation actively plays its part in its community, exercising social responsibility and reinforcing sustainable business practice. The positive impact of CSR is being seen in communities worldwide. Attracting and retaining competent people is a good example of the business driver for CSR.

HR can play many roles with respect to CSR: leading and educating their organisations about its importance and actively introducing HRM practices that support company business and CSR goals (SHRM, 2004). Sustainability often requires organisational and cultural change (both activities that are within HR's remit) but if HR does not understand sustainability issues, they will not be able to contribute to the organisational and cultural changes required (Wirtenburg et al., 2007).

The notion of service to the community is a common motivator for many of the HR leaders in this book. Most participate as board members in the work of charities and social enterprises. Anne Minto, for instance, has chaired the Institute of Employment Studies and has also been on the National Employers Liaison Committee for the Reserve Forces.

David Fairhurst is leading McDonalds' contribution as an employer to the national skills agenda: 'We are supporting the sector skills council People 1st (I am Vice-Chairman) and the Confederation of British Industry - the CBI - (our CEO Steve Easterbrook chairs the CBI's Education and Training Affairs Committee) to change attitudes towards the service sector and to play our part in ensuring that we have sufficient high-quality customer service skills available in the workforce.' As an industry leader, David was responsible for contributing to both the formulation of policy and the delivery of employer-led qualification initiatives, and McDonalds now runs a training company offering a variety of business relevant 'A' levels, degrees and other qualifications. His contribution to improving the skills of young people is therefore on a national scale.

Spotlight on Angela O'Connor: Building a Diverse Culture at the Crown Prosecution Service

When Angela O'Connor arrived at the Crown Prosecution Service (CPS), she recognised that this was an organisation in distress. Trust was at an all-time low. Staff survey results showed that there were dysfunctional issues relating to equality, diversity and performance which needed to be dealt with. On performance, in particular, it was clear that improvement was needed. There were no rewards for success, nor were there any sanctions for failure. The organisation had become a 'soft touch'. Angela personally went through the many employment tribunal cases and sorted them into those cases where the organisation had messed up, in which case they should make things right, settle or sign agreements; and those cases where the CPS had no case to answer, which they decided to defend, using the best employment lawyers rather than settle. The large number of cases against the CPS was significantly reduced and morale in the organisation drastically improved, as was evident in exceptional improvements in staff survey results.

On diversity, to bring about change in a highly intellectual organisation, Angela saw the importance of approaching the issues using evidence. She published statistics and facts which raised key questions such as why are there no black Chief Crown prosecutors in England and Wales? Angela's assumption was that this was partly because potential candidates were de-selecting themselves on the basis that they had no chance of being appointed to such posts, so she set about radically overhauling the system. She charged the Crown Prosecutor as leader with developing people as a key part of their role. There was to be no tokenism; in fact, the bar was raised. She worked with groups of people across the organisation and focused on building a diverse talent pipeline.

Continued

Spotlight on Angela O'Connor: Building a Diverse Culture at the Crown Prosecution Service—cont'd

One initiative introduced by Angela's team was the legal 'scholarship' scheme. These were people who aspired to a legal career but came, like herself, from less conventional backgrounds, such as administration. For instance, one scholar was a single mother; another had multiple sclerosis. The scheme received the backing of the then Solicitor-General Harriet Harman and the Director of Public Prosecutions (DPP). It was launched at a summer reception hosted by Cherie Blair. This scheme alone helped change the face of the law to one based on merit and equality. By the time she left the CPS after 4.5 years, the CPS had the best diversity levels across Whitehall and a 33-year-old Asian woman had become Chief Crown Prosecutor and was the first of many BME Chief Crown Prosecutors.

ACTIVELY BUILDING HEALTHY ORGANISATIONS

Beyond being custodians of values, HR leaders must be culture-builders, working actively and persistently to build healthy and sustainable business cultures. Their task is essentially an organisational development (OD) task. OD is concerned with developing organisational effectiveness and sustaining organisational renewal. OD is '... *a process (and its associated technology) directed at organisational improvement' (Margulies, 1978).*

> '...all the activities engaged in by managers, employees and helpers that are directed toward building and maintaining the health of the organisation as a total system.' (Schein E., 1988)

OD recognises that organisations do not exist in a vacuum but are part of an 'open system'. OD focuses on ensuring that the organisation is responsive to the world it operates in and that its internal capacity matches its strategic ambition. It is:

> '... a system-wide process of planned change aimed toward improving overall effectiveness by way of enhanced congruence of such organisational dimensions as external environment, mission, strategy, leadership, culture, structure, information and reward system, and work policies and procedures.'(Bradford and Burke, 2005)

Environmental factors (input) affect what the organisation exists to deliver (output), and how the organisation in turn affects the environment.

OD looks, too, at how the total system can work well together to serve the outside world. OD looks at the total system and the linkage between all the parts of the organisation, and on how change in one part will affect the other parts. OD also works to ensure that during turbulent change, organisational capability is maintained, aligned and improved through a planned change effort. It is:

> '...a long-range effort to improve an organisation's problem-solving and renewal processes...with the assistance of a change agent, or catalyst, and the use of the theory and technology of applied behavioural science, including action research.' (French and Bell, 1999)

As a discipline, therefore, it is fundamentally strategic, even if OD activities may be practical and occasionally tactical. It is the systematic application of behavioural science principles and practices to understand how people and organisations function and how to get them to function better within a clear value base. It is shamelessly humanistic and has strong value drivers.

Core Values of OD

What held the OD field together from the beginning are its core values which focus on the following:

- *Process* – this is as important as content, if not more sometimes;
- *Organisational effectiveness* – making an organisation a 'better' workplace for its employees and those the organisation serves;
- *Balancing individual and organisational needs* – aiming for multiple wins for those who work in them and depend on them for their services; and
- *Humanistic values* – believing that individuals should be given opportunities to become all that they can become, reflecting a humanistic striving for optimal alignment between organisational and individual goals and needs.

These core values – as manifested in participation, openness to learning, equity and fairness, valid information, informed choice, shared ownership and commitment – are vital in shaping processes which help organisations to become and remain healthy.

The role of the OD practitioner is to 'help'. Skilful help involves using diagnostic data (organisational, behavioural and psychological) and intervening within the system, using structured interventions to achieve the development of the organisation.

Intervention Tools and Levers

HR has many tools and levers to use to build healthy, ethical cultures. As HR's role becomes more strategic, OD will become intrinsic to Strategic HRM. One of the reasons why OD may be less well understood than other disciplines is that OD transcends functional boundaries. HR professionals have traditionally practised within the fields of HRM and HR development (HRD). These functional fields are much more clearly articulated than that of OD, even if an overall model for HR may still be lacking.

HRM deals with all activities traditionally linked with the personnel function except training. For instance, according to McLagan (1989), all HRM efforts are to increase organisational production by using the talents of its current employees and are associated with talent management, including Recruitment & Selection, Resourcing, Compensation & Benefits, Employee Relations, Appraisal and other Performance Management Systems, and HR

Information Systems. HRD, defined as 'Organisational learning and development to bring about the possibility of performance improvement and/or personal growth' deals with all activities related to Training, Education and Development. All HRD efforts are to bring about the possibility of performance improvement at individual or team level and/or personal growth. These disciplines make a powerful combination but stop short of being able to build organisational capability.

This is where OD fits and provides a foundation for current and future organisational success. While Learning and Development (HRD) focuses on human learning, OD focuses on human dynamics. This is why solutions to the quest for employee engagement will not be found in single remedies – a more systemic approach is needed. The rich field of knowledge in OD helps us understand how people and organisations function, and how to help them function better within a clear value framework. It's about getting the organisation's total system to work coherently.

OD – in contrast to HRM or HRD – is an eclectic, relatively new and emerging field which borrows from many other disciplines and theories – strategy, systems thinking, behavioural science disciplines such as psychology, social psychology, sociology, anthropology, systems theory, organisational behaviour, organisational theory, culture and management literature – to name but a few.

OD's Role in Sustainable Competitive Advantage

From the beginning, OD developed and applied its theories of people and change to organisational life and functioning. Many of the interventions originally pioneered and practised by OD professionals have now become mainstream, shaping the way we all think about how organisations work, as Edgar Schein (2006) points out:

> '...how many elements of OD have evolved into organisational routines that are nowadays taken for granted: better communications, team building, management of inter-group relationships, change management, survey research, meeting designs, feedback and learning loops, organisation design, effective group processes, conflict resolution ...to name but a few.'

Typically, OD practitioners use a framework of diagnostics to link the environmental factors which affect the organisation, its strategic imperative and the organisation's 'throughput' (i.e. linked to both the external customer's experience and employee satisfaction and behaviour), working back from implementation. OD practitioners have to deeply understand how groups work, why certain groups bring out the best or the worst in people – find out what needs fixing – how to influence the 'shadow' system of the organisation – its internal politics and power bases. While interventions can focus on any part of the organisational throughput system, they increasingly focus on upskilling leaders, turning them into strategists and organisational leaders, not just senior technocrats.

Much has changed since OD's humble beginnings in the 1950s. Technology, globalisation, competitive pressures, trends and changes within industry, worldwide markets, increasing workplace diversity and a host of social and economic forces have all altered the world of work and the ways we organise work groups. However, despite the changing challenges, the following concerns remain constant. How do we:

- Build a sustainable high-performance organisation in which individual workers take an active part in achieving the required output, i.e. they are appropriately engaged, proactive, empowered and accountable?
- Solve the problems of aligning and integrating diverse cultural elements?
- Get information to flow upwards within hierarchies?
- Help organisations to be externally sensitive?
- Get organisations to be agile and flexible?
- Release human potential at work and foster learning and renewal within organisations?

In the past few decades, OD has evolved to meet these challenges, continuing to grow and defining new concepts and tools to tackle ever-tougher problems of change and organisational dynamics in an increasingly complex, global and diverse world. Human capital, and the quality of relationships between people, and between people and organisations, will be more important than ever in predicting organisational success. We must, therefore, continue to build and strengthen the field of OD and maintain its core values while seeking innovative solutions to resolve the new sets of challenges facing organisations.

Leaders as Commissioners of OD

And HR can best deliver effective OD through line managers; these are the primary practitioners of OD. Leaders hold the custodian role of safeguarding and improving organisational health and performance. HR leaders need to work closely with senior leaders, turning them into commissioners of OD who are able to diagnose and understand their impact and role in improving organisational health: who appreciate that an organisation is a human system, not just a technical system. HR needs to ensure that leadership capabilities are transformational, not just transactional. Leaders need to be able to interpret the data on the horizon, form effective strategies to manage the environment, ensure that the vision, mission and culture of the organisation are aligned and inspire people to come along with them. Misalignment could mean pressure to fulfil business objectives in ways which could lead people to compromise their own or the organisation's ethical standards. In other words, leaders need to ensure that the organisation's internal capability matches with the strategic ambition.

Executive Concerns

Encouragingly, MLab's management innovation agenda (LabNotes 9, 2009) suggests that some executives recognise the need to build new work cultures which seek to bring out the best in people. These forward-thinking executives have identified goals to create for more participative and honest work cultures, together with their suggested OD solutions (my italics):

- Create more space for emergent strategies *by relying more on variety/experimentation and less on analysis/focus for strategy.*
- Dramatically diminish the influence of (formal) hierarchy *by eliminating silos and collapsing the distance between the centre and periphery; decoupling power and position.*
- De-politicise decision-making by surfacing conflict, *by allowing minority views to be heard and exploiting the wisdom of the crowd in critical decisions.*
- Enable communities of passion *by rebalancing the use of extrinsic/intrinsic rewards and motivations for those at work, using social networking technologies and other means to create work environments that enable employees to innovate beyond the boundaries of their job.*
- Humanise (the language of) business by *using words like love, beauty, honour, truth and justice to engage with humankind's loftiest ideals.*

When executives are identifying the issues and looking for solutions, HR leaders should be integral to the process of finding and implementing these.

Leadership Practice

Countless surveys indicate that leadership is perhaps the key factor affecting employee engagement and performance. Leaders and the practice of leadership are a particular focus for HR leaders since culture and leadership are closely associated. For Sarros et al. (2002, p.7) 'it is likely that the way a leader provides leadership for an organisation will affect behaviour, values and style of the organisation (its culture) and these factors in turn will affect the attitudes towards the organisation (the job outcomes) of those who work at every level within it.' A cynical culture results when employees perceive mismatches between what leaders espouse and how they actually behave.

Ulrich and Smallwood (2007b) suggest carrying out a leadership audit to assess whether leaders deliver value to key stakeholders in terms of the following deliverable:

- Employees: competence and commitment;
- Line managers: strategy implementation;
- Customers: service, customer share; and
- Investors: financial returns, intangibles.

Of course, employee cynicism is likely to be all the greater if HR leaders themselves behave hypocritically or are self-deluded or power crazy. Such approaches can destroy employee engagement and undermine the fabric of common purpose and trust. Employees and managers really then have no one who can genuinely be their advocate. HR leaders therefore must model the values the organisation embraces. For Boltz Chapman (2006), this is about *service* over self-interest. It's authentic, nurturing, mentoring and selfless.

DESIGNING CUSTOMER-FOCUSED ORGANISATIONS

HR leaders build customer-focused organisations working back from what is needed to provide customer-intensive service. And as previously stated, HR has both internal customers (i.e. executives, managers and employees) and external customers (those buying the organisation's services and products). Building customer-focused structures involves taking the needs of the key customer groups into account in the organisation design. Linder and Brooks (2004) suggest that high-performing organisations (HPOs) have flexible and decentralised structures to empower internal customers, i.e. employees, and stimulate innovation. They redesign processes and new technology to stimulate new ways of working. Anne Minto argues that building a customer-focused organisation is about listening to your customers and finding out what they need and want, then designing a product to meet the customers' need – not over-designing the product.

Clemmer (2001) argues that HPOs have this intense customer and market focus, with internal systems, structures and processes facilitating this. The organisation is designed in such a way to allow daily contact with customers by frontline staff and line managers:

- They are designed for teamwork, having both operational and improvement teams;
- They are highly autonomous and decentralised, with teams able to adapt the way they work to better serve their customer;
- They have support systems that are designed to enable employees to meet the needs and demands of the customer, rather than being designed for management and bureaucratic purposes;
- There is partnering and working across boundaries, learning and collaboration with other teams. Focused professionals with specific skills can be drawn on throughout the organisation. There is a flatter organisational structure and fewer people whose only contribution is 'leading, directing and developing'; and
- They tend to have a single point of contact for customers, which would enable a rapport to be built with the customer.

And such organisations balance the needs of internal and external customers. Leaders of the 'people dimension' are expected to be creators of value across the organisation. For Geoff Armstrong, the people dimension centres on:

- The 'willing contributor' i.e. creating and enabling discretionary effort, knowing you put the boundaries around that, where the organisation needs to overlay that with compliance;
- Skills development;
- Knowledge sharing;
- Effective teams; and

The big challenge is how to craft an organisation where people feel motivated, respected and expected to deliver - and turn that into a sustainable organisational strength rooted in shared values and practices at all levels – and coincide with optimum collective effort as an organisation.

Blanchard (2007) advocates the importance of developing organisations which are people-oriented, customer-centred and performance-driven. He highlights flexibility, nimbleness and responsiveness as key features that will enable HPOs to succeed in the future. He uses the acronym SCORES to represent the six characteristics of HPOs:

- **S**hared information and open communication;
- **C**ompelling vision;
- **O**ngoing learning;
- **R**elentless focus on customer results;
- **E**nergising systems and structures; and
- **S**hared power and high involvement – 'participation, collaboration and team work as a way of life'.

In my own research into high performance (Holbeche, 2005) I found similar characteristics. High performance organisations build trust and ensure that decisions made are aligned with the organisation's goals and values. Employees know how they fit with the organisation's vision and personal values are aligned with organisational values. Such organisations facilitate the building and sharing of knowledge and focus relentlessly on delivering high standards of quality and service to customers. Systems and structures are designed to allow rapid response to external challenges and opportunities. HR leaders need courage, vision and clarity to work on this agenda. They have to demonstrate from business evidence that what they do works in practice, makes a difference and is sustainable – something which can be replenished and built on, making people management the source of competitive advantage. And they have to keep on re-winning this particular battle.

Leaders can start by focusing on the needs of the people who work for them and move on to the communities in which they operate. As we saw in Chapter 5, what employees need may vary according to their age and other aspects of diversity. For instance, Deloitte's (2006b) study of manufacturing firms found that what Generation Y valued most included:

- Sense of purpose and meaning in work;
- Long-term career development and multiple experiences within a single organisation;
- Availability of and access to mentors across the company;
- Work/life flexibility;
- Tech-savvy work environment; and
- Open social networks that embrace open and honest communication.

And although these needs are primarily focused on the aspirations of Generation Y, older generations of workers also appreciate them, although they may not always have articulated them, or expected them to be met by their employer.

Spotlight on: Jon Sparkes, CEO of Scope

Jon Sparkes joined Scope as HR Director from his previous role as HRD at Cambridgeshire County Council. Within a short while, Jon was appointed CEO, at a challenging time in Scope's history. As CEO, part of his job is about fixing an organisation that was struggling. This brief case study outlines how Jon has gone about putting Scope on a firm financial footing, improving Scope's ability to campaign successfully and provide better services to service users.

About Scope

Scope is a charity working on behalf of disabled people. It provides education and support to 20,000 service users (telephone/internet/email) of whom 1500 are supported by 24-hour care. Scope runs five schools, a Further Education college, 40 adult residential facilities, and 15–20 domiciliary/day services. There are 3500 staff, 8000 volunteers and 270 shops. Scope has a turnover of £100 million.

In addition to providing these core services, Jon describes Scope's role as follows. 'We campaign on a local and national basis. We ran a survey which suggested that 85% of UK think disabled people are treated as second class citizens. We want to campaign to bring an end to that situation. We lobby about regulations. It's about being fair to people.'

Scope has significant campaign objectives. 'We measure the number of people who support our campaign by giving us money, or writing to their MP. Our vision and target is one million people supporting us (currently we've reached 500,000). We provide reports to the Board Trustees (Volunteers who are a subset of members and appointed by members who pay a subscription).'

Jon has also focused on improving governance, by slimming down what was a very large board structure, much of which had been in place for a long period, and introducing processes to raise the calibre and quality of board contributions: 'We are trying to appoint trustees based on their skills and experience versus popular support.' As in other member or volunteer-driven organisations, bringing about

Continued

Spotlight on: Jon Sparkes, CEO of Scope—cont'd

such a change was not without its difficulty, but the changes at the top made possible faster and better decision-making and other improvements.

5 year plan 2007–2012

1. Recovery
   Jon inherited some big problems when he became CEO. In 2005–2006 Scope made an operating loss of £9m. As Jon suggests, this was an unsustainable position: 'Huge losses, services failing inspections, lack of investment in buildings, which were crumbling (these were people's homes!); fund raising was static (at best) and in decline in real terms. We have free reserves of £10m but the organisation's finances were in terminal decline. Over 15 years profits from shops had declined until they are loss-making. This was commercially not viable. As an employer too we were failing. We did not meet Investors in People (IIP) criteria. Sickness absence averaged at 16 days per person per annum. We have tried "quick fixes" i.e. cost-cutting £4m in 6 months back in 2006, living within our means, as well as longer-term investments. We are restoring the business, putting in place better people practices.

   In 2006 only 16% had appraisals; now (2009) 100% have. To sustain our recovery we have been working on regulation and finance, in particular costing, pricing for services, investing in decent information technology (IT), going for IIP. We have put in place a platform of good practice, carried out a complete review of governance. We have a clear view of the culture of the organisation we want to develop. We have gathered a wide range of views about what we feel we want to be like to be sustainable. For me that's an organisation which is financially sound and where people enjoy and are fulfilled by their work.'

2. Aspiration
   Going back to the vision of one million people supporting us to change the perception of 85% of UK population that disabled people are treated like second class citizens, we've been asking ourselves – what would success look like? Our vision is about transforming the service.
   a) Empowering disabled people to have control and choice in their lives versus others feeling sorry for them.
   b) Being exemplars of how you deliver empowerment services. We had a special school in Cornwall which was not viable and it closed in 2004. We took the skill-base of the school and unleashed it externally, supporting disabled kids at home or at day school, providing all the support needed to help kids to lead normal lives. We provide baby-sitting, speech training and language therapy, etc. All of these have been funded by the state. We're now providing for twice as many children (120) and their parents as when we ran the school ourselves. The service will break even in the near future. We have an headquarters (HQ) office which has a training room in Saltash, Plymouth. Most of the staff work from home – they are nurses, therapists, carers. Our motto is 'we're here to empower young disabled children and make the service pay for itself.'

Spotlight on: Jon Sparkes, CEO of Scope—cont'd

As HRD, Jon was very much involved in the consultations about the closure. In 2004 he did a road-show, holding a meeting with staff in Cornwall over the school closure, and another in Cardiff where an adult service was closing down.

Jon has also focused on recruitment as a strategic activity. He recruited the Education Director – an innovator who created the Cornwall service. Jon believes in allowing innovators to do what they are good at, based on the track record of the individual. He recalls his learning from the Generics Group – that a technically brilliant person who knows how to make a business work does not always do what you want them to do. Business leaders need to be technically brilliant and business competent – they need balancing with good systems.

As CEO he is very much involved in fund-raising, as well as improving margins from existing sources of income, such as shops, and driving down overheads. Another part of his role is about inspiring and motivating people with his belief: 'I can do that'. Jon sees his role as selling the vision – about having a go at changing the entire landscape. Externally, Jon deals with politicians, runs policy campaigns, is a spokesperson in the media and drives marketing campaigns. He has spoken at all three party conferences. Stakeholders include government ministers, and leaders of other disability charities and Disabled People's Organisations.

And does Scope's internal capability match the strategic ambition? Internally, Jon runs the Executive Management Board and a Strategy Group, which includes Directors' direct reports and 'special guests'. He sees his task as being about 'unleashing what we've got and acting as steer and guide'. Jon feels fortunate to have been in the organisation for 18 months as HRD before he became CEO. He had been involved in appointing all the top team (from outside) with the previous CEO. The new top team have mixed sector, political, commercial and functional backgrounds. All have proven themselves and all want to make a difference.

Jon recognises that these appointments signalled that promotion possibilities from within were limited. Now he has succession plans in place for the tier below his direct reports. He believes the next CEO could be any one of them.

Postscript

And since this short case study was written, Jon has agreed to take up the position of Director of Workforce Development for NHS Cornwall and Isles of Scilly with effect from the beginning of January 2010. Jon led Scope through a period of significant financial turnaround over his three years as CEO and drove forward the development of Scope's long-term strategy which provides a clear vision and purpose for the future. Under his leadership, Scope moved from a substantial deficit position to a small surplus in the last financial year, at the same time as seeing considerable improvements to the quality of Scope's services and their ongoing modernisation and transformation. In addition to this considerable achievement and many others, Jon was instrumental in securing a £5.9 million investment (a loan of £5.3 million and grant of £600,000) from the government fund Future-builders. This will be used to develop and diversify Scope's services for disabled children and young people.

TACKLING THE 'SHADOW SIDE'

HR leaders need to reconcile dilemmas around:

- How to build and maintain corporate reputation – what will need to stay the same and what will need to be challenged and to change?
- How to learn from the past and anticipate tomorrow?
- How to build leadership and management fit for today's and tomorrow's challenges?
- How to build a climate where employees are right to trust management and each other?

By their nature all organisations are political. They are beset by conflict, anxiety, favouritism and protectionism. Yet healthy organisations operate across boundaries, build relationships and trust and collaborate even while competing. The 'shadow side' of organisations gets in the way of their effective functioning. HR leaders must be prepared to challenge and fight to put right what goes wrong. As Anne Minto points out, such behaviour can be profoundly counter-productive: 'I just cannot stand duplicity. Incompetence I can almost cope with, but duplicity, I really can't stand that in business. When I worked as a commercial negotiator if you had duplicitous people, it was very difficult to strike deals or feel that these people had a measure of constancy about them. Having strong business ethics is important in the workplace'. In particular, HR leaders must ensure that the organisation and its leaders 'walk' the 'talk'. This authenticity must extend to the implementation of policies in diversity and equality.

Corporate Reputation

Successful organisations can become complacent and blind to poor practice, so HR leaders need to be good at spotting when things need challenging and be prepared to stick their heads above the parapet. They need to be bold – and create the environment for their team to challenge. One HR leader who has done just that and fought to establish a positive employer reputation for his company in the face of negative press coverage is David Fairhurst.

> **Spotlight on: David Fairhurst, Senior Vice-President People, at McDonalds**
>
> One of the greatest challenges to business success is when an organisation's brands become tarnished – and that is what was at risk for McDonald's a few years ago. This is a people-intensive business, with staff serving two million customers per day. As David Fairhurst says: 'People are at the heart of the business – at McDonald's it's our people that make the difference between a good customer experience and the kind of customer experience that makes somebody's day. Our business model is a simple People-Profit chain, so if we don't get the people piece right, the whole model breaks down.'

Spotlight on: David Fairhurst, Senior Vice-President People, at McDonalds—cont'd

Fast food establishments typically employ relatively young people – generally between school-leaving age and late twenties – and tend to have high levels of staff turnover. Retention for almost all such businesses is, therefore, a vital business driver since the cost of recruitment and training can be very high. As David says, 'My role is to create an environment which enables our people to do the job which needs to be done. This applies as much to my role in heading up the People team (HR) as it does to the role the People team has in supporting front-line restaurant staff.'

David joined McDonald's from Tesco and he found 'an organisation with a heritage of over 30 years of great HR practice in the UK. As a result, the business had an enormous amount of evidence which proves that McDonald's is a progressive employer offering jobs which give people workplace skills which will last them a lifetime. And if people want to develop their career with us, the opportunities we can give them are outstanding too.'

But that is not what was reported by the press. A sustained campaign began over the infamous 'McJob' which sought to vilify McDonald's practices as an employer – in particular the lack of opportunity for employees to develop or have a meaningful work experience. The press campaign started to be very damaging, both in terms of making recruitment more difficult because young people were starting to be embarrassed about saying they were thinking of working for McDonald's, and for the brand itself.

David decided to do something about this and he went on the counter-offensive. He decided to get together some evidence which would lay the 'McJob' myth to rest and asked Professor Adrian Furnham of the London School of Economics to carry out some research amongst a random sample of staff, and their personal stakeholders, i.e. parents, former schoolteachers, etc. The research proved that employees found working for McDonald's both enjoyable and fulfilling. In particular, they valued their opportunities for training and career progression – many of them had become restaurant managers. Their parents and schoolteachers also commented on how much the employees were benefiting from being employed by McDonald's, including the way in which the training and discipline of work were improving the social skills and overall motivation of the young people.

Armed with this data, David went on the offensive and formed a team to focus on establishing a correct reputation for McDonald's as an employer. The Reputation team includes people from HR, training, corporate affairs, and internal communications as well as external PR and communication consultants. Without exception, they all say they've learned an enormous amount from each other. And while the press generally prefer a bad news story, the reputation team has applied ethical approaches to influence and shape opinion proactively and positively, rather than waiting to be the victims of fate or vicious slander.

Continuing to dispel the negative and inaccurate myths surrounding what it's like working for McDonald's and the wider service sector is an ongoing challenge and the work continues, but the team's efforts are being crowned by success when it comes to recruiting and retaining staff. As David says, 'Over the past 3 years, therefore, our approach to tackling the perception gap has been to simply take this

Continued

Spotlight on: David Fairhurst, Senior Vice-President People, at McDonalds—cont'd

evidence to a wider audience and, having seen that evidence, they make up their own minds about the jobs we offer.'

Tackling the McJob myth and seeing growing pride and confidence of employees is one of David's proudest achievements. The best part for David is 'when we've helped someone achieve something that's meaningful to them. We encourage our people to send us their "iStories" ... stories which capture how working for McDonald's has made a difference to them. For some it's as simple as time off at short notice to see their favourite band or flexibility around a student assignment. For others, however, we have been able to make a profound difference to their lives and their futures, and that is immensely rewarding.'

In particular, David has focused on making sure that the employer brand is real in its delivery of the promise of development. McDonald's is helping employees develop the skills that will equip them for success now and in the future. David's main regret is in not seeing quickly enough the potential opportunities the Internet would provide for McDonald's. Initially he saw the Internet as simply a communication channel. It was only when Facebook and MySpace took off that David saw it as a *community* – a place of support and encouragement and a place to share ideas and co-create. This led to OurLounge (our staff social networking site) – the first of its kind, but David thinks they could have got there a year, maybe 18 months earlier '... the implication is that we might have missed the opportunity to change hundreds more lives by giving them important Basic Skills.'

However, David's other successes have already changed many lives and his work continues at a national scale. In his own words: 'Over 3000 of our staff are currently studying for Maths and English qualifications via OurLounge.co.uk at the moment. That's over 3000 people whose lives will be positively changed as a result of working for McDonald's – and we're only 18-months into our Basic Skills programme. The scale of things at Coats, D means that our People initiatives can have an enormous impact and that is immensely satisfying.'

One topic which is affecting many organisations at senior levels is the contested and sensitive issue of executive compensation – in particular Director bonuses.

EXECUTIVE COMPENSATION

Top-level reward and performance is a key responsibility of HR leaders. The challenge around executive remuneration has arisen in the wake of the banking crisis and subsequent inquiries into City bonuses. This is a moral issue, and is being treated as such, rather than purely a pragmatic market issue. HR leaders have choices about how they address the market forces argument for paying people huge bonuses 'many HRDs may have just gone with the fad. They've paid huge bonuses to keep up with the competition and lost sight of "felt fairness" within the organisation. As a result they can be blown off course by one decision taken in isolation and then the repercussions are terrible. Some of the banks which are now tarnished are companies which we used to laud for their people practices.

There is a real need for a stronger sense of fairness within organisations and broader society. We have moved a long way from the days when an organisation's highest earner earned ten times as much as the lowest earner -in the US four hundred times is a more common ratio. Even though G20 governments have failed to act in a concerted way to curb executive bonuses, with the banking crisis we have perhaps crossed the rubicon and it is to be hoped that the days when traders would happily pay £10,000 on a bottle of wine with lunch are over. With respect to addressing the executive compensation issues of today, as Geoff Armstrong points out, there are previous lessons we could draw on: 'Of course in the UK we have been through this before. In the motor industry in the 1970s and 80s we found that escalating pay did not work, with the toolmaker at the top of the pay chain and production makers who were envious beneath them. We also found that simply paying everyone the same does not work either – it simply ratchets up the costs and is unfair. The same is true of both society and organisations. The concept of fairness is crucial: being capable of being understood and measured. A brave HRL will tackle this.'

Geoff argues that we must learn the lessons from this banking crisis and transform HR leadership by doing so – 'we did not think through what we were doing in the context of the long-term or the bigger picture. HR's role is joining the dots – making the big picture clear, showing how actions result in impact.' Members of an HR leader network also advise: 'never be paid too much you can't afford to leave'. The table stakes can be high and act as tests of personal integrity.

The huge bonus culture has been characterised by executive excess and lavish hospitality. Executives have treated the company chequebook as always open. The nature of targets which triggered bonuses before the crisis was often so short-term that people would be paid before the targets were delivered. This creates a cynical organisation – one which writes about one set of values but practices another. HR leaders must question how value is created within the organisation itself – it is not just the rainmaker at the top who makes the profit; success relies on contribution from the whole organisation. If employees are asked to change continuously while others behave differently and are rewarded disproportionately. HR has a lead role in expressing the problem openly, then scrutinising and reconciling how behaviour matches up to what is wanted.

Geoff Armstrong urges HR to challenge assumptions about reward: 'Everyone assumed that there was just the one lever in the talent war – money – but this is only one of the features which cause people want to work effectively for you or not. HR fell into the trap of thinking that money was the main thing. They'd say, "You have to pay what you have to pay", but it's proved counter-productive, especially when the behaviour that has been encouraged by such payments causes the business to go broke. HR leaders need to ask themselves if there are other things that make working for an organisation more motivating than just money.' Geoff urges HR leaders to create and lead the debate about over how long a time period should targets be measured - to ensure that profits made are sustainable.

HR and reward professionals need to figure out how to pay for real success – what does a good reward look like?

This has led to a new relationship for Head of HR with the Board's compensation committee. One question that this raises is where a Board gets guidance from on matters of corporate pay, etc. Does it have to rely on its own externally appointed consultants or the internal HR function? HR needs to be doing this analysis and bringing this information to the Board as a strategic partner to the Board, not just the CEO. This 'business focused HR' (Ephor Group, 2008) involves working with the Board to confirm regulatory compliance of compensation and stock programmes.

Top-level reward and performance is a key responsibility of HR and leading thinking on this requires HR to segment both the work and the workforce across the company and to treat people differently according to business needs, individual preference and performance (Wharton on HR, 2007). This allows differences to be defined and valued but the key principles of equity and transparency must be the guiding light.

MAINTAINING TRUST – STAYING TRUE TO THE EMPLOYER BRAND

HR executives can play an important role in helping their companies address the very real challenges that they face today and to prepare them for when the recovery eventually comes. My own research suggests that many employees, regardless of age, consider that an organisation which is desirable to work for is one where people:

- Have a degree of job security and can progress in their career;
- Feel involved;
- Feel equipped to do their job;
- Are appropriately rewarded;
- Can balance work and home life;
- Can learn and develop;
- Are ethically led;
- Are supported and coached through periods of change; and
- Can work flexibly to suit their lifestyles.

Right now the focus should be on relevant and actionable policies. There should be regular workload reviews to avoid people being 'burned out', adequate resources and support systems must be put in place and there should be a sustained commitment to building career tracks and work/life balance policies, even if these require some innovative thinking. The focus should be on engaging employees by remaining true to the employer brand.

Of course, the real test of authentic values is what happens when times are tough, and in today's challenging environment, how are employers remaining true to their employer branding promise? Are they maintaining their focus and determination to live their values, to build their talent base and improve the quality of management and leadership, or will short-term expediency push these out of the frame?

On the whole the CIPD Employee Outlook survey (2009) reveals some encouraging and serious attempts by employers to keep employees both in jobs and engaged. Practices that seem to matter most to help survey respondents through the downturn include:

- Development
  Continuing to actively manage talent will be important, providing development opportunities, including training and upskilling on the job floor, rather than sending people on external training courses. These will help make people more employable within the organisation in preparation for the recovery. It will be essential that organisations in a 'strategic holding pattern' find ways of stretching and motivating key talent, preferably in ways that prepare the organisation for the upturn. This may involve giving employees short-term project goals and team goals linked to potential longer-term improvements and opportunities.

- Management development
  As one senior HRD describes, it is vital that managers have the skills they need to manage people through turbulent times. Yet as he points out, this is difficult to achieve: 'It's very difficult to do consistent and structured management development training when you're in so much turbulence, there just isn't the time or the focus, there's too much change going on. It's different when you're growing, I mean growth and change, fine you can structure stuff in there and get it all going in the right direction, but when you're in this turbulent stage you're likely to end up with a neglected cadre of managers. We are laying off our more experienced people, and we're bringing through some of the new people in order to change the business model. But some of those people are profoundly inexperienced and profoundly poorly trained actually. And they have lots of bright ideas, they may have lots to offer, but actually managing is another challenge and HR has to help with that process. And HR leaders have a very, very important task in that by getting alongside line business leaders and getting them to consider these people implications of their decisions. It is not always easy; some leaders get it very well but relatively few; some can talk to it quite well, but actual practice is different.'

- Improving communication
  Many respondents reported that they do not feel there is enough communication, that there is a lack of direction from the top, and that the absence of communication is adding to their feelings of uncertainty and anxiety. Leaders need to be honest with managers about the current economic climate and encourage managers to have open discussions with employees about its effect on the business. Frequent and honest communication will be vital for building the resilience needed to help organisations through the downturn.

- Providing employee assistance
  Many employers' initiatives relate to providing meaningful support for staff and managers to help them deal with issues arising from the recession. It not only shows employees that they are valued, even if their own job may be at risk, but also can help 'survivor' employees remain productively focused on their work. Providing employee assistance to help people cope with the impact of the recession is important, whether or not employees are directly affected by redundancies.

Example: Major Supermarket Chain

One major supermarket chain is thriving in the current circumstances, and its budget lines are doing particularly well. Employees, as a whole, are in little danger of losing their own jobs. However, HR is aware that many employees are anxious about the possibility that their friends and family may be at risk of losing theirs. The company has provided a range of paper-based and online tools to help employees and those they care for obtain the advice they need for everything from financial matters to applying for jobs.

- Adapting engagement programmes to reflect the current climate

---

Example: Simplyhealth

In uncertain times like these, it might be all too easy to forget about employee engagement; after all, some might argue, people are just happy to have a job. One company which remains very focused on engagement is the group of healthcare businesses known as Simplyhealth whose business aim is to make more people feel better.

Mark Day, Executive Director, HR and PMI of Simplyhealth believes that now it is more important than ever for organisations to keep their people engaged. Leaders need to establish the key areas they need to focus on to maintain engagement, which may be different now from before the recession. Day proposes that the only way to do this is to remain close to staff and ask what really matters to them.

Example: Simplyhealth—cont'd

He believes that engagement is not a static process, but that engagement programmes need to be adapted as employees need change.

Leaders need to be seen to lead and employees must feel they are part of a wider, united group, facing the downturn together. Day believes communication and open dialogue are keys to engaging his staff at Simplyhealth. Empathy is a key ingredient and he recognises that employees will be facing the effects of the recession in their personal lives. In reaction to the current situation, Simplyhealth's engagement programme has been refocused on the health and financial well-being of employees. This low-cost but innovative initiative shows staff that their employers empathise with their current pressures and should build a committed workforce.

Based on Day (2009).

- Taking a leadership stance

By this, I mean employers remaining true to their values and (having the courage to do this) in the face of many short-term challenges to save costs.

Example: John Lewis Partnership

John Lewis Partnership or its supermarket chain Waitrose usually come at or near the top of 'favourite retailer' categories of customer polls. The Partnership's 'spirit' is based on four principles:

- Ensuring that the happiness of partners is at the centre of everything we do;
- Building a sustainable business through profit and growth;
- Serving our customers to the very best of our ability; and
- Caring about our communities and our environment.

At a time when other organisations are freezing bonuses and pay rises as a result of current conditions, the John Lewis Partnership remains true to its partnership principles, paying 70,000 staff their annual bonus in 2009, despite the challenging trading conditions. Staff members ('partners') were delighted to receive the news, despite the bonus pot having decreased by a third, from £180 million in 2007 to £125.5 million in 2008, due to the effects of the recession on profits which are reported to have fallen by 26% in 2008 to £279.6 million. As they collectively own John Lewis Partnership, all staff will receive the same percentage annual bonus which is reported to be 13% this year, but will be equivalent to just under seven weeks' pay for Waitrose and John Lewis department store employees.

Employees have been rewarded for their hard work and the bonus they receive is based on the profit-sharing philosophy of John Lewis. By being true to their principles, John Lewis Partnership is likely to maintain employee trust.

Based on source: Wood and Wearden (2009).

- Senior managers' role modelling/sharing the pain

Example: The BBC

The BBC have stopped paying bonuses and frozen the pay of around 400 of its senior managers. The decision will remain in effect until at least July 2010 when it will be reviewed. The rest of the 24,000 strong workforce will undergo a 'modest' pay review.

This action is part of the BBC's aim to step up its cost cutting as a result of the downturn. Traditionally, senior managers could have received up to 10% of their salary as a bonus. These measures will save the BBC 20 million pounds and it is hoped they will stave off redundancies.

Based on source: Holmwood (2009).

CONCLUSION

So the current economic crisis raises more questions than it answers. In a very real sense we may be moving into a new era, one in which governments, business and institutions are more closely scrutinised and held to account. And there are no easy answers to questions such as the following:

- Are there bigger shifts in society and what people expect of politics, institutions and organisations?
  - Will organisations have a wider group of stakeholders than shareholders alone?
  - Will leaders have to be more value-led than just market-led?
  - How will greater transparency in business and organisational life be achieved going forward, including how people are rewarded?
- When the recession ends, what will differentiate those organisations able to return to growth mode faster and more successfully than others?
  - Will the shape and operation of business be different from before? Will business models be more flexible? Will organisations need to collaborate more both within and beyond their own boundaries?
  - Will new models of leadership and management be needed?
  - Will the way organisations have dealt with their employees during the crisis determine the nature and effectiveness of their recovery?
  - Will employees want and expect different things from their employer?
  - Will organisations have a wider group of stakeholders than shareholders alone?

The question 'How best can HR contribute to providing answers to some of these questions'? does deserve an answer. HR can contribute to building sustainably healthy organisations by ensuring better corporate governance and risk management – taking on a proactive stewardship role, practising humanistic values – and working to build accountability, trust, truth and transparency into every aspect of organisation. HR must work to create customer-focused organisations using all the tools and levers at their disposal to stimulate employee engagement with customer purpose. Employees need a fair deal, opportunities to participate and authentic leadership if they are to remain engaged. Building the structures, systems and policies which support diversity, employee well-being and flexibility is only part of the process. The other part is ensuring that people have the tools to do their jobs, including the right communications and management support. In a very real sense, HR must be willing to act as both employee advocate and organisational advocate, and manage the dynamic tension between the two.

HR will have to work with stakeholders to define what good leadership looks like now, at the top and at other levels too. In particular, HR needs to tackle the 'shadow side', challenge poor practice and develop the quality of leadership, building future leaders and succession plans which look beyond 'the usual suspects'. Fairness must be the watchword and new approaches to executive compensation must be found – not simply using market-driven criteria; more effort and imagination will be needed to find ways to reward people for real and sustainable results, not just fantasy performance.

All of these activities represent choices for HR leaders – it is perfectly possible, after all, to focus on compliance and risk management in a 'tick-box' way. But if that is all an HR Senior does, in my view they are not leaders, no matter how senior they may be. To lead this dynamic agenda for the organisation requires, an HR leader who has courage, a strong personal values base and the willingness to challenge and the ability influence with integrity. They need to be driven by a desire to create healthy and sustainable organisations in which people can do 'good work'.

And with its powerful and influential heritage, solid core and evolving applications and approaches, OD will continue to play a vital role in today's competitive, turbulent and constantly changing world. And as Professor David Cooperrider (1998) states, OD's focus on building healthy organisations contributes to society as a whole: *'The best path to the good society is the construction of great organisations that nurture and magnify the best in human beings.'*

Chapter 9

Developing HR Leader Capabilities

'The troubling gulf between the needs of the business and the ability of HR to respond will force many companies to rethink their approach to the recruitment, training and development of HR employees.'

Lawson et al. (2005)

The HR leaders featured in this book have by and large come through an HR career route, though many started in other functions or business areas. In some cases they are reaching the end of their personal career, having reached the heights of the profession. Others are midway through their career journey. And for all of them, the development process continues – even those on the verge of retirement plan to continue their personal development journey.

In this chapter, we consider what capabilities are required by HR leaders and how these can be developed. We also look at how our HR leaders have developed themselves and their teams – and continue to do so.

But first, we need to consider how the HR leader role may well develop in the future in order to deduce what might be the most relevant forms of capability and how these might be developed.

HR'S CHANGING ROLES

Dave Ulrich's thinking about HR roles has largely led the rapid evolution of thinking about the HR role. In the mid-1990s, Dave identified the need for the Employee Champion role. By the mid-2000s, this role had become that of Employee Advocate (EA) and Human Capital developer (HC). This reflects the fact that employees are increasingly critical to the success of organisations. EA focuses on today's employee; HC developer focuses on how employees prepare for the future. In both cases there is an acknowledgement that employee well-being and chances for development are central to employee engagement and performance.

By the mid-2000s, Ulrich's (1990) 'Administrative Expert' had become the 'Functional Expert', since HR practices are central to HR value. Some HR practices are delivered through administrative efficiency (such as technology), and others through policies, and interventions, expanding the 'Functional Expert' role.

The 1990's 'Change Agent' role later became the 'Strategic Partner'. This role has multiple dimensions: business expert, change agent, knowledge manager and consultant. Being a Change Agent represents only part of the 'Strategic Partner' role. The overall focus of original 1990's 'Strategic Partner' role remained the same, although many organisations implementing the 'Ulrich model' recognised that there were clear distinctions between 'business partners' (BPs) who were essentially internal consultants to line managers and commissioners of services, and Strategic Business Partners (SBPs), who work with executives on major strategic initiatives such as mergers and acquisitions. However, as Dave Ulrich himself points out, business partnering as a relationship approach applies to all the HR roles, not only that of Strategic Business Partner.

It was in the mid-2000s that Dave Ulrich really emphasised the importance of the role of HR leader for the first time. The sum of the first four roles equals leadership, but being an HR leader also has specific implications for leading the HR function, collaborating with other functions, ensuring corporate governance and monitoring the HR community. In addition to looking at HR roles, Ulrich and his colleagues have also periodically carried out exhaustive studies of the competencies required for strategic HR (2008). They found that the top four human resource competencies - credible activist, culture and change steward, talent manager/organizational designer, and strategy architect - account for more than 75 percent of the success of a human resource professional.

And the Next Step?

Given its rapid evolution, the HR profession seems poised to transform itself still further and HR leaders themselves have many views on what this transformation might look like. Over the last year or two there have been many debates, surveys and network meetings between HR Directors to discuss where HR is heading and what the HR profession's future looks like. Though not everyone agrees, there appears to be a growing consensus amongst senior HR professionals that the HR function may be splitting into two parts – the 'people bit' and the 'strategic group'. Jon Sparkes, for instance, considers there will always be two HR professions.

1. *Generic* – payroll, dealing with line managers' queries, employee benefits, training administration and procurement. These transactional tasks can be done at the end of a phone. In the future you will get 'back-office' people morphing into one – if a computer breaks down, or you don't understand a spreadsheet, have staff off sick, you want to book a conference room – you have to phone different people. In future you'll have 'helpline/hotline' professionals.
2. *People who can sit at the top table* – at the shoulder of the Chief Executive Officer (CEO) and Senior Executives and help them run the business. They

might not be anywhere else. The value they add is in knowing the whole thing – not doing it. For instance, a Chief Technology Officer is responsible for keeping the top team sharp on technology. At Scope there was for a time a Disability Commissioner on the top team who keeps the team sharp on what disabled people want. HR professionals should be similar.

For Jon, BPs are in between the two categories, neither one thing nor another. There will come a point where line managers manage people and the need for the business partner role disappears. Other HR Directors argue that most HR practitioners (80%) are doing operations and that the 'top end' of the profession is much smaller. They suggest that HR will always be a contact sport – and cannot be separated out into 'people who do' versus 'people who think'.

And it is not only HR roles which are changing but the nature, access to and value placed upon HR knowledge. HR specialist's functional knowledge used to be regarded as the main differentiator between HR professionals and other people managers. Now, everything can be done by someone else. With outsourcing and increased commoditisation of knowledge, people can get HR information and advice online. Over recent years much of what HR has focused on was previously the responsibility of line managers. As the tide flows back towards line managers taking on responsibility for basic human resource management HR needs to reskill line managers for these responsibilities, without driving too quickly to a structural solution. Moreover, since about half the HR professionals surveyed by the CIPD described their role as 'specialist', this raises the question, 'what is relevant HR knowledge'?

The CIPD has consulted with practitioners and academics to create a professional 'map' which details the knowledge, skills and behaviours required by HR professionals over the next few years. This map will be the basis of new HR professional standards and qualifications and will help clarify routes into CIPD membership for non-specialists or for senior practitioners who have amassed relevant knowledge and experience.

The 'Zone of Inconvenient Truth'

What HR Directors do agree on is that the limiting factor for the next stage of development of HR is the capability of HR professionals to carry out the new emerging roles. As Lawson et al. (2005) report: 'The (Ulrich) model is fine, but what it fails to mention is that a critical success factor is people.' The role of the HR generalist appears at a crossroads. There is a general shortage of good candidates for business partner roles. HR needs employees with cross-functional, service-focused skills in order to become a true partner of the business. However, it must provide higher-quality services at a lower cost. As Lawson comments, 'An effort to accomplish these complementary roles with the same individuals, within the same career structures, and with the same HR leaders, is almost bound to fail.' Ulrich and Brockbank (2008) agree: 'As with all support functions, it is undoubtedly the case that some HR professionals may never become business partners. They are mired in the past administrative roles where conceptually or practically they cannot connect their work to business results'.

The general argument is that for the more strategic and leadership roles, the calibre of potential candidates is not impressive and that there are insufficient high-potential candidates who are being attracted into the profession. And while there is no shortage of people wanting to get into HR, as Anne Minto says, 'It's the quality issue. Recently we found it challenging to fill a senior HR role for a large part of our business. We had to search for some considerable time before we met someone who met our capability standards. We have been very demanding with our search consultants and our internal recruitment team as well who were certainly not always getting people from the first round of search'. Anne's view is that it is important to hold out to get the right person: 'We'd rather do without for 3 months and cover it whichever way we can to keep on searching. Usually that strategy has paid off.'

Moreover, there is tremendous variability at senior levels of HR, and no common agreed standard about what 'good' looks like for an HR leader. David Fairhurst, for instance, says that one of the worst aspects of his job is: 'The sinking feeling you get when you meet lacklustre HR people who damage the reputation of HR by complaining that the profession is not being taken seriously enough. Conversely, the best is spotting a rising star and watching them soar!'

Attracting and Recruiting High-Calibre Candidates

So ironically, the profession which is charged with leading on talent management itself has problems in attracting high-calibre individuals capable of delivering 'next generation HR' effectively. This gives the profession as a whole the challenge of repositioning itself to be able to recruit people who might not have previously considered a career in HR as a compelling proposition. Again, there is a circular character both to this issue and its solution. The more that graduates see HR leaders being influential, and adding something unique, exciting and relevant, the more likely it is that they will want to have an HR career. Unless HR leaders are leading in such ways, they are unlikely to attract in the people they need to move the function forward.

IDENTIFYING HIGH-POTENTIAL HR

Given that the various HR roles are still in a process of evolution, defining what 'high potential' looks like in a business partner can be difficult – but many HR Directors say 'you know it when you see it'. Anne Minto describes what she would look for when recruiting a high-calibre HR business partner: 'I would be looking for somebody with fantastic employee engagement skills, somebody who is able to create good people agendas that meet the needs of the business units they are working in and somebody who is prepared to network across the divisions. I look for people who have demonstrable intellect and financial capability to work in our business. We have an extremely complex upstream, midstream and downstream business.'

For Anne, when it comes to applying that potential in the job, it's not just enough to excel in your own area: 'I want you to be taking leadership of a particular project or an issue that is important to Centrica, demonstrating that you can pull that together right across the businesses and are clearly respected by the management team you are part of.' Moreover, she would expect successful BPs to gain their understanding of Centrica's business by getting exposure from working from different parts of the business.'

Sourcing Candidates

Where to find high-calibre potential HR candidates? Opinion differs, and increasingly potential HR leaders come from many backgrounds. Many are bright management trainees who enjoy their experience of working in HR for a short period and return to the function later after experiencing other business roles. Some HR professionals consider a background and qualification in HR essential to future HR leaders. They build links with institutions offering HR qualifications to provide a key source of potential business partner candidates. For instance, Infosys has partnered with 60 universities running its own Business Partner outsourcing module. This has allowed the company to build its skills agenda flexibly around future demands.

Others look more widely, aiming to pull in capable candidates by developing an appealing employer brand. Again the Infosys operation in Bangalore, India has tried to understand what existing staff consider to be the main differentiators in its employment proposition. They found that seemingly small factors – such as the quality of the canteen, being able to trade off various benefits for pay – made all the difference. They are then able to make use of this insight when appealing to potential recruits. Another company which knows that flexibility appeals to graduates has been very successful in attracting potential recruits by playing up the project-based nature of its work.

Continuing Professional Development

Lack of a high-calibre field of potential recruits is part of the reason for Centrica having created its own career development scheme which it runs with the CIPD and the Institute of Employment Studies. Anne is keen that her team retain their professional level of competency in relevant areas, because things are changing all the time: 'We run a whole series of hot topics internally which people can sign up for and many are run by the Principals within those speciality areas. It might be the head of policy running something, or the head of reward or the head of pensions. Of course there is so much for people to learn and keep up with, and if you don't keep up with your professional development, before very long you are not such a good employee any more.'

How Will HR Careers Develop – Specialist or Generalist?

There is a growing debate about whether HR leaders need to be deep functional experts to be effective HR leaders. Many HR Directors argue that this is not necessary, as long as they know what kinds of expertise are required for different situations and how to access and use that expertise. What matters is that HR leaders have a sensible, pragmatic approach, especially about managing people. Geoff Armstrong contends: 'The HR function should be led by people who understand the people dimension fully – you can learn to do "people".' As Jonathan Evans points out, 'If you're not spending 90% of your time dealing with queries, you can learn the rest. If you have a lifetime in organisations managing and leading people then HR is not that hard.'

Other HRDs do not agree. They take the view that you need a specialist level of skill before you can meaningfully contribute as a generalist. Wayne Cascio (2005) suggests that these skills should include a firm grasp of functional areas within HR: legal requirements, recruitment, staffing, training and development, performance management, compensation and benefits, labour and employee relations and occupational safety and health. CIPD's own research into the current shape of the HR profession found that about 50% of respondents described themselves as specialists.

This depth of understanding in one or two disciplines is what some describe as a 'professional' approach over that of a general line manager who is 'helicoptered in' to HR as part of their career development. Alex Wilson of BT, for instance, argues that board level HR leaders need a good understanding of organisational development. In particular, there appears to be a dearth of skills in industrial/employee relations, which are very likely to be in demand again in the next few years. Jackie Orme argues that while HR leader capabilities are not distinctive to HR leaders alone, anyone aspiring to be a leader of the people dimension needs well-developed 'hip pocket' HR skills and knowledge, and an understanding of how to deal with HR issues.

IS THERE A NEW SKILL SET FOR HR LEADERS?

However, breadth must be maintained as well as depth. To have impact, future leaders need to develop a broader range of business and leadership skills – from the outset of their careers. And they will also need a business partnering mindset to equip them for their leadership role.

Business First, Function Second

What is clear is that specialist knowledge must be allied to commercial nous and be applied to real business issues. Geoff Armstrong argues that leaders of the people dimension are business leaders first and functional specialists second. They are expected to be creators of value across the organisation. They need to understand and be motivated by the commercial realities. They have to demonstrate from business evidence that what they do works in practice, makes a difference and is sustainable – something which can be replenished and built on, making people management the source of competitive advantage.

Cascio (2005) argues that HR leaders need the skills of a Strategic Business Partner, i.e. the ability to:

- Create an HR strategy that aligns people, processes and systems;
- Assess talent during the due diligence phase of a proposed merger or acquisition; and
- Ensure that ethical standards are practised.

But HR leaders must also be able to create an overall talent or people mindset: 'The emerging role for HR requires professionals to understand and identify the key drivers of individual, team and organisational success that are consistent, or aligned with the strategy of an organisation.' These drivers become the basis for human capital metrics that are connected to the strategy of the company and can be used to assess work unit or organisational performance. The challenge is to link metrics to the behaviour of customers and important financial outcomes for the business and to build a coherent management system around the whole business.

Cascio (2005) argues that the basic capabilities of SBPs must include deeply understanding your organisation's business model – how it competes for business in the product or services markets it operates in, understanding the constraints that managers face, as well as the needs of external and internal customers.

David Fairhurst agrees that when recruiting potential BPs he looks for HR professionals who see HR in context, i.e. they put business issues first and HR technicalities second. Then David looks for individuals who 'don't work in isolation... who see themselves as a part of the wider business and not in a silo.' Other business leaders commenting on the capabilities of peers whom they consider to be HR leaders describe them as follows: 'his influence drives the culture'; 'He operates as a business leader' and 'She's about leveraging resource, motivating'.

Business insight can be gained in many ways – through taking an MBA or other business qualification, developing their strategic thinking by working on major business challenges and projects, exposure to different functions, operations, businesses, sectors – or simply through experience, curiosity and practice. David Smith of Asda, for instance, believes that exposure to many different contexts is important and himself regrets not having moved around more earlier in his career. Gaining this insight involves mastering basic business literacy: corporate finance, marketing, accounting, information technology and general management. It's about getting into the field and working with the managers and employees responsible for operations, and by serving on a management team with other executives to gain maximum experience.

As Liane Hornsey points out, understanding a very complex business like Google's can be hard but you've just got to do it: 'You learn through reading; you learn because you're at the board, so you and through board meetings; and through reading board papers; you're always invited to all the business planning meetings because "people" is the one thing that transcends every area of every business. So you go to every business plan review, just like the finance guy – you are the other most senior guy. And you listen and you ask questions and you watch and you learn. I think it's pretty damn tough, but if you can't understand the business then you can't really make any sensible decisions or suggestions.'

Speaking the Language of Business

But insight without action does not count for anything. HR professionals sometimes fail to be influential because they insist on speaking in HR jargon which results in their being seen as irrelevant to business, or they act as if they see line managers as the problem, rather than part of the solution to issues the businesses are facing. Geoff Armstrong reminds us that the vast majority of people come to work to do a good job and points out that often it is management action that turns them into toxic assets. But he argues: 'We can't accept line manager recalcitrance as an excuse: most line managers are very pragmatic, and if HR leaders can demonstrate value, they will snatch it from us willingly.

We need to be able to say:

Here's where we are in business performance.

Here's what our competitors are achieving in share price and productivity.

If we're going to overtake them we need a different approach:

- Here are the practices we'll use.
- Here's how we'll measure progress.
- Here's what we'll do.

Business first, functional specialist second. HR leaders need business orientation, to be courageous and bold. HR leaders need to articulate a set of measures the business can relate to, not just functional ones. Their thinking needs to take the organisation to different places than others could.'

Capability Builders

HR leaders need to be good capability builders – of individuals, teams and the organisation. They need to understand capability, how things need to change and provide insight into how the organisation needs to develop. They also need a strong change leadership background. In particular they need a perspective on how sustainable high performance can be built – which capabilities will need to be developed and how.

They need to pay attention to their own and their team's development. For Anne Minto, the measure of success of a good HR Director is their ability to create a diverse team that can bring the skills to the business as in her view there is no HR Director who will have every single skill you require around the HR table.

HR leaders need a strong people orientation and to be interpersonally effective using their emotional intelligence and listening skills to get underneath the issues to understand the drivers for individuals. Martin Ferber sometimes tells people that in HR you have to be a bit nosey and inquisitive. You need to probe into things and be aware of what's going on around an organisation and around the people in the organisation at all levels, including the executive you support and the management team. You often need to be the ears and the eyes of the organisation.'

HR leaders need to be willing, able and confident enough to build effective leadership, especially at the top of organisations. They therefore need the courage to raise difficult issues with senior executives based on what they have learned by listening. And as Martin Ferber points out: 'You need to be loyal and dedicated but be prepared that tomorrow you may not be needed!'

COMPETENCIES

Ulrich suggests that HR needs key competencies, to which I have added HR leader characteristics in italics as follows:
Business Knowledge
Personal Credibility

- Achieving results
- Effective relationships, *especially with decision-makers*
- Personal communication

Strategic Contribution

- *Future-focus and able to balance the long- and short-term*
- *Strategic progenitor*
- *Strategic insight and influence*
- Culture management *and change management capability*

- *Leadership*
- Fast change
- Strategic decision-making
- Market-driven connectivity

HR Delivery

- People (*also using their diagnostic ability*)
- Performance *with customer-intensive focus*
- Information
- Work

HR Technology

- *Using data to create insight and effective action*
- *Seamless transformation*
- *Upskilling the line*
- *Analytics – using data for the purposes of workforce (talent) planning, employee segmentation and understanding the drivers of employee engagement*

KNOWLEDGE

HR's knowledge base is rapidly moving on. Much of the information an HR leader needs can be gleaned through the general business press and specialist HR, management and economics journals. CIPD's professional map outlines in detail the professional *knowledge* which HR professionals need to access if they are to deliver an 'expert HR' contribution. HR leaders must keep their working knowledge of HR related developments, for instance in employment legislation, up to date. And HR leaders need some level of knowledge about:

- What is coming round the corner – *scenario planning, business, economic, political and environmental trends, strategic modelling, demographics, workplace trends*
- Insight into how thinking is developing about for instance (leadership, target employee segment expectations and reward practice)
- How to draw conclusions based on evidence – *insights into data modelling processes, including how these are used in workforce planning, tracking possible causal links with respect to employee engagement, value chain modelling and employee segmentation techniques*
- Knowledge of processes which produce change and how these can be used – *organisational design and development, behavioural processes, internal communications and ergonomics*
- Techniques learned from other functions – *branding, segmentation, effective use of social media and customer engagement techniques*

BEHAVIOURS

CIPD's research with HR professionals and line managers suggests that behaviours and the way technical knowledge is used are more important than the technical knowledge itself. These behaviours cluster into three areas: setting the agenda, doing it the right way and making it happen.

Setting the agenda is about being curious to learn and understand, being a powerful thinker, confident to challenge and a wise decision-maker.

Doing it the right way is about being personally credible, a trusted partner, relationship manager and a skilled influencer.

Making it happen is about being driven to deliver, a collaborative team player, a clear communicator and change agent.

DEVELOPING CAPABILITIES FOR HR ROLES

Many HR leaders have developed their capabilities by a combination of experience, taking on challenging projects, executive education and a professional qualification, such as CIPD. As Liane Hornsey suggests, the best approach to prepare for an HR leader role is to do good internal consultancy job as a business person. One example of an HR leader who moved into an HR role part way through her career is Philippa Hird.

Spotlight on: Philippa Hird, Formerly HR Director at ITV

Now a Non-Executive Director and Writer, during the period 1990–96 Philippa Hird was in general middle management at Granada TV and was taking on more responsibility. Two significant influences helped shape her career direction at this time. Stephanie Monk was then HR Director of Granada Group Plc which was the parent company. She demonstrated what assertive HR could be like. Philippa was impressed by Stephanie who became something of a role model. Monk joined the main board and helped to professionalise the organisation.

Philippa also worked closely with, and was heavily influenced by Granada Television's CEO Charles Allen who encouraged change. Philippa learned a lot and fast and grew in confidence. Prior to this, the company had been relatively unsophisticated in organisational terms. There was a split between the general management cadre and the unions and between the unions representing the cameramen and the 'creatives', such as producers.

Following the ITV franchise renewal process at the beginning of the 1990s, the company changed a lot. Gerry Robinson became the CEO of Granada Plc and, in the Television Division, regulatory change paved the way for dramatic structural and corporate change to create a more flexible and competitive business. Granada Television, supported by its parent Company, chose to be in the vanguard of this change and so a decade of fierce consolidation battles took place.

The first of these was the closely fought Granada take-over of London Weekend Television (LWT). By the time this was concluded, Philippa had met her husband

---

Continued

Spotlight on: Philippa Hird, Formerly HR Director at ITV—cont'd

and wanted to move to be in London to be with him. The back office of both organisations was pulled together and, having seen the role Stephanie Monk had shaped for HR during the merger, Philippa formally moved into HR in order to provide HR services for Granada. She felt it important to be qualified in professional HR, given her management background and was awarded CIPD membership on the basis of accreditation of prior learning. In common with many people who take on HR roles following general management careers, qualification was Philippa's way of 'stopping thinking that there's a bunch of stuff that you don't know'.

Philippa started to clarify the kind of HR service she wanted to supply. Her personal interest was not in administration, and Philippa was clear that she wanted HR to be in the business, delivering for the business for HR to be influential, relevant, respected, powerful and in fluential. As she sees it, 'there's no point being there unless you matter and make useful things happen'. Her own philosophy has guided her through the ups and downs of business life: 'You've got to have an incredibly clear moral compass. "Do as you would be done by" is in fact quite a tough message for many HR teams and is much less sentimental than it sounds'.

Consolidation

Meanwhile, acquisition continued and before long Yorkshire TV and the Television Division of United News and Media were acquired and the merger with Carlton took place. Philippa acted as HR Director in each acquisition or merger and became increasingly clear about how to successfully integrate businesses.

Between each acquisition, Philippa restructured HR. She introduced a shared service for administration, called 'HR Direct', based in Manchester. She introduced three streams – administration, BPs and specialists – which operated between United and Carlton.

Philippa insists on one 'golden rule': 'The client never sees the join', i.e. that only one answer should be given rather than confusing the client with contradictory messages. This means that the combined HR teams need to be very aligned about what they think and it is the need for alignment which drives communication in HR. For Philippa, clear communication is the absolute rule: 'if you're clear about the headlines, they get on with it'. Philippa comes down hard on people if they break this rule.

About Business Partnering

Philippa is a resolute supporter of centrally managed HR and sees this as absolutely consistent with business clients feeling that they have their own team. It is essentially a professional service model. The HR partnership team consists of four people, including two who are operationally focused and two specialists. The central core team is very customer-focused and responsive. It is best practice professional services model rather than acting simply as a service function. BPs come mainly from the line and Philippa hires on the basis that these are people who can not only do the job but also become role models.

> **Spotlight on: Philippa Hird, Formerly HR Director at ITV**—cont'd
>
> Philippa does not believe in HR doing the line managers' role for them. She recognises that there can be a dangerous symbiosis – line managers who sabotage efforts to help themselves and HR professionals who like being needed. Philippa's approach is to coach line managers – once or twice, but not three times. Good HR is never threatened by effectively making their roles redundant because line managers are fully capable. For the best Leaders, the issue of who they hire to do what will always be their most difficult issue to resolve, and so they will always make great use of good HR.

HOW DO OUR CONTRIBUTORS DEVELOP THEMSELVES?

One characteristic shared by all our HR leaders is their ongoing quest for development. Some of the many routes they are taking to develop themselves are as follows.

Taking on Challenges

- *Public and/or non-executive roles*
  Angela O'Connor's hunger for development led to her being elected the President of the Public Sector People Managers' Association – the PPMA. Anne Minto has been involved in the governance of other organisations through roles such as being a non-executive director at Northumbrian Water Group, a non-executive director of SITA UK, chairing the Institute of Employment Studies, and the Engineering Development Trust, and has been on the National Employers Liaison Committee for the Reserve Forces.

- *Challenging roles*
  For instance, at several points in her career Angela O'Connor has taken stock of what she wanted to do next in her life and this has led her to changing career direction, often taking on significant and very challenging roles.

Keeping up to Date

- *Reading*
  Most HR leaders appear to read prolifically. Martin Ferber reads and the Economist, both of which he considers very important, and often shares good articles, he comes across and finds useful sending them in PDF form to someone. As he says, 'I do read the FT because I think as an HR director you're obliged to be aware of business at that kind of level.' He particularly looks for refreshing views on HR, such as those of the journalist Lucy Kelloway. Martin also comments on generational preferences with

respect to how people like to keep up to date, in particular, the preference for younger people to keep up to date with immediate events via the Web and Google in particular.

- *External speaking*
  David Smith gets on speaker circuits and is often involved in question and answer sessions. Graham White has also been on some of the European speaking circuits, so he gets to go to a number of conferences and meets what he describes as 'some fantastic people doing some amazing things'.

Peer Networks

Martin Ferber prefers to keep up to date by engaging with the professional body, the CIPD, and getting out to meetings. David Smith tries to stay in touch as much as possible with a network of best companies in the UK and Europe. Graham White invests quite a bit of time in networking. He goes to a number of HR technology sessions, networks with the CIPD and with some HR fraternals, such as a Surrey local government group. Graham thinks that you can never network enough in all those circles as this is a great way to get access to some interesting new thinking: 'What I do is I listen to what others do, I put it together in my mind and apply it.'

Anne Minto occasionally meets with a small network of peers over dinner, which is not only socially pleasant but helpful in other ways: 'These dinners afford us the opportunity to discuss sensitive issues in strict confidence, exchange views on the latest people policies, legislation and best practice'. The group has provided job opportunities through its network. Anne approached three of her colleagues with respect to one of her team whose project role had come to an end. She couldn't offer the person another job because she didn't have another project so, as she says, "I particularly wanted to help this person get another job. I wrote to three of my colleagues and all of them came back to me expressing interest in the individual. The individual was interviewed by all three and has now successfully gone to join one of those companies. This was a fantastic result". Members of the network knew that Anne would not be writing to them about a person who was not a quality person, so this was a win-win situation. As Anne comments, a network like this can be very useful because it can be lonely in a top level HRD role. "We know that we can discuss issues in complete confidence and we know that it is not going to go anywhere else".

Some HR leaders are using every means at their disposal to both develop themselves and put that development to good use. David Fairhurst, for instance, gets involved in all of the following.

- Speaking at and attending conferences (especially Harrogate)
- Chairman – Centre for Professional Personnel Practice, Manchester Metro-politan University (MMU)

- Vice-Chairman – People 1st
- Honorary Fellow Lancaster Business School
- Fellow Sunningdale Institute
- Columnist with HR Magazine (800 words on a different topic every month is a great discipline)
- Networking. David believes in proactive rather than reactive networking ... 'I was advised many years ago to have "Loyalty to my Rolodex". It taught me that there is more to networking than mass-emailing your contacts inviting them to join your LinkedIn network!'

All of these leaders make the time and space to pursue their organisations' interests and their personal development needs at the same time.

DEVELOPING HR TEAMS

Most of the leaders featured in this book have gradually built the 'dream team', but this has involved making changes on the way.

Team Composition

When David Smith first started at ASDA, most of the HR department were pure HR professionals, and almost exclusively female. There's now a better mix of people who have worked in the line and people who have worked in both retail and non-retail. He sought to hire people with new ideas, from other sectors and other parts of the economy. So it's a much more eclectic group of people than ever it was in those days and as David says: 'it's a very experimental culture. Retail likes to have a go and try things and I think that's very healthy in terms of building a new way of working.' The Bank of America (BofA) has assembled an HR team that includes managers with degrees in business, HR, psychology and engineering. According the HR Director: 'our team looks very similar to any other high-level team in BofA so when HR sits around a table with other departments we don't talk HR we talk business.'

One early lesson for Anne Minto was the importance of having a mixture of people on your team who have worked in line management as well as people who have committed their lives to the function: "I did change the team a bit, but I have done it perhaps more gradually rather than going in and changing everybody out because I do not believe that's right. I think you have got to have a period of time in which you evaluate the capability that you have in a new team that you take responsibility for. What I did find was that the team was a bit dysfunctional and pretty desperate for leadership and direction. She lost some good people through acquisitions and changed a few people out. There's only one person left doing the same job. As Anne recalls, "The biggest challenge was ensuring that the team could deliver against the business agenda – that was the bottom line against which our peers would judge us".

Development

All the HR leaders place a great emphasis on developing their teams. Many are keen to celebrate the skills and successes of their team members and are clearly pleased with what their teams have achieved.

- *Sharing practice and ideas*
  Anne Minto for instance, gives credit to members of her team for their significant achievements which are shared at team meetings. Anne also describes the two internal HR conferences held each year – in June and November. 'We bring around 70 of our top HR people together and that's a pretty action packed, fun-filled day. We have a 2- slot at each of these conferences where we display the best practice cameos from around the group, so people compete for a slot and we always have more people who want to display their project than we have space or time for. Our Chief Executive is a regular attendee and other members of the top team make presentations or take part in panel discussions'.Those are some of the most popular parts of the conference.

- *Career pathways*
  Anne focuses on upgrading and up-skilling the whole function, not just future HR leaders. She has put team members on to executive leadership develop-ment courses as well as business skills courses. Anne also encourages her team to accept opportunities to speak at external conferences or attend external networking seminars. At Centrica they have done a lot of work in delivering career pathways within HR and defining the learning they want their people to go through and setting the milestones for the capabilities and competencies that they want their HR staff to have. Business acumen and financial awareness play heavily on the skills agenda for all the function.
  During his time as HR Director of Microsoft UK, Dave Gartenberg clarified the roles of BPs, who were embedded in the business, and SBPs who were off-line tackling major projects and strategic change. Dave encouraged the SBPs to act as mentors to some of the high-potential BPs, gradually exposing them to some of the corporate-level activity as a means of helping business partner career development.

- *Coaching*
  Martin Ferber considers coaching and developing his team to be a very important part of his role: 'I remember when one of my HRDs went into a new job, it really was a big step up for them and they needed a lot of coaching and help to make it in that job. They were faced with a new MD, new relationships had to be built and it was quite a testing time for them in terms of developing that relationship.' Indeed, Martin believes that it was his job as functional head to ensure that this person could succeed. Martin has helped various members of his team get non-executive

director's jobs which are very good for developing their broader awareness. Martin encouraged a line manager to become director on a Health Board. So these are all things people can do to develop their skills both within the work environment and outside. Such opportunities give people the chance to see how other organisations operate and they can bring a lot as well in these roles.

Liane Hornsey spends at least 20% of her time coaching her team, listening, just letting people blow off steam and helping them sort out organisational issues: 'We're growing so fast that there are lots of questions for me all the time about organisational structure, organisational design, talent. I probably spend another 20% of my time working on the learning and development agenda: how do we develop people, how do we make sure that we keep learning as an organisation, how do we make sure that some very, very capable people in this organisation get the opportunity to learn and grow?'

- *Development planning*
  While Graham White was HR Director at Surrey, he operated a model whereby staff members throughout the organisation enhanced their development by 'stepping up'. The same was true for HR, for while Graham represented HR at the very highest level, he often put his second tier people into all the major activities to expose them to broader business issues.

  He has a personal development plan for each member of his team and holds reviews with each person four times a year. As well as personal development plans there are HR team plans detailing what the whole HR team needs to develop, looking at issues such as their visibility in the organisation, how they are operating, how they move around in their functions and so on. Graham consciously tries moving people around as well. He thinks the danger with HR people who have stayed in local government all their lives is that they may follow a very narrow path; for example, just working in pay and reward and although they will become experts they will never actually be capable of leading the totality of the HR function.

- *Changing responsibilities*
  Liane Hornsey believes it is important for her to do to people what someone always did to her, which is to put her in roles where she had things to learn. Consequently, she has broadened the remit of some of her team's roles. She thinks that bright, high-potential people just want to keep learning and contributing and knowing that what they do really contributes to the business goals.

  When Liane arrived at Google there were four or five people working for her – on the recruiting side, in people operations and HR itself. Staffing was separate from HR – which is the Californian model – and the staffing team was run out of Mountain View in the US. Out of the four or five people who worked for her, three really shone over time and they have become the staffing managers at Google EMEA. Liane has developed them by giving them real clarity of goals, because previously they didn't know what they were supposed to be doing, or what they were being measured on. They've been given the responsibility to build their own teams and promoted in terms of breadth of their job. One of them has taken on internal resourcing, another has taken on a whole pan – EMEA role, where previously he just had a Swiss role, and the third has taken on programme management.

- *Creating room for action*
  When Angela O'Connor started at the Crown Prosecution Service (CPS) she found the HR service delivery to be poor: *'They were wonderful people, hard working, but many were gifted amateurs – they did not know they were anything to do with HR. I had an early conversation with my boss and I said, "let me help turn HR into a professional community. They will need to study and work at building their professional skills. If that's not for them, we'll give them help to get something elsewhere".* 'I was grateful for the support of colleagues in HR in creating a team approach to excellence'.

  However, HR's internal clients were highly articulate and damaging in their criticism of HR. Lawyers for instance, were polite to Angela's face but would criticise the HR unit behind her back. Angela needed to build her team's confidence to deal with the issues and the people. She told her own management team, *'Trust me. You're going to feel very uncomfortable but what we're going to do will work.'*

Angela used a public occasion – a big conference – to get the clients to vent their spleen openly so that the issues could be brought into the open and worked on. Her team facilitated table discussions and anonymised feedback was collated and shown on screen. Even the highly critical head of the Department of Public Prosecutions (DPP) was staggered by the level of criticism: *'I can't believe someone could say that.'* Angela's team response was non-defensive. Instead, HR gave their own version of why they were criticised: *'we said we'd do this, but we didn't.'* The room went quiet.

Then collectively the twelve most important things that HR needed to work on were identified and measures of success and performance indicators agreed in response to the prompt: 'What does good look like?' Angela was prepared to stake her job on achieving what was needed, saying 'We'll deliver in 12 months or I'll resign'. In the bar that evening there was a lot of chat, friendly this time, with people asking 'are you mad?' Afterwards, no-one challenged what HR was doing but instead let them get on with the key activities required 12 months later no resignation was required.

NEXT GENERATION HR CAREER DEVELOPMENT

Most of today's executives have come up through the ranks in-house. They have acquired their skills through a mixture of training on the job, specialising in HR disciplines or demonstrating mastery across disciplines. However, with in-house HR departments increasingly consisting of specialists or small numbers of HRBPs – this conventional career path is likely to disappear. Similarly, with many of the disciplines outsourced to specialist firms, the entry point for HR careers will be increasingly with vendors or consulting firms, creating more specialists than generalists in the future. So what will next generation HR careers look like and how can they be developed?

Jackie Orme argues that the path to HR leadership starts early. In the early stages of their career, professionals should aim to achieve breadth, through the variety of activities they are involved in and the organisations and sectors they work in. They need to be hungry for learning and keen to get on. It does not matter if they start in shared services, or reward, or aspects of resourcing. They need strong, finely honed capabilities and will all become generalists in due course. They need to be willing to take calculated risks.

While the 'ideal' career development path does not exist, some contexts may be more useful from a career development standpoint than others. If HR professionals have what it takes they can use every experience to develop their thinking and practice.

Spotlight on: Victoria Bird

Victoria Bird was recognised by Personnel Today as a 'young HR Professional to watch' a few years ago. This was at a time when Victoria had moved from Time Warner to Electronic Arts (EA) in order to gain international experience (Europe, South Africa and the USA) and become part of the technology / dot com boom. Her achievements in both roles brought her to the attention of head-hunters and the HR press but Victoria had some unfulfilled ambitions which she was keen to pursue. One of these was running a yacht in the Caribbean, in order to do this Victoria completed a vigorous 6 month training to become an Ocean Yacht master (a commercially endorsed skipper with celestial navigation skills!) and also took PADI scuba diving and Cordon Bleu chef courses to enhance her skills.

She and one other ran a 50ft Catamaran called 'Top Secret' and provided all inclusive sailing / water sports holidays for mainly American guests in the British Virgin Islands.

After returning to the UK Victoria went through a challenging time personally which resulted in a bout of glandular fever. Victoria believes that looking back she learnt from this episode in her life and that it helped her develop a deeper empathy for others.

After some interim work Victoria joined Whitbread PLC and her experience expanded as she became involved in restructuring, outsourcing, acquisitions and the selling of the pub restaurants and David Lloyd Leisure businesses. It was at

---

Continued

> **Spotlight on: Victoria Bird**—cont'd
>
> Whitbread that she also gained further international experience and was Interim HR Director for the start up of Costa Coffee in Shanghai, a joint venture with a local Chinese Partner
>
> After an Executive role working for TSL Education (publishers of the Times Educational Supplement and Times Higher) as HR Director Victoria has decided that she wanted to take some time out to develop her mind further - she is just about to start a Masters in Social Anthropology at the School of Oriental and African Studies (SOAS) at the University of London and has taken part in an intensive meditation retreat to help sharpen her focus. Whatever Victoria does in her next role, she will bring added depth of insight to her contribution, having stepped off the career ladder to gain breadth of experience and take the opportunity to reflect. Whatever Victoria does in her next role, she will bring added depth of insight to her contribution having stepped off the career ladder to gain breadth of experience and take the opportunity to reflect.

Learn by Doing

Developing careers can be a matter of luck, but more often the old cliché about 'luck' = 'preparation meeting opportunity' comes true. However, I believe that there are some very practical things which HR practitioners can do to develop themselves for future leadership roles. If you want to really excel as an HR professional you need to learn from on-the-job experience in a planned and structured way:

1. *Use influence in an appropriate way*
    Develop your influencing skills by deliberately working to understand the needs of different stakeholders, and influence them to recognise when they need to change their behaviours themselves.

2. *Continuously review priorities*
    With ever-growing workloads and fast deadlines, being able to prioritise well is essential in delivering to the needs of the business, particularly as individual remits get wider and more demanding. *Especially during a period of fast change it is vital to be constantly reviewing and prioritising the urgency and timing of tasks throughout the day to ensure deadlines are hit and the needs of the business met.*

3. *Gain line management experience*
    Working at the 'sharp end' gives people better insight: '*You must understand the business model and the financial and marketing side, and it's difficult to do that as an HR staffer. 'You come across with a lot more credibility if you are in touch with the business, how it functions and operates, and after you have had some line manager experience.' Anne Minto also thinks that it's important, developmentally, for people to have worked somewhere outside*

of HR in their career; not necessarily for a long time but Anne argues that having experience of running a different function gives you a different dimension on life, because you've been there in the role of a front line manager. It gives you more empathy with line managers.'

4. *Keep things in balance Life in HR requires resilience*
   You have to be clear about what you want to achieve. You have to be resilient and not be diverted. Also, you have to be prepared to take on the big issues that others may not be comfortable with.

5. *Develop your emotional intelligence*
   When conflict or a sensitive situation arises, managers should listen and be more of a coach, not a counsellor. Learn too how to give feedback in a way that people can receive it.

6. *Spend time in a customer-facing role*
   Spending time to work outside HR helps you not only to see HR from a customer perspective and how HR can really tick a customer off, but also how HR can really add value.

7. *Make friends with the financial director (FD)*
   The FD sees the business in terms of cost, of course, but if you can get him or her to understand social cost and understand people benefit not in a financial sense, but in an overall business health sense, then you have the basis of a real partnership.

8. *Take the initiative*
   Be proactive – don't always wait to be given tasks by your manager – think what needs to be done and do it before being asked.

   And HR leaders agree that HR leadership is more a mindset and orientation than a specific set of skills. First and foremost HR leaders are business enablers. Mike Campbell, People Director at easyJet (with its orange logo) offers the following pointers to help would-be HR leaders achieve success:

Instead of Being a Business 'Preventer' You Need to be an Enabler

- You have to understand the business – you can't have impact without that. You have to understand:
  - The key business drivers.
  - The motivations of people you are partnering – they expect you to understand what matters within the business and how to manage risk.
  - Be able to work alongside them, including leaders – you need to be able to say, 'if you want that outcome, this is the best way to get there'.
  - You need to be numerate, business-aware, have commercial acumen.

- Be bold, don't compromise on quality.
- You've got to have good judgement and be able to take macro- and micro-issues quickly – take 10 decisions and expect that at least 8 are right. Your judgement should show that you:
  - Understand what the business is trying to achieve.
  - Align with the value set.
  - In easyJet everyone knows what needs to be achieved and their part in it. Over the first few years we aligned the business around five key areas of focus and three simple outputs/measures: 15% growth; 15% return on equity; £5 profit per seat – and safety is our first priority: no compromises.

Be Tough on Building HR Quality

- We're 'turning Europe orange'. We need talent magnets to attract high-quality people to work for them. While there is huge value for specialists in any aspect of HR, you really need to be generalist and able to learn enough about the specialisms that you know when to call in a specialist.
- As a leader of an HR team you face a big challenge. While you will have a view that the best thing is to develop people, sometimes people can't make the transition in the time frame or at all, so don't be seduced by the challenge to develop everybody. You have to take the right decision quickly.

Leadership involves taking decisions, not only about HR issues

- Take advice, make recommendations and stand by your judgement. Sometimes they'll expect you to take the lead. For instance, we've been debating whether we should continue with part of our business – we've learnt that we need to be bolder.
- It's important that you and your team have access to all the tools you need such as assessment and psychometric methods, employment law across Europe, etc., but you don't burden the line with too much of these – think of them as *features* (e.g. features of a PC could include a 200 Gb hard drive, Intel centrino chip, flash memory, etc. But really the benefits are how quickly it works, how well it runs the software and can I store all my documents and/or play my games and get fast broadband links).
- *Sell them the benefits*. It's like providing them with a car – they don't need to know the details under the bonnet; you don't need to educate people about the sophisticated HR techniques – just that they deliver the benefits.

CONCLUSION

As organisations compete to attract and retain the best employees and strive to develop high performance capability, so the need for effective leaders of the people dimension grows. Attracting high-calibre individuals to HR roles can be a key challenge, but as Liane Hornsey says of Google, 'you've got to offer the employee a proposition that is sufficiently different to make the great employee, the high-potential people, really want to associate with that company.'

HR leaders must deliberately develop themselves and their teams in order to keep at the forefront of their field. The skills, competencies and knowledge required to be an HR leader are burgeoning as the scope of the role rapidly expands. But potential HR leaders should not be put off by that. As Graham White suggests, you could bring an individual off the street and turn them into a superb HR person very quickly if they have the right competencies. For Graham these are about engaging with people and having good interpersonal skills. He argues that in reality there is nothing HR does that you can't read in a book. If you have the capability and the desire to engage with staff and to value that contribution then anyone could be a good HR person.

The HR agenda is a fast-moving one and requires HR leaders to have a strategic mindset and skill set. To become an HR leader, you must have the vision and the drive to deliver the strategic agenda. You must be a business person first and a functional leader second. There can be few roles more exciting and worthwhile than one that marries the individual and the organisation, today's and tomorrow's agenda, that requires deep insight and effective, innovative delivery, in other words, one that builds sustainable performance through people.

Chapter 10

The Future of HR?

"Has HR been taken by surprise by changing demographics, and a growing need for accurate employee data and does HR have the strategic capability to tackle business leaders' priorities? How business leaders approach the challenge – and how HR responds – will determine who takes the lead on managing People Strategy and HR Operations to address tomorrow's most significant people priorities."

Aijala et al. (2007)

It will be clear from the content of this book that I believe the HR profession to be potentially the most exciting, worthwhile and value-adding business function since its 'raw material' is people. Yet, many managers respond to the very notion of HR leadership as if it is a contradiction in terms. How can HR lead, some might ask – it is a service function after all? And how can HR provide organisational leadership if it does not have its own functional house in order?

I would argue that strong HR leaders lead the function and more beside. Like David Fairhurst, I see HR as a key driver of business and not only as a technical function anymore. Cascio (2005) sums up the future role of HR as follows: 'In a nutshell, this encompasses three broad areas: to ensure compliance, to gain commitment and to build capability.' But in many organisations the perceived value of HR hangs in the balance. Partly, this reflects the way an HR leader approaches the functional leadership task and therefore how HR operates. So does HR act as the function that turns compliance into a rule book, or an art form? Does it focus on doing the basics or on getting them delivered well? Does HR blame line managers for the problems in organisations or develop line managers? In other words, HR's own approach will determine whether HR is perceived to be part of the problem or part of the solution.

Given that HR is integral to organisational success, not apart from it, HR leaders must define HR's role and contribution together with key stakeholders. Many HR leaders have been reorganising their function for years now in order to better drive forward the people agenda, and in some cases they have failed to deliver major improvement. If senior management are to derive the greatest benefits from HR transformation, they have to know what they want from HR. This requires the HR leader to be part of the inner circle, influencing strategy, shaping thinking, raising awareness and delivering effectively.

As Martin Tiplady suggests, many HR teams need to raise their game: 'I believe in successful HR. Properly focused, it adds value to the bottom line. Deep down, most organisations know that. The trouble is, there are not many who know exactly what they want from their HR. And in many cases, HR is the whipping boy of sloppy administration and doer of deeds not fancied by managers.

I'm fortunate to work in an organisation that does know what it wants from its HR. And mostly – though not always – I agree with it. But I certainly have a boss and am part of a board that knows what it wants. The other members welcome my views on the business, and they want me to help drive it. Their vision is mine, and vice versa.

If HR is to survive its current doldrums, we need to get a whole deal wiser to the business and start using our muscle to drive serious organisational reform.'

WILL THERE BE A FUTURE FOR HR?

From a selection of comments from our contributors, the consensus answer to this question is firmly yes – but different from the past. As Geoff Armstrong comments, 'We've still a long way to go, but I'm optimistic. In the 1970s HR was purely reactive, fire-fighting, trying to keep the show on the road, rather than making roads. When I started at British Leyland the things we were doing were ground-breaking, enabling things to happen that couldn't otherwise.

Now we're seeing a lot of HR leaders emerging who see the role in business terms – they have "nous" in behavioural sciences, sociology and business administration – they understand how people become the differentiating factor. There are more sophisticated interventions, such as organizational development (OD) and coaching which are now seen as mainstream and make a difference. But the majority of organisations are untouched by these – they're still carrying on and on. Too many people are just administrators, and the same is true in finance and marketing.

There's a divide between international organisations operating at a tough global level and a lot of public sector organisations who have not moved as fast as they need to – they need to learn. Younger people and women are adopting non-conventional thinking and practice – it's less about prerogative practice, more about the people dimension and what works sustainably.

Business first, functional specialist second. HR leaders need business orientation, to be courageous and bold. They need to articulate a set of measures the business can relate to, not just functional ones. Their thinking needs to take the organisation to different places than others' could. It does not matter what we call the Function. The key is how you turn people into the drivers of success without which we can't succeed.

David Smith agrees that businesses are going to be more about people than they've ever been because technology is widely available so it's no longer going to be a differentiator in the way it was in the previous century.

Anne Minto sees HR becoming more professionalised, very involved in the shaping as well as the execution of the business agenda and adding value to that business agenda. Anne believes that the customer base will become much more discriminating about the value that it will place on what HR delivers, and HR has a definite future if it can deliver those things to benefit the delivery from the overall employee basis and reduce bottom line costs.

As Anne suggests, 'HR has got to be smart and sharply focused. HR has to have the courage of its convictions to stand up for what it believes. It shouldn't be the moaning and whinging voice of the organisation. Whether or not you're on the board is a 1990s issue. If you are doing a good job with your voice being heard at the top of the organisation and doing your job with the remuneration committee and the nominations committee then that is where your influence lies.'

Martin Ferber thinks that HR has become more project-driven, and more expert-driven. He wonders if whole process of work hasn't become too scientific and perhaps taken the humanity out of it. Martin a believer in the Ulrich model, since it's allowed people to dissect the function quite neatly, and led people to think properly about the foundations of the function. Martin argues that HR needs to think about its own function and how it can work more closely with other functions in the support arena, – Finance, IT etc- to deliver value.

Graham White thinks that the HR profession is definitely here to stay, but is going to evolve into something else. He wants HR to drive into a new and different role in organisations. He wants HR to wake up and realise what's ahead. He's concerned that currently people are blind to a fast growing tide of change and that HR is hanging on to a belief that no one else can do the things HR does. The trouble is that HR can't do anything else. In future even more of the functionality of what HR does is going to separate out and become very much more 'self-service' and a lot of what HR has been known for doing will disappear. The operational aspect can be made slicker and more efficient, available on the desktop of the manager. At the same time HR should retain a service, develop lots more real business partners, probably with a set of skills that most HR professionals don't currently have around project management and consultancy. Consultancy houses have developed skill sets that the HR profession could definitely use, beg, borrow, or steal and bring into that leadership role.

It's up to HR to grab a new purpose!

A NEW PURPOSE FOR HR

HR's purpose is to build sustainable high performance and that this is achieved through people. Geoff Armstrong argues that the traditional differentiators – IT, customer service, etc. – are both antiquated and replicable. Looking ahead the people dimensions will be more central than ever to business success. Since HR's business is people and organisations, I believe the HR Function is in pole position to bring extraordinary value to organisations if it does its job well.

The global crisis gives HR leaders a major opportunity to make a difference to the long-term health of their organisations. This will mean dealing with the short term challenges with this in mind, for instance avoiding wiping out generations of talent through overly stringent cost-cutting programmes.

For Jackie Orme, HR must be clear that it is not there just to support the people management role, but beyond. It's about how to make organisations capable for the future. To be credible to operate in this space, HR can't only just be advocates of employees, but also of the organisation and its customers, the community and investors. At the same time we must not lose our focus on employees. As Jackie points out, 'HR is in a better shape to do that now than in the past but not everyone will make it.'

The challenge is that others can also rightly say that people and organisations are their responsibility. No debate about that. The question is what can HR leaders bring that differentially moves the people agenda forward and builds the basis of organisational sustainability?

FUNCTIONS OF HR LEADERSHIP

Returning to the functions of leadership we began with, the specific leadership focus for HR leaders makes their role very special. They are the people experts, but they must also develop the organisation to equip it for a sustainable future. They will continue to deal with the traditional challenges of managing talent, and providing infrastructure processes for performance and compliance. They will create HR organisations and processes which are effective and cost-efficient and free up HR professionals for more value adding work. Administrative work – pay and other transactional issues-will be delivered through shared services or outsourced. These will be fantastic and seamless.

Jonathan Evans believes that there will always be a need for HR – specialists in reward, OD thinking, etc. – but the HR function will be smaller and more influential. HR professionals will be more and more into the business, more business savvy, more professional and specialist. They will use their understanding of the human dimension to train line managers and give them confidence to believe in themselves as people managers. HR will go ahead and do things without needing to be asked. They will be true experts that people will listen to rather than work around.

Moreover, HR leaders will drive ever more evidence-based and insightful approaches to motivate and retain employees and customers. Their stakeholders are not only internal to the organisation – management and employees – but also external – customers, investors, communities and society at large. They will be acutely aware of the need to drive value, but not for the purposes of justifying existence, more to highlight key linkages in the process of delivering value and where these can be improved.

They must be change agents and capability builders. Since no organisation is a static entity, they must be alert to the many context drivers which will affect their organisation, pre-empt risk and help create opportunities for the business. HR leaders will understand where and how to intervene in the organisational system in order to build speed, adaptability, the ability to operate effectively across boundaries and stimulate innovation. They will hone in on leaders and managers developing them to be key culture builders who can create ethical, sustainable businesses and turning senior managers into effective commissioners of organisational development. They will drive management innovation to create forms of leadership which are fit for the future.

They will also build the capability of their team. The HR leaders featured here have all worked hard to develop their teams as individuals and as teams, often helping individuals pursue their careers in other organisations at the right time.

To sum up, how do HR leaders carry out the functions of leadership outlined at the start of the book?

1. *Providing direction*
   - Their perspective, which is future-oriented, balances the short and the long term and is intensely customer focused. This perspective is derived from their vision to build sustainable high performing organisations.
   - Their judgement is informed by their deep understanding of their business, where it is going and what it needs in terms of capability in order to succeed.
   - Their people management and organisational development strategies are aligned to, and support both the short-term and the long-term goals of the organisation.
   - They work with stakeholders to design structures and processes which bring out the potential for high performance, innovation and shared learning.
   - They use tools to identify, recruit, retain and build talent, including within HR itself.
   - They provide direction to their own teams as line managers, and also to the organisation as business leaders. They operate as business people first, functional specialists second.
   - They build their own team to be high performing professionals. They also create collaborative cultures capable of balancing risk and innovation, value and efficiency, stability and change.
   - They earn the respect of their colleagues by having the skill and confidence to contribute to the broader business agenda, not sticking within the comfort zone of the HR agenda.

- They proactively contribute to business strategy development, often acting as strategy initiator and innovator.
- They use high leverage change methodologies to involve employees in the strategy process and create ownership of the outcomes.

Spotlight Example: Mike Campbell – Aligning HR to Business Strategy in easyJet

'When I joined easyJet this was fast moving, making itself a European brand. It had a fabulous front-end Web advantage. The aim was to become a European (from British) airline within 3–4 years. It was a complex business with a simple business model. Over the last few years we have greatly improved the professionalism of the business; maintaining easyJet as a great airline and made significant strides in moving us to become a great business too. We wanted to provide a straightforward framework of how we would operate with a view to "turning Europe orange" as the world's best low fares airline.

We expressed this in measurable ways around 5 pillars of: *Safety* – Our Number 1 priority, *People* – making easyJet a great place to work, *Operations* – the world's best operator, *Customer* – low cost with care and convenience and *Investor* – a superior return. As well as stating what we wanted to achieve and what our goals were – we also talked about the *how*. A simple value statement summarises this: Safety (no compromises), Pioneering, Passionate, Teamwork and Integrity. We engaged with, and involved all of our people in this process, in relatively low key ways through surveys, focus groups, etc. and the result was actually a refreshment of what already existed – sharpening it up, professionalising it and making the picture a movie as opposed to a still image; the still photo becomes dated, the dynamic one adapts and refreshes with time – whilst staying to true to the brand and culture.

From an HR perspective we talked about our goals as focused on:

- Getting the right people in the right place at the right time – *Talent*;
- Making sure our people perform better for us than they would for anybody else – *Engagement; and*
- Building our organisation and processes to make sure all of these individual contributions are aligned to the business strategy – *Organisation.*

We achieve this by having strong leadership that ensures behavioural values are congruent with the brand values and that we as an HR team are a role model for all of this.

So what are the specifics from this? Well we didn't have a huge launch of a whole new brand philosophy. Our culture was a distillation of the orange pixie dust, it was already present – so we have built the image from the inside out, reinforcing orange values through the usual methodologies around recruitment, performance management, etc. but also strong personal communication and involvement from each of us on the management team. We want to keep legacy creep away from the business, to stay fresh and psycho-graphically young – and ensuring we retain the small business, almost family-feel, despite our becoming a large operation.'

2. *Leading with courage*
   - They are clear about their own values and will promote and defend them, rather than opt for the easy option. They stand up for what's right.
   - They act as champions and stewards, taking responsibility for building a healthy business culture within their organisation.
   - They focus intensely on developing ethical leadership practice and challenge where appropriate. They work hard to stimulate constructive rather than divisive politics.
   - Fairness and transparency are the principles which underpin their approach to rebuilding trust with employees. They develop reward, development and other elements of employee value propositions which are 'felt fair'.
   - They pursue better governance, and find ways to improve decision making at all levels, meetings, standards and norms, performance management and accountability, line management capability and leadership behaviour.
   - They challenge organisational practices that undermine sustainability. They change such practices where they can, such as addressing executive compensation issues head-on.

3. *Influencing others*
   - They act with integrity and are honest in their dealings with all stakeholders.
   - They handle their special relationship with chief executive officers (CEOs) and finance directors (FDs) with discretion, and act as a sounding board, contributor and challenger.
   - They avoid playing political games which destroy trust, and discourage such behaviour in others.
   - They use their insights into people and organisations to help people. They deliver initiatives and services which matter and which build support.
   - They act with confidence, and win credibility for their intellect, their contribution and that of their team.
   - Their's is a whole business perspective. They speak the language of business and avoid jargon.
   - They are forward looking and proactive, producing innovative solutions to operational problems and strategic challenges.
   - They deliver and are true to their word.

4. *Fostering team working*
   - They focus on building the organisation as a community, where the customer is the key focus for innovation, knowledge sharing and performance.
   - They ensure that the organisation is engaged with the community, leading corporate social responsibility initiatives not only to be good corporate citizens but also because they enhance brand.

- They embed diversity in recruitment and management practices. Similarly, they place corporate social responsibility at the heart of the employer brand.
- They understand how to build effective collaboration across cultural boundaries. They manage integrations in such a way as to ensure that $1 + 1 = 5$.
- They work constructively with trade unions and staff groups, building firm foundations for partnership and mutual respect and trust.
- They stimulate their own teams to be high performing, acting as a coach and mentor, role model and leader.
- They use OD methods to address conflict issues and to create employee ownership of change.
- They contribute to management teams and executive groups, ensuring that these function effectively and developing them when necessary.

5. *Motivating others*
   - For the organisation, they develop talent practices and employee value propositions which reflect different employee needs while still remaining fair to all.
   - They develop reward and recognition processes which are equitable and reward good performance not just good results.
   - They work hard to make sure that the employer brand is real, and that people's expectations are well-founded.
   - They give their team credit where it's due.
   - They provide people with stretching roles where there is scope for real achievement and development.
   - They celebrate success.

6. *Developing others*
   - They ensure that the HR development agenda is closely tied to organisational goals and also enables employees to meet their personal development needs.
   - They focus on developing leaders and find new ways to support line managers with the skills they need for their challenging roles.
   - They ensure that their team members are exposed to new insights – by attending conferences, visits to other companies etc.
   - They share good ideas, circulate interesting articles, make time for discussion as well as task.
   - They act as coach and mentor – to the CEO and their peers as well as line managers and their own team.
   - They find challenging project opportunities across the business to provide stretch for talented people.

7. *Continuous learning*

As we saw in Chapter 9, all the HR leaders have a huge appetite for learning and keeping up to date. In one example of how learning can be shared, Anne Minto describes her own approach to team development: 'I join my HRDs on a regular basis at their team meetings. I have sandwich lunches in my office – brown bag lunches– half a dozen people at a time at different levels in the function and from different parts of the company. So it's their lunch and they can raise any issues they like. They want to hear what their colleagues or I might be doing and that just helps to create a better communication line.

I do a monthly message which covers the business, and what we've done in our HR team. It gives them a potted version of what I have been doing in the month – so businesses I have visited, people I have met, both internal and external. I'll write up a little bit – almost like a blog – and people find that incredibly interesting. I get great feedback from that because people feel now that they know what I do on a monthly basis. Of course they don't know everything but they really feel they have had a good look at my diary so that they know what the head of HR has been doing in the month of October.

And we have a great Website – "My HR" it's called – and people can go in there. It's also where we keep all our policies and procedures and helpful processes that you can click through and it helps the customer to get to the answer that they are looking for. But our own HR site – we keep that regularly updated with stories, events, and who's been winning awards – that sort of thing. For instance one of the team did a fantastic job with our age discrimination last year.'

8. *Championing change*
- They act as change agents, taking a global perspective, scanning the environment, anticipating problems and building new opportunities.
- They focus on building flexible mindsets, behaviours and structures.
- They involve executives in leading change, getting them to be commissioners of OD initiatives.
- They transform HR functional delivery so that administration works reliably, faster, better and more cheaply than before.
- They help line managers have confidence to take on their human resource management responsibilities by providing training and coaching.
- They recruit high-calibre people into HR and give them chance to accelerate their development and responsibility.
- They improve employee communications and deliberately embrace participative methods of communication.
- They also build on the culture's strengths, act as guardians of appropriate continuity, identifying and building on what works well, reinforcing brand identity and employee commitment.

- They are able to prioritise and reprioritise, giving clarity to, and energising the team and the organisation. They make clear what can be stopped in order to make other more important things happen.

Spotlight Example Continued: The Challenges of Change at easyJet

Any HR leader will face significant challenges in their role. easyJet, for instance, has clear ambitions to shift from its original position of being a British airline operating internationally 7 years ago, to becoming a European airline, and best at short haul. This aim is pursued through a business strategy which needs to take account of the fast-changing marketplace.

The range of strategic activities to be pursued is staggering. At the same time, the airline industry is a highly operational, to the minute, high volume, low margin business, with both manufacturing and retail aspects. The pace of activity is fast, the Website gets 12 million unique customer visits per month. In common with many businesses, systems are always being stretched to cope with the volume and pace required. The challenge is no different for HR. As Mike Campbell says, "We need to be responsive to operational needs, while buying time to be strategic and deal with the bigger issues. The question is how do you cope? How do you prioritise? What does it mean if you don't make progress?"

For easyJet's senior management, challenges come thick and fast. The only business issues which Mike does not deal with directly are the procurement of aircraft, the new bag charge, launch of speedy boarding, and change of onboard catering supply. Mike recalls just some of the business challenges which easyJet's management team, including Mike himself, has had to deal with over the last 12months:

- 'Buying and integrating an airline with a clear view of becoming one brand within 2 months of completion.
- Shifting employment in Europe to employ our crew in France, Spain and Italy on local contracts with all the associated employee representation aspects.
- Managing a relatively newly established (in its second year) ground handling operation in Spain.
- Handling two massive legal cases in France, one involving a pension claim, which was won by easyJet, and another in which easyJet is currently defending itself against accusations of illegal employment in France.
- Hiring local HR managers in France, Germany and Spain to handle "business as usual" and sourcing local payroll providers.
- Dealing with the issue that UK managers based in Europe have suffered a reduction in income in real terms because of the poor value of the £ against the Euro.
- Addressing 25% staff turnover rates in administrative roles and improving productivity.
- Outsourcing our call centre with 120 roles to Poland and Germany.
- Carrying out a redundancy exercise cutting 10% of jobs within the central team.
- Buying an engineering company employing 120 engineers on different terms and conditions.
- Closing a base in Dortmund with over 100 jobs transferring elsewhere in Europe.
- Carrying out a cost-cutting programme, producing a £50 m saving.
- easyJet has opened new bases in Charles de Gaulle, Lyon and Manchester.

Spotlight Example Continued: The Challenges of Change at easyJet—cont'd

- We've gone to our suppliers asking them to share the pain of rising prices, in order to save costs.
- We've closed GB Airways head office and their Overseas operations in France, Spain, Portugal, Morocco, Egypt and Tunisia.'

Mike's responsibilities have involved him for example, in opening the new easyJet base at Charles de Gaulle airport, Paris. His facilities team is responsible for making sure that the base is ready to operate from day one, while his HR team recruits cabin crew locally. Mike took the decision to employ pilots from Charles de Gaulle rather than positioning them from the UK. As Mike recalls: 'This meant negotiating with the Works Council on why we were doing what were doing. It was time-consuming but it was something we had to get right. You have to deliver on your promises.'

Another aim is to increase crew productivity by 10% over the next few years. Part of the focus is on increasing the proportion of work carried out on a seasonal basis, changing contracts, looking at every penny, taking costs out of the business. And if that was not enough, the economic crisis has added to the challenges as Mike outlines.

The big issues

'We had a clear strategy of 15% growth, which current circumstances are causing us to rethink. In the current economic situation it is obvious that we should review it. What will the right strategy be? There is a clear interdependency with the employment model. easyJet's reward policy reflects the product strategy – no frills – and it is highly geared, i.e. the greater part of people's income is variable pay, and this is geared to individual and business performance. When external factors such as fuel price results in pay reductions, at senior levels this can affect significantly our ability to attract and retain people. Also the level of growth has a direct correlation with the number of people and promotion prospects. So how do we grow, become more European without taking the worst of country practices, and produce market competitive packages which are also affordable?

As an HR team our resources are stretched. The organisation consists of 19 bases with 19–20 cabin crew managers and a total staff base of 4000. HR is provided on a 1:300 ratio; there is one HR Business Partner and a service centre of 10. Given the ongoing challenges of absence, performance, etc., when you are this lean, people could soon burn out, if they didn't have the ability to deal with pressure and ambiguity.

As a management team we need to have a clear recommendation we all subscribe to. It ought to be easy to explain to our cabin crew. For instance, they understand that with tight margins, every extra cup of coffee sold can help us improve our performance. But the brand stands for more than the cost. *Turnaround times* – when we turn our aircraft round on average in 25 minutes, every minute counts. *Customer care* – we smile, we support the customer. Our cabin crew are our major asset. They have a 4-week induction. We train them about safety on board, passenger sales (we encourage passengers to part with their money in a way that they don't feel ripped off). We encourage people to *bring their personality* to work, within the orange framework. It's great when people are confident enough to do this in a way that's customer-centric.'

By keeping people focused on the business essentials, Mike and his peers are keeping the business on track and employees engaged despite the pressures.

WHERE ARE HR LEADER CAREERS GOING?

Increasingly, what used to be the top of the HR career ladder, i.e. Personnel or HR Director, is becoming only one route – and typically for capable people this is a junction rather than a terminus. At the more senior levels, HR roles tend to broaden out considerably, especially at Group level. Typically on the way up the career ladder HR Directors will find themselves responsible for not only employee relations, pensions and executive compensation, but also for strategy, corporate social responsibility, reputation management, internal communications, branding, facilities management, and more besides. And as workforces become more diverse, and human capital challenges more complex, it is likely that the scope of an HR leader's role will continue to expand still further.

And as we have previously discussed, effective HR leaders do not restrict their contribution to functional policy areas only. They will be actively engaged with the business as a whole, not only understanding the issues but also identifying how and where to build competitive advantage.

A National Stage

Moreover, the level of influence of some senior HR leaders, such as David Fairhurst, extends way beyond their own organisation. In David's case his influence is likely to have a national impact since he has contributed to the building of national public policy and practices with respect to skills and employment. His company is one of the first to develop and offer employer-led qualifications under the current Government's skills policies. Other HR leaders are contributing to the development of thinking around people practice by steering think tanks, research bodies and University centres specialising in the field. Many are actively contributing to the success of other organisations by sitting on boards and trusts, helping with the development of professional standards and taking part in government consultations.

Shaping New Employee Relations

Given that change is likely to be a permanent feature of the workplace, some HR leaders, like Geoff Armstrong earlier in his career, are helping move forward new forms of employee relations which are appropriate to the knowledge age and its workers. As Geoff says, 'This is every bit as necessary for the people dimension – it's more critical. We won't revert to collectivism – the whole business of talent, securing willing contribution, innovation – these are more and more essential and increasingly critical. In the loose organisations of the future these temporary alliances of skill will be important for employers to secure. Hopefully employee relations won't be as dramatic or brutal as industrial relations in the 70s when we were betting the company on a daily basis, removing impediments to progress and making those early steps to moving forward.'

One example of someone who has worked to establish a positive basis for employee relations is Jackie Simmonds, HR director for TUI Travel for the UK and Ireland. In September 2007 two of the UK's largest travel companies, First Choice and TUI (which had recently formed from the combination of Thomson Travel Group and My Travel) merged to become TUI Travel Plc. Previously HR Director for First Choice, Jacky was appointed as HR Director for the combined organisation in the UK and Ireland, and was responsible for the people outcomes of the merger.

A key objective was to build a positive culture for the new business and Jackie worked closely with Balpa, the pilots' union, to find a partnership solution to pressing issues arising from today's challenging environment and the merger.

The combined operation had almost 100 surplus pilots. But instead of going straight for redundancies, the company asked pilots' union Balpa to look for a joint solution – an unusual and welcome approach, according to Balpa's general secretary, Jim McAuslan.

By the end of 2008, it was clear that the measures agreed with the union – which included voluntary redundancies, part time working and sabbaticals – were not enough. So TUI went back to Balpa for more savings.

At the end of February 2009, the two sides announced a 'pain-sharing' deal and as Jim Mc Auslan says, 'This was a managed process, a joint approach, instead of the company just announcing redundancies and us having to pick up the pieces.' Based on sources Finney and Jefkins (2009) and Syedain (2009).

Ensuring that employees have 'voice' and the means to participate, requires HR leaders to directly intervene in internal communications, guiding and steering both process and message. They will have their finger on the pulse of employee morale and satisfaction through surveys and other means; they must act on key issues which emerge and produce positive change through their initiatives.

Beyond HR?

Ultimately HR will become a philosophy, not a department, according to Graham White, and there are already signs of this starting to happen. Graham predicts that we'll then see more senior HR people taking on Chief Executive roles. Business has been through eras when CEOs were predominantly production people, then marketing people. David Smith also believes that as organisations become more human capital oriented this could lead to more CEOs coming through the people route than has been the case in the past.

And there are already signs of this trend in the growing numbers of CEOs with HR backgrounds. HR leaders who are strategic progenitors are increasingly considering other seats in the boardroom as possible career goals. As Hesketh and Hird (2008) suggest: 'These individuals are highly politicised, understand and possess leadership traits of empathy and wider forms of social capital and convert/commodify their economies of experience into executive leadership signalling devices. Their influencing ability is as much testimony to their increasing political skills as to the rising status of people issues.'

Indeed several of the leaders featured in this book are already CEOs of organisations, and many also sit on the boards of others. And this trend seems set to continue, with two-way moves also possible. Jon Sparkes, for example is moving back into a very senior HR role from being CEO at Scope as his career develops into its next stage. Mike Campbell believes he could become a CEO, after all he was doing some of that at Wedgwood – but knows that he can contribute fully as a member of the management team in any case. As he says, 'If an outsider looked at the Management Team today they probably would not be able to tell who did what – which is the mark of a good management team. If need be, I would be able to cover for several different roles. For me, it's ultimately about making a contribution and enjoying myself.'

Creating a Legacy

Some of the HR leaders featured in this book are on the verge of retirement while others are midway through their career. What they all have in common is a desire to carry on contributing, developing and using their knowledge and skills in a value-adding way.

And all our leaders want to leave behind a positive legacy when they finally move on from their organisations. Mike Campbell would like people to say of easyJet:

- easyJet is a European airline;
- Learning is institutionalised; and
- The business thinks systemically.

And about himself:

- He brought in and developed some really great people;
- He helped to ensure the business always over-performed;
- He made our business simple to understand and easier to deliver; and
- He was really 'orange'.

AND FINALLY...

Organisations will have to reposition themselves to deal with customer demands – and in today's emerging economy, they are more reliant than ever before on the discretionary contribution of people. Organisations will have to change in ways that enable them to maintain competitive advantage and create opportunities. In today's knowledge and service-based organisations, HR leaders are the vital intersect between business and people needs. They must master the art of building change-able cultures in which workforces (not just employees) are engaged and giving of their best. Organisations with a customer-intensive purpose are likely to be most capable of bringing the best performance from employees. With an energising purpose employees are willing to feed back what customers think, create innovative ways of delighting the customer and building customer loyalty. HR leadership is about ensuring there is clear line of sight for people in their day jobs.

It is going to be from people in organisations that most differentiation and sustainable performance is derived. The new organisation will be a collection of contributions that people can't be obliged to give. What will distinguish 'winning' organisations from the 'losers' is the ability to cause people to want to work for you, to do discretionary things that can't be decreed. HR's job will be to equip the organisation with the people, talent, skills and learning to make a winning difference for it. HR leaders will need courage, vision and clarity to lead that agenda. They are expected to be *creators* of value across the organisation, not just tinkering with processes to 'add' value.

They must lead thinking and practice on people and organisation. While HR leaders should keep themselves up to date and ahead of the game in terms of where they seek inspiration, they should not simply follow fashion. They should set up a clear process for gathering evidence and build their knowledge base around the practice of people management to determine what is needed. It has to be an explicit, ongoing process – about how to position ourselves to be sustainable, and get customers coming back to us; how to craft an organisation where people feel motivated and respected. HR leaders need to know how this evidence coincides with the optimum collective effort as an organisation and the maximum return for the business.

HR leaders have to demonstrate from business evidence that what they do works in practice, makes a difference and is sustainable – something which can be replenished and built on, making people management the source of competitive advantage. It will be a continuous process – HR will have to recraft policies continuously. There will need to be more flexibility to accommodate individuals – their talents and changing work patterns such as home working. This is a big challenge, and we have to keep on re-winning this particular battle. Would-be HR leaders will need to embrace the fields of strategy, organisational design and development and turn their knowledge into applied expertise.

Leaders of the people dimension are business leaders first and functional specialists second. HR leadership is best exercised by people who understand the people dimension fully – and you can learn to do 'people'. The HR profession is in a strong position – it has the tools and methods to elicit willing contribution, to be the primary driver of value as we go forward. I am confident and optimistic that HR leaders will be able to build these sustainable futures for their organisations and by doing so contribute to the creation of health, wealth and happiness of society as a whole.

References

Aijala, A., Walsh, B., Schwartz, J., 2007. Aligned at the Top. Deloitte Development LLC.

Alexander, M., Korine, H., 2008. When you shouldn't go global. Harvard Business Review 86 (12), 70–77 (December).

Allen, A., 2008. Taking in the views. People Management Magazine, 12 Feb.

Augier, M., Teece, D.J., 2005. Reflections on (Schumpeterian) leadership: a report on a seminar on leadership and management education. California Management Review, February 1.

Badaracco Jr., J.L., 2002. Leading Quietly: an Unorthodox Guide to Doing the Right Thing. Harvard Business School Press, Boston, MA.

Barling, J., Kelloway, E.K., Weber, T., 1996. Effects of transformational leadership training on attitudinal and financial outcomes: a field experiment. Journal of Applied Psychology 81, 827–832.

Beatty, R.W., Ewing, J.R., Tharp, C.G., 2003. HR's role in corporate governance: present and prospective. Human Resource Management 42 (3), 257–269 (Fall).

Becker, B.E., Huselid, M.A., 2006. Strategic human resources management: where do we go from here? Journal of Management 32 (6).

Bennis, W., O'Toole, J., 2005. How business schools lost their way. Harvard Business Review, May.

Bennis, W., 2004. Lessons of leadership. CIPD Conference, London.

Bens, I., 2007. The ten essential processes of facilitative leaders. In: Global Business and Organizational Excellence. Wiley & Sons, pp. 38–56, July/August.

Blanchard, K.H., 2007. Leading at a Higher Level: Blanchard on Leadership and Creating High Performance Organisations. Pearson Education, Harlow.

Boltz, Chapman, M., 2006. Higher calling: will stewardship to your company bring better returns? Chain Leader, 1/1/2006.

Boudreau, J.W., Ramstad, P., 2007. Beyond HR: the New Science of Human Capital. Harvard Business School Press.

Bradford, D.L., Burke, W.W. (Eds.), 2005. Reinventing Organization Development: New Approaches to Change in Organization. Pfeiffer Wiley & Sons.

Bridges, W., 2003. Managing Transitions: Making the Most of Change. Da Capo Press, New York.

Brockbank, W., 1997. HR's Future on the Way to a Presence. Human Resource Management, Spring, 36, No.1, 65–69

Brown, T., 1995. Life without job security. Business Credit, September 1.

Bunker, B.B., Alban, B.T., 1996. Large Group Interventions: Engaging the Whole System for Rapid Change. Jossey Bass, San Francisco.

Burns, J.M., 1978. Leadership. Harper & Row.

Cappelli, P., 1997. Change at Work. Oxford University Press.

Cappelli, P., 2005. Is Your HR Department Friend or Foe? Depends on Who's Asking the Question. Available from: <Knowledge@wharton>, August 10.

Cappelli, P., 2008. Talent management for the twenty-first century. Harvard Business Review, March 4.

Cascio, W.F., 2005. From business partner to driving business success: the next step in the evolution of HR management. In: Losey, M.R., Meisinger, S.R., Ulrich, D. (Eds.), The Future of Human Resource Management. Wiley & Sons.

CIPD, 2008. UK Highlights, Global Leadership Forecast 2008–09, Research by Development Dimensions International. CIPD, London.

CIPD, 2009. Learning and Development Survey. CIPD.

CIPD/Penna, 2009. Gen Up: How the Four Generations Work. CIPD.

Clark, P.A., 2000. Organisations in Action: Competition Between Contexts. Routledge.

Clark, M.C., Payne, R.L., 1997. The Nature and Structure of Workers' Trust in Management. John Wiley & Sons.

Clemmer, J., 2001. High Performance Organization Structures and Characteristics. Available from: <www.managerwise.com>.

Coats, D., 2005. An agenda for work. The Work Foundation.

Collins, J.C., 2001. From Good to Great: Why Some Companies Make the Leap…and Others Don't. Harper Collins.

Cooperrider, D.L., 1998. An invitation to organizational wisdom and executive courage. In: Cooperrider, D.L., Srivastva, S. (Eds.), Organizational Wisdom and Executive Courage. Lexington Books.

Corporate Leadership Council, 2004. Driving Employee Performance and Retention Through Engagement. CLC.

Covey, S.R., 2004. The 8th Habit: From Effectiveness to Greatness. Free Press.

Covey, S.R., Crawley, J.D., 1999. Leading corporate communities. Executive Excellence, June, 6.

Crabtree, S. (2004). "Getting Personal in the Workplace." The Gallup Organization (Gallup Management Journal) 1–4.

Davis, B.L., Skube, C.J., Hellervik, L.W., Gebelein, S.H., Sheard, J.L., 1992. The Successful Manager's Handbook: Development Suggestions for Today's Managers. Personnel Decisions Inc, Minneapolis.

Day, M., 2009. Engagement requires a rethink. Management Today, 1st Feb.

DDI/CIPD Research Insight, 2007. Leadership Transitions – Maximising HR's Contribution. CIPD.

DDI/CIPD, 2008. Global Leadership Forecast 2008–09: the Typical, the Elite and the Forgotten. CIPD.

Deloitte, 2006a. Global HR Transformation. Deloitte Research.

Deloitte, 2006b. Generation Y: Changing the Face of Manufacturing. Deloitte Research.

Edwards, P., Geary, J., Sisson, K., 1998. New forms of work organisation in the workplace: transformative, exploitative, or limited and controlled. In: Murray, G. (Ed.), Work and Employment Relations in the High Performance Workplace. Routledge, pp. 72–120.

Engineering Employers' Federation, 2009. Unprecedented drop in manufacturing pay settlements. In: EEF Press Release, 19th Feb. Engineering Employers' Federation.

Ephor Group, 2008. White Paper: Outsourcing Best Practice. Ephor Group.

Erickson, T., 2008. Plugged in: the Generation Y Guide to Thriving at Work. Harvard Business Press.

Flade, P., 2002. "Great Britain's Work Force Lacks Inspiration." The Gallup Organization (Gallup Management Journal): 1–3.

Finney, E., Jefkins, C., 2009. Best Practice in OD Evaluation, Roffey Park.

French, W., Bell, C.H., 1999. Organization Development: Behavioral Science Interventions for Organization Improvement. Pierson.

Gardner, H., Laskin, E., 1996. Leading Minds: an Anatomy of Leadership. Basic Books.

George, B., 2007. Where have all the leaders gone? (Part 2). Business Week, October.

Godard, J., 2004. A critical assessment of the high-performance paradigm. British Journal of Industrial Relations 42 (2), 349–378.

Goffee, R., Jones, G., 2005. Managing authenticity, the paradox of great leadership. Harvard Business Review, December.

Gratton, L., 2007. Making virtual teams more productive – ten golden rules. Marketing, June 17.

Guest, D.E., Conway, N., Dewe, P., 2004. Using Sequential Tree Analysis to Search for 'Bundles' of HR Practices. Human Resource Management Journal 14 (1), 79–96.

Hagler, C., 2008. Global companies struggle to find long-term solutions in 'War for Talent'. Available from: <resourcesglobal.com> (accessed 11.08.08).

Hamel, G., 2009. HBR at Large: Moon Shots for Management. Harvard Business review. February, pp 91–98.

Hamel, G., Breen, B., 2007. The Future of Management. Harvard Business School Press.

Heger, B.K., 2007. Linking the Employee Value Proposition (EVP) to Employee Engagement and Business Outcomes. Organization Development Journal. July 1.

Hernez-Broome, G., Hughes, R.L., 2004. Leadership development: past, present, and future. Human Resource Planning 27 (1), 24–32.

Hesketh, A., Hird, M., November 2008. The Golden Triangle: How relationships between leaders can leverage more value from people, CPHR White Paper 09/03, January. In: Paper Derived from an Article in Human Resources Business Review vol. 1 (no. 2).

Hewitt., 2008. Perspective: next generation HR. HR Connect Issue 7, March, Nasscom.

Hiltrop, J.M., Udall, S., 2008. Managing core talent and positions: key questions and recommendations. In: Developing HR Strategy, May. Croner.

Holman, P., Devane, T., 1999. The Change Handbook: Group Methods for Shaping the Future. Berrett Koehler, San Francisco.

Holman, P., Devane, T., Cady, S., 2007. The Change Handbook: the Definitive Resource on Today's Best Methods for Engaging Whole Systems. Berrett Koehler, San Francisco.

Holmwood, L., 2009. BBC scraps bonuses and freezes pay for senior managers. The Guardian, Jan 27.

Huselid, M.A., Jun. 1995. The impact of human resource management practices on turnover, productivity and corporate financial performance. Academy of Management Journal 38 (3), 635–672.

Jamrog, J., 2008. Cultivating Effective Corporate Cultures: a Global Study of Challenges and Strategies. American Management Association.

Jentz, B.C., Murphy, J.T., 2005. Embracing confusion: what leaders do when they don't know what to do. Phi Delta Kappan 86 (5), 358–366.

Joni, S.-N.A., 2004. How Successful Leaders Use Outside Insight to Create Superior Results. Portfolio.

Joyce, W., 2005. What really works: HR's role in building the 4+2 organization and an introduction to the case studies in the HR leadership forum. Human Resource Management 44, 67–72.

Katz, D., Kahn, R.L., 1978. The Social Psychology of Organizations, 2nd ed. John Wiley & Sons, New York, NY.

Kochan, T.A., Osterman, P., 1994. The Mutual Gains Enterprise: Forging a Winning Partnership among Labor, Management and Government. Harvard Business Press.

Kransdorf, A., 1998. Corporate Amnesia. Butterworth-Heinemann.

Lambert, A., 2009. Configuring HR for Tomorrow's Challenges – Post Meeting Review. Corporate Research Forum Report.

Lawler III, E.E., Mohrman, S.M., 2003. Creating a Strategic Human Resources Organization: an Assessment of Trends and New Directions. Stanford University Press.

Lawson, E., Mueller-Oerlinghausen, J., Shearn, J.A., 2005. A dearth of HR talent. The McKinsey Quarterly, May.

Leroux, M., 2009. Lego proves itself a blockbuster once again. The Times, February 24.

Linder, J.C., Brooks, J.D., 2004. Transforming the Public Sector. Accenture.

Locander, W.B., Luechauer, D.L., 2006. Leader as inquirer; change your approach to inquiry. Leadership Journey 16 (5), 46.

Logica Management Consulting and the Economist Intelligence Unit, 2008. White Paper: securing the value of business process change, Logica Management Consulting.

Losey, M.R., Meisinger, S.R., Ulrich, D., 2005. The Future of Human Resource Management. Wiley & Sons.

Loubier, C., 2002. Sustainable Learning Systems: a Model for High Performance Organizations (A keynote presentation given at Collaborative Learning 2002 a virtual conference held November 19–22, 2002, online). iCohere, Walnut Creek, CA. Available from: <http://http://www.icohere.com/cl2002/program.htm>.

Margulies, N., 1978. Organization development. Academy of Management OD Newsletter, Winter.

Markides, C., 2009. Speaking at CIPD's Human Resource Development Conference. London, April.

Marshak, R.J., 2006. Covert Processes at Work. Berrett Koehler, San Francisco.

Mayo, A.J., Nohria N., 2009. Zeitgeist leadership. In: Harvard Business Review on Managing Through a Downturn. Harvard Business Review, pp. 123–159.

McCartney, C., Willmott, B., 2009. The UK Employee Outlook. CIPD.

McEwen, W.J., Fleming, J.H., 2001. Stress resistant customer relationships. How smart asset management can boost your stock payoff. The Gallup Management Journal, Oct 22.

McKinsey Quarterly Surveys, 2009. <mckinseyquarterly.com>

McLagan, P., 1989. The Models – a Volume for Models of HRD Practice. American Society for Training and Development, Alexandria, VA, p. 6.

Mirvis, P.H., Gunning, L.T., 2006. Creating communities of leaders. In: Gallos, J.V. (Ed.), Organization Development – a Jossey-Bass Reader. Wiley & Sons, pp. 709–729.

MLAB, 2008–9. Management 2.0: Labnote 9, MLab at London Business School.

Moore, M.H., 1995. Creating Public Value: Strategic Management in Government. Harvard University Press, Cambridge, MA.

Pearce, C.L., Manz, C.C., 2005. The new silver bullets of leadership: the importance of self and shared leadership in knowledge work. Organizational Dynamics 34 (2), 130–140.

Pfeffer, J., O'Reilly, C.A., 2000. Hidden Value: How Great Companies Achieve Extraordinary Results with Ordinary People. Harvard Business School Press, p. 255.

Pfeffer, J., Sutton, R.I., 2000. The Knowing–Doing Gap: How Smart Companies Turn Knowledge into Action. Harvard Business School Press.

Pomeroy, A., 2006. (April). The ROI of Succession Planning. HR Magazine, 51(4), 16, RHR International.

Prahalad, C.K., 2009. Speaking at the Hay Mt Conference in Valencia, May.

Purcell, Kinnie, Swart, Rayton, Hutchison, 2009. People Management and Performance. Routledge, London.

PwC Saratoga, 2008. Managing People in a Changing World: Key Trends in Human Capital: a Global Perspective. PwC Saratoga.

Raelin, J.A., 2005. We the leaders: in order to form a leaderful organization. Journal of Leadership and Organizational Studies 12 (2).

Global Professionals. 2008. Global HR Survey. resourcesglobal.com.

Rooke, D., Fisher, D., Torbert, W., 2000. Personal and Organizational Transformations: Through Action Inquiry. Edge\Work Press.

Sarros, J.C., Gray, J.H., Densten, I., 2002. Australian Business Leadership Survey: Key Findings. Australian Institute of Management.

Schein, E.H., 1988. Process Consultation, Volume 1: Its role in Organization Development. Addison-Wesley.

Schein, E.H., 1992. Organizational Culture and Leadership, 2nd ed. Jossey Bass, San Francisco, CA.

Schein, E.H., 2006. In: Gallos, J.V. (Ed.), Organization Development. Jossey-Bass.

Society of Human Resource Management (SHRM), 2002. The Future of the HR Profession. SHRM.

Society of Human Resource Management (SHRM), 2003. HR Role Models. SHRM.

SHRM, 2004. Research quarterly corporate social responsibility: HR's leadership role. HR Magazine, December.

Sforza, L., 2009. HR Barometer. Hewitt Associates.

Sparrow, P., Brewster, C., 2008. Global HRM. CIPD.

Sparrow, P., Hesketh, A., Hird, M., Marsh, C., Balain, S., 2008. Reversing the Arrow: Using Business Model Change to Tie into HR Strategy. CPHR, Lancaster.

Spears, L.C., 2004. Practicing servant–leadership. Leader to Leader.

Stalk, G., 2009. Five Future Strategies You Need Right Now in the 'Memo to the CEO'. Harvard Business School Press.

Strack, R., Dyer, A., Caye, J.M., Minto, A., Leicht, M., Francoeur, F., Ang, D., Bohm, H., McDonnell, M., 2008. Creating People Advantage: How to Address HR Challenges Worldwide Through 2015. Boston Consulting Group/World Federation of Personnel Management Associations.

Strack, R., Caye, J.M., Thurmer, R., Haen, P., 2009. Creating People Advantage in Times of Crisis. Boston Consulting Group/European Association for People Management.

Sujansky, J.G., 2003. 20 Keys to leadership. Healthy, Wealthy and Wise, September.

Sujansky, J.G., 2006. Leadership challenges for challenging times. Business Credit, January.

Syedain, H., 2009. A smooth landing. People Management Magazine, 26 March.

Taleo, 2009. Talent Retention: Six Technology Enabled Best Practices. Taleo Research.

Tate, W., 2009. Search of Leadership. Triarchy Press.

Tiplady, M., 2007. The Future for HR: Get an attitude – or get your kit and get outta town. Personnel Today, 17 April.

Towers Perrin, 2003. HR Effectiveness Survey Report. Towers Perrin.

Towers Perrin, 2006. Global Workforce Study – Executive Report, Winning Strategies for a Global Workforce. Towers Perrin.

Towers Perrin, 2007. HR Service Delivery Survey. Towers Perrin.

Towers Perrin, 2008. Closing the Engagement Gap, Global Workforce Study 2007–8. Towers Perrin.

Truss, K., Soane, E., Rees, C., Edwards, C.Y.L., Wisdom, K., Croll, A., Burnett, J., 2006. Working Life: Employee Attitudes and Engagement. CIPD.

Truss, C., 2008. Continuity and Change: the Role of the HR Function in the Modern Public Sector. Public Administration.

Tubbs, S.L., Schultz, E., 2006. Exploring a taxonomy of global leadership competencies and meta-competencies. Journal of American Academy of Business, Cambridge, MA. No.2, March.

Ulrich, D., 1997. Human Resource Champions: the Next Agenda for Adding Value and Delivering Results. Harvard Business School Press, Cambridge, MA.

Ulrich, D., Brockbank, W., 2005. The Bottom Line Lent: HR's Value Proposition. Harvard Business School Press, Boston, MA.

Ulrich, D., Brockbank, W., 2008. The Business Partner Model: 10 Years On – Lessons Learned. Human Resources Journal, 1 December.

Ulrich, D., Brockbank, W., Johnson, Sandholz, Younger, 2008. HR Competencies: Mastery at the Intersection of People and Business. RBL/SHRM, Alexandria, VA.

Ulrich, D., Smallwood, N., 2007a. Leadership as a brand. Leadership Excellence, Jan. 2007.

Ulrich, D., Smallwood, N., 2007b. Building a leadership brand. Harvard Business Review (July–August), 92–100.

Van Velsor, E., McCauley, C.D. (Eds.), 2004. The Center for Creative Leadership Handbook of Leadership Development, 2nd ed. Jossey-Bass.

Weisbord, M., 1978. Organizational Diagnosis: a Workbook of Theory and Practice. Basic Books, Reading, MA.

Wheatley, M., 1999. Leadership and the New Science: Discovering the Order in a Chaotic World. Berrett Koehler, San Francisco.

Williams, H., 2009. Recession roundtable: retooling for the recovery. Personnel Today, 30 June 2009.

Wirtenberg, J., Backer, T.E., Chang, W., Lannan, T., Applegate, B., Conway, M., Abrams, L., Slepian, J., 2007. The future of organization development in the nonprofit sector. Organization Development Journal 25 (4) Winter.

Wharton on Human Resources, 2005. Is Your HR Department Friend or Foe? Depends on Who's Asking the Question. Available from: <Knowledge@Wharton> August 10.

Wood, Z., Wearden, G., 2009. John Lewis staff delighted with 13% bonus. The Guardian, 11th March.

Index